MARYAM JAMEELAH AND THE GLOBAL MUSLIM IMAGINATION

Maryam Jameelah and the Global Muslim Imagination

JUSTINE HOWE

PRINCETON UNIVERSITY PRESS
PRINCETON & OXFORD

Published by Princeton University Press
41 William Street, Princeton, New Jersey 08540
99 Banbury Road, Oxford OX2 6JX

press.princeton.edu

GPSR Authorized Representative: Easy Access System Europe - Mustamäe tee 50, 10621 Tallinn, Estonia, gpsr.requests@easproject.com

ISBN 9780691249469
ISBN (pbk.) 9780691249452
ISBN (epub) 9780691296555
ISBN (PDF) 9780691249681

Library of Congress Control Number: 2026939483

British Library Cataloging-in-Publication Data is available

Editorial: Fred Appel and Tara Dugan
Production Editorial: Mark Bellis
Cover Design: Katie Osborne
Production: Lauren Reese
Publicity: William Pagdatoon
Copyeditor: Lachlan Brooks

Cover Credit: photograph of Maryam Jameelah, creator unknown, 1962. Manuscripts and Archives Division, New York Public Library. Courtesy of Momin Khan.

This book has been composed in Arno

For Liam and Rory

CONTENTS

ACKNOWLEDGMENTS

I AM pleased to express my gratitude to the many people who supported the publication of this book. The New York Public Library staff made this scholarship possible through their meticulous care for Jameelah's materials, from her first deposits in the early 1960s to their stewardship of her legacy to the present day. When I began this project during the COVID-19 pandemic, NYPL archivists generously responded to my questions and scanned key materials, enabling me to make progress while the building was closed to the public. Once the library reopened, Cara Dellatte ensured that my archival visits were smooth and productive.

Research for this book was made possible by generous support from several funding sources: a National Endowment for the Humanities Summer Stipend, an American Academy of Religion Individual Research Grant, a Baker-Nord Institute for the Humanities Research Travel Grant, a W. P. Jones Development Grant, and a CWRU Finish Line grant.

I would like to extend my gratitude to several colleagues at Case Western Reserve University. I deeply appreciate Timothy Beal's support and encouragement over the years, and especially in facilitating my progress on this book. Thank you to Jue Liang, Alanna Cooper, Ananya Dasgupta, and Maysan Haydar for the lively discussions about Jameelah and her legacy, and for suggesting many helpful sources. I am very grateful to Lee Thompson for her mentorship.

This book benefitted from the research assistance of Olivia Weiss. I would like to extend special thanks to Ussaid Ishaq, who provided nuanced translations of Mawdudi's Urdu correspondence.

I would like to thank several colleagues for their exceptional feedback. Brian Clites, Matthew Cressler, Rachel Gordan, Brannon Ingram, Maggie Popkin, and Jonathan Sadowsky all offered extensive suggestions for how to improve the manuscript. Several fruitful conversations also facilitated this work. Many thanks to Kambiz GhaneaBassiri for his insightful comments and advice. I want to thank Kecia Ali and Ilyse Morgenstein-Fuerst for encouraging me to consider Jameelah's story for a book-length study. I am grateful to Shari Rabin for our discussions about American Jewish history. Many thanks to Elora Shehabuddin for illuminating conversations about feminism and Jameelah's impact in South Asia. Kathryn Lofton offered both wise counsel and incisive reflections at a critical stage.

To my writing group, Amanda Baugh, Kate Dugan, and Michal Raucher, aka the BLS, I cannot thank you enough for your brilliant feedback on many, many drafts of this book. More importantly, your friendship sustained me throughout the writing process.

Thank you to Brook Wilensky-Lanford for helping this project take shape. I would like to extend special thanks to Catherine Osborne for her exceptional developmental editing and insights into American religions in the Cold War period. As the project neared completion, this manuscript benefitted tremendously from Kaersten Janene-Nelson's editing skills.

I had the opportunity to present this scholarship at many venues. I deeply appreciate the generous and constructive feedback that I received from colleagues at Elon University, Oberlin College, University of Florida, Universität Freiburg, Rutgers University, the International Quranic Studies Association, and the American Academy of Religion.

Working with Princeton University Press has been a fantastic experience. Fred Appel saw this book's potential in its early phase and provided exceptional guidance throughout the writing process. Tara Dugan and Mark Bellis expertly shepherded the manuscript into publication. Many thanks to Lachlan Brooks for her superb copyediting. Thank you to the two anonymous reviewers for their astute comments and suggestions. I am grateful to Momin Khan for granting permission to use images of his grandmother's drawings and letters.

To our Cleveland friends and chosen family, we are so lucky to have such a close-knit and interwoven community. Thank you for the patio gatherings, walks to school, themed soirees, and camping trips.

I owe a profound debt of appreciation to my family. Thank you to Vicki, Steve, Amber, and Tori Clites for the special visits and sweet treats. I am forever grateful to my parents, Richard and Susan Howe, for their unconditional support and love. My grandmother, Tina Theurkauf, inspires me with her grace and wisdom. I am lucky to have the encouragement of my wonderful siblings, Ellen Kueterman and Warren Howe, and their families.

To my sons, Liam and Rory, I am very proud of the people that you have become. You are confident, principled, empathetic, and hilarious. Cheering for you on the field and on the stage is such a joy.

Brian, thank you for being my person. Over the past two decades, we have learned, grown, and loved in ways that I did not know were possible. I am so fortunate that we found each other.

MARYAM JAMEELAH AND THE GLOBAL MUSLIM IMAGINATION

Introduction

IN 1962, Maryam Jameelah (1934–2012), formerly Margaret Marcus, left New York City for Lahore, Pakistan, at the invitation of the prominent Muslim political and religious leader Abul A'la Mawdudi. In the decades that followed, Jameelah eschewed her American Jewish upbringing to become a leading voice of the global Islamic Revival.

Three portraits of Jameelah capture her unlikely trajectory from a middle-class Jewish child in suburban New York to a global Muslim intellectual (figs. 0.1, 0.2, and 0.3). The first is Jameelah's self-portrait, drawn in pastels in 1944, when she was ten years old. The bright, cheery colors and the half-smile on her face portray the optimism of postwar middle-class Jewish life in the United States—a vision that Jameelah would come to reject, but never quite leave behind.

The second is a photograph taken of Jameelah in 1962, soon after her conversion to Islam and around the time of her emigration to Pakistan. Her hair is loosely covered in a white headscarf; she smiles directly at the camera as she sets off on a completely uncharted path. Though she would never return to the United States, she actively capitalized on both her insider knowledge of being American and her reputation as such.

The third image, taken on the streets of Lahore in the 1960s, is Jameelah as she wished to be seen by her readers—the embodiment of pure Muslim femininity. While the photographer and

FIGURE 0.1. Maryam Jameelah, *I Am in My Room Making a Model Airplane*, 1944. Pastel drawing. Manuscripts and Archives Division, New York Public Library.

FIGURE 0.2. Photograph of Maryam Jameelah, 1962. Manuscripts and Archives Division, New York Public Library.

FIGURE 0.3. Photograph of Maryam Jameelah, 1965. Manuscripts and Archives Division, New York Public Library.

original purpose of the image is unknown, it served an important function in Jameelah's career, appearing at the beginning of her books, articles, and pamphlets, signaling to the reader that *this* female author lived out the prescriptions for modesty and piety that she demanded of all Muslim women.

The circumstances that undergirded her dramatic transformation are fascinating. In 1960, before converting to Islam, Jameelah published her first article in the South African magazine *Muslim Digest*. Soon after, she wrote to Mawdudi (1903–79), the enormously influential Islamist Pakistani leader. Mawdudi led the Jamaat-i-Islami movement, a political and religious organization founded in 1941 that was dedicated to the Islamization of society and the creation of an Islamic state. After a substantial exchange of letters, and at Mawdudi's encouragement, Jameelah formally converted at the Islamic Mission in Brooklyn, NY. In 1962, Mawdudi invited Jameelah to relocate to Pakistan and start a new life. With her parents' support, she departed New York harbor for Lahore, arriving in July 1962 with her Smith Corona typewriter and a suitcase of clothes. In 1963, she married Muhammad Yusuf Khan, a Jamaat-i-Islami worker who also became her publisher. She was Khan's second wife, and together they had five children. After she moved to Pakistan, Jameelah began publishing books and pamphlets through Jamaat-i-Islami imprints, which gave her work much wider distribution in Pakistan, the United Kingdom, South Africa, the United States, and Canada.

As is the case with many female intellectuals and religious figures, Jameelah's biography and publications have received limited scholarly attention. Yet her oeuvre is significant for understanding the role of affect in creating, solidifying, and sometimes subverting religious and political boundaries during the Cold War. Her work was translated into Arabic, Urdu, Persian, and Turkish, and was reprinted and published widely, especially among Muslim communities in Anglo-American contexts like the US, UK, and South Africa. Jameelah's more than twenty books and pamphlets gained prominence due to their unrelenting critiques of modernity and arguments for the superiority and distinctiveness of Islam in opposition to "the West." Jameelah became a prominent author in the global Islamic Revival—the multifaceted, diffuse twentieth-century movement aimed at reinvigorating individual Muslim piety and enhancing the public presence of religion in politics, culture, and education. She was instrumental in the revivalist project to restore Islam as the center of contemporary politics and culture. Jameelah has been described as one of Mawdudi's "most important disciples," and she was one of few female Muslim writers to make a name for herself on a global scale in the mid-twentieth century.[1]

This book explores the role of affect, especially negative emotions, in cultivating transnational religious imagination. Jameelah harnessed negative affects—shame, disgust, anxiety—not only to critique what she saw as the catastrophes wrought by Western modernity, but also to generate a global Muslim solidarity that could be mobilized toward a reinvigorated Islamic future. The transnational appeal of Jameelah's work came from her ability to rouse collective emotions that resonated across geographic boundaries and established universalistic aspirations of the *umma*, or global Muslim community, that could serve as a third way between Western capitalism and Soviet communism. Women and gender norms became the key affective flashpoints through which she sought to bridge differences among Muslims with a variety of loyalties. Jameelah's corpus is thus critical to understanding how gender and affect are at the center of contemporary religious politics.

Threads of Revivalism

This book demonstrates that Jameelah came to revivalism, and many of her non-liberal views, through a distinctly American Jewish set of concerns about rising materialism and assimilation. What she feared above all else was her community's abandonment of religious distinctiveness to the crushing power of modernity. This trepidation animated her lifelong project of convincing other Muslims to feel that same fear and to respond by committing to preserving that distinctiveness.

Jameelah's rise and impact can only be understood by examining the intersecting histories of postwar America and global Islamic revivalism. In fact, I first discovered Jameelah's writing through research I was conducting on the Muslim Students Association (MSA). In the 1960s and '70s, the MSA reprinted many of Jameelah's articles and helped to disseminate her ideas back to the country of her birth. I was intrigued by the global circulation of Jameelah's ideas and what her transnational trajectory could teach us about the crossing of religious and cultural boundaries. Her Jewish inheritances and chosen Muslim identity inextricably informed one another, resulting in a female religious figure who made use of racial and religious alterity to advance her transnational project of Muslim unity.

Jameelah's early religious outlook was shaped by, and forged in reaction to, a religious revival that expanded the institutional scale and congregational dimensions of American Judaism.[2] Her oppositional stances toward Western capitalism and cultural imperialism developed out of disenchantment with her affluent, Reform Jewish background, and later grew during a period of spiritual seeking in the late 1950s, which included stints with the Baha'i and the Ethical Culture movement. Although Jameelah was an affluent, educated woman in postwar America, she refused to submit to the expectation that she would marry young and pursue a life of caregiving and other domestic responsibilities.

Beginning with her earliest reflections on her childhood, and continuing through her later corpus, Jameelah argued that most American Jews had abandoned their faith's essential truths in favor of material comforts. An affect of loss, anguish, and anxiety, combined with an intense conviction that religious solidarity was the only antidote to the ills of modernity, permeated Jameelah's assessments of both American Jewish communities and Muslim-majority societies. "Why I Embraced Islam," the opening essay of her 1965 collection *Islam and Modernism,* illustrates this persistent thread in her work: "My parents' philosophy was that one must avoid contemplating the thought of death . . . the purpose of life is enjoyment and pleasure achieved through self-expression of one's talents, the love of family, the congenial company of friends, combined with the comfortable living and indulgence in the variety of amusements that affluent America makes available in such abundance."[3] In describing her childhood, Jameelah lamented that the High Holy Days were mere occasions for socializing rather than solemn rituals of sacrifice and remembrance. She argued that the "congenial" character of these holidays portended Judaism's collapse into an American civil religion and the end of Jews' status as God's chosen people. Resonating with deeply held anxieties over what it meant to be Jewish, her critiques of suburban communities ran against the affective currents of the postwar era that celebrated capitalist plenty as the pinnacle of human progress.

Many Reform Jews of this period experienced buoyed optimism over their rising status in the American matrix of religion, race, and class.[4] At the same time, other American Jews experienced collective anxiety over which religious and cultural practices they had to give up to become more fully accepted into the American mainstream.[5] Jameelah came of age in the transition from the postwar and Cold War eras, and experienced this period as a fraught transition from being a racial, minoritized other toward a closer affinity to ascendant whiteness marked by material wealth.[6]

Determined to help Muslims avoid a similar fate, Jameelah sought to preserve Islam as a "total system." Jameelah understood Islam to be distinct and separate from other religious systems. It was also a bulwark against the threats posed by modern capitalism: "Islam demands the Muslim's total allegiance. A Muslim is a Muslim every minute of the day. Islam is rigorous to a degree inconceivable to a person of any other faith. Its laws control very aspect of his life from birth to death. Awake or asleep, Islam is always with the Muslim. He is never for an instant allowed to forget what he is."[7] For Jameelah and many other revivalists, retaining Islam's pure and elevated status demanded constant vigilance on the part of committed Muslims against that which is "un-Islamic." In her eyes, many Muslims had become such in name only, swayed as they were by the allure of Western materialism.[8] These two strains—that is, an emphasis on the distinctiveness of Islam and a vigilant attention to boundaries around Islam—became key features of revivalism in American Muslim communities.[9] Jameelah's writing was an important conduit for these two dimensions of revivalism: her writings reached transnational religious communities, and, in a twist of historical irony, deeply resonated with Muslims in the country of her birth.

I show that Jameelah's formative years were shaped by several trends associated with "big religion," which was characterized by mass institutionalization of American religious communities, increasing professionalization of clergy, governmental entanglements, and the rise of a civil religion.[10] Religious congregations were bigger, more visible, more public than ever—mobilizing huge numbers of laypeople and clergy alike.[11] At the same time, a new vision of "tri-faith America" emerged that recognized Protestant Christianity, Catholicism, and Judaism as equal yet discrete groups making up American civic life.[12] Promoting the value of tolerance, the tri-faith ideal placed a high premium on national unity to combat the Soviet threat.[13] From living through the postwar realignment of faith and American national identity, Jameelah discerned the power with which religiously inflected nationalism could structure politics and everyday life. She saw herself as taking on the descent into materialism and nationalism that she observed in American society. What Jameelah imagined as the salve for the problem of modernity was the revival of Islam—what she called an Islamic awakening—one powerful enough to counter religious revivals of postwar America, both Christian and Jewish. As she cultivated a distrust of the intertwining of nationalism, materialism, and faith, Jameelah came to see the revival of Islam as the necessary antidote to the catastrophes of modernity.

Jameelah's religious imagination offers an important window into how the Islamic Revival emerged in relation to twentieth-century American pluralism while also highlighting key convergences between global Islam and American religious thought. I use the term "Islamic Revival" broadly to encompass the multifaceted, transnational, diffuse movement aimed at reinvigorating Islam from the 1960s to the 1990s. Jameelah represents an early figure in this longer trajectory. Several key elements of her thought became prominent as the twentieth century went on: an unabated embrace of Muslim universalism; a focus on individual piety as the basis for social change; and a catastrophizing outlook on modernity.

While scholars have long recognized the growth of revivalism after the Iranian Revolution in 1979, there is scant literature on how postwar and Cold War developments shaped revivalism outside the Middle East and South Asia. Current scholarship on Islamic revivalism tends to focus on its emergence within postcolonial contexts. In Egypt, for example, twentieth-century authoritarian regimes sought in many ways to manage and repress Muslim authorities and practices, but their efforts ultimately spurred new Muslim revivalist and reform movements that sought to restore Islam to its "rightful" status.[14] Other accounts of revivalism emphasize how new religious authorities helped to both displace traditional Muslim scholars and pave the way for alternative interpretations of Islamic texts.[15] Relatedly, some scholars explain revivalism as part of the broader "objectification" of religion—in which religion is no longer taken for granted.[16]

These important accounts do not fully capture the transnational pathways through which Jameelah established herself as a leading revivalist voice. As a young girl, she found herself drawn to the music of Umm Kulthum, the iconic Egyptian singer and actress, which sparked her imaginative and affective relationship with Arabs and the Middle East. As a teenager she read a lot of Sayyid Qutb (d. 1966), the Egyptian Muslim Brotherhood ideologue and inspiration for many revivalist thinkers. But it was Abul A'la Mawdudi who shaped Jameelah's trajectory most profoundly. She first encountered his writings in English translation at the New York Public Library. Jameelah spent many hours of her youth there, especially in the Oriental Division. A few years later, she was probably reintroduced to his vision through her deep involvement in the transnational Black Sunni community at the State Street Mosque in Brooklyn, where she converted in 1961.[17] At the center of Mawdudi's vision was what Humeira Iqtidar calls a "conservative anti-colonialism" that centered on a critique of Western materialism and a corresponding insistence on the necessity of Muslims to act to oppose it.[18] It was this combination of activism and anti-colonialism that captivated Jameelah's attention, particularly Mawdudi's insistence that you had to know your adversaries—who were often fellow Muslims.

Although invoked less explicitly, Jameelah's critique of modernity also echoed that of Traditionalism—a loose, diffuse twentieth-century philosophical movement that condemned materialism as the undoing of civilization. In *Islamic Culture in Theory and Practice,* she writes:

> While the evils of atheism and materialism, supported by all the forces of modern technology, are working day and night to destroy us—spiritually, culturally and politically—rather than hold fast to faith in Allah, unite and combat our real enemies, we foolishly choose to tread the path of an alien civilization, hoping thereby in vain to attain social prestige and the comforts and pleasures of this transitory world in utter forgetfulness of the eternal Life Hereafter . . . this is not the way to "Progress" but can only result in our failure, degeneration, and doom, both individually and collectively![19]

Here Jameelah employed two hallmark elements of Traditionalist thought as developed by René Guénon, the late nineteenth-century thinker who combined elements of Catholicism, occultism, and Sufism to diagnose modernity's ills. First, she followed Guénon's diagnosis that the West had destroyed "tradition," the timeless beliefs and practices that had previously ensured civilizational flourishing but were now drowned out by materialism. Second and more importantly, Jameelah adhered to Guénon's proposal that modernity constituted the end of civilization—not its apotheosis, as its proponents would have it. As Mark Sedgewick describes it, "Inversion was seen as an all-pervasive characteristic of modernity. While all that really matters is in fact in decline, people foolishly suppose they see progress."[20] Jameelah made ample use of Traditionalist inversions, particularly the idea that the comforts of modern life were in fact the opposite of how they were sold in glossy magazines and political rhetoric. Leisure and ease only generated an unending desire for more, which in term produced inevitable malaise.[21] Progress, equality, and freedom were far from aspirational ideals; instead, any society that celebrated them was well down the path to "doom" and "degeneration."[22]

Affective Economy and Revivalist Publics

In reconsidering the relationship between American postwar religion and twentieth-century Islamic revivalism, I incorporate affect theory to conceptualize the transnational contours of religion and politics. Drawing on the work of Sara Ahmed and Donovan Schaefer, I use "affect" to refer to collective emotions that accomplish important religious and political work as they circulate among bodies, objects, and communities.[23] As a case study, Jameelah's work provides exceptional insight into a strain of 1960s and 1970s revivalism that sought to harness negative affects centered around women, the family, and sexuality in order to generate global Muslim solidarity. Scholars have tended to portray Islamic revivalism as an "ideological" version of Islam that seeks to make a simplified set of beliefs and practices universal and normative for all Muslims.[24] For example, Omid Safi calls such attempts "pamphlet Islam," identifying this orientation in short books, guides, and other prescriptive literature popular in American mosques during the 1980s and 1990s.[25] Safi criticizes this genre as excessively reductive because it erases the historical and cultural diversity of Islam while also marginalizing important strains of Muslim piety, such as Sufism. Jameelah's work could be seen as potentially falling into this genre. She primarily wrote short books and pamphlets that aspired to create internal uniformity among Muslims; she repeatedly politicized Muslim identity and decried any changes in Islamic practice that she considered to be immutable. *But why would such reductionism be appealing, and to whom?* I argue that we cannot understand the vast appeal of revivalism writ large without analyzing collective emotion.

Foregrounding the role of affect in religious politics offers key insights into how communities form attachments over and against "others." Ahmed's concept of affective economy hinges on what she calls the "objects of emotion" that circulate through cultural production—as opposed to emotions being the preserve of individuals. Collective emotions are often harnessed to forge communities through relations of "difference and displacement."[26] As they move through social texts and practices, emotions forge powerful bonds between individuals and their identities. For example, Ahmed explores how hate, as a collective emotion, catalyzes white British and Australian citizens to imagine themselves into a "discourse of pain" in which outsiders threaten to destroy the social fabric.[27] Hate is not simply "out there" as an emotion waiting to be tapped, nor is it an internal emotion generated from within an individual self. Rather, hate is produced through the relationships cultivated between white citizens and groups such as immigrants that are marked as "undesirable."

Jameelah's writings contributed to an affective economy that connected Muslims to broad civilizational imperatives and transnational religious belonging. Affect does more than just attach individuals to others in community; it also binds Muslims to grand narratives of Islamic and global histories, creating a "felt sense of us."[28] Shenila Khoja-Moolji makes a similar point regarding the construction of Muslim and Pakistani identities. She demonstrates how the cultivation of affect around certain bodies, or what she calls "figurations," produce "ambivalent attachments" to the state and to the Taliban, who compete with one another for sovereignty in contemporary Pakistan.[29] Gendered affective attachments play a key role in forming what Khoja-Moolji calls "feeling publics."[30] As Schaefer argues, "The chunky raw materials making up the contact zone between bodies and worlds—the membrane between bodies and power—include not only a range of unnamed forces, but the named affects or emotions."[31]

While these examples demonstrate how affect cultivates attachments to the nation-state, this book focuses on how affect shaped transnational Muslim revivalist publics in the 1960s and 1970s. I argue that the umma, as Jameelah conceived of it, is a *feeling public.* By emphasizing the role of affect in generating attachment to the umma, I underscore its contingency and flexibility as a theological and political concept. The idea of the umma has a long history, dating to the origins of Islam, but its meaning depends on the context in which it is imagined and acted upon. Jameelah's notion of the umma was highly politicized, and closely related to her use of another term, "Muslim civilization."[32] Jameelah's insistence on the primacy of Islam as a total way of life was by no means a framework that other Muslims universally shared. As she herself lamented throughout her writings, contemporary Muslims attached themselves to all sorts of other political and religious communities, particularly national and ethnic identities. Within this context of competing allegiances and identities, Jameelah's aim was to make her audiences *feel* like they belonged, first and foremost, to a *universal* Muslim community.

By generating disgust, shame, and outrage, Jameelah contested and inverted the universalist claims of the West—the teleological narratives of modernization theory, the triumphalist ideology of "tri-faith" America, and the neocolonial justifications for economic and cultural interventions in Asia and Africa. I show how Jameelah's aspirational project emerged from an idiosyncratic braiding of ideologies, communities, and practices.[33] Her work engages with a broad range of religious and political frameworks of the postwar and Cold War eras, enabling us to see the global circulation of universalist Islamic projects. As Jameelah understood it, her life's mission was to extricate a pure Muslim way of life away from the corruption wrought by colonialism and capitalism. By focusing on Jameelah as a singular figure, I illuminate how transnational religious imagination is rooted in smaller scales of local religious networks and individual lives.[34]

For Jameelah, Muslims had to *feel* the collective weight of modernity's destruction. This book traces Jameelah's lifelong attempt to pull Muslims' attention back to Islam by stirring a constellation of negative emotions, or what I call an "anti-modern affect." At times she targeted specific affects such as disgust or shame; at other times, Jameelah employed an "affectsphere," a term that I use to refer to the constellation of emotions that Jameelah used to enhance Muslim attachment to her vision for an Islamic politics.[35] Jameelah attempted to build solidarity through what Sianne Ngai identifies as "ugly feelings" around the catastrophic effects of modernity.[36] By excoriating the destructive effects of modernity, Jameelah sought to drive her audiences toward the revivalist cause. For Jameelah, existential threats required constant iteration and repetition: "The Muslim divides the world into two opposing camps—Dar al-Islam, or the 'Abode of Islam' and Dar al-Harb, the 'Abode of the Unbelievers.' The worst affliction of mankind is not poverty, disease or illiteracy, but Kufr [state of unbelief or ingratitude]. Teen-age pregnant brides, unwed mothers, venereal disease, abortions, rapes, illegitimate children, drunken derelicts, and chauvinistic nationalism—all reflect the consequences of Kufr."[37] Jameelah's writing conveyed an urgent sense of impending destruction: the rot at the heart of modernity that derives from the condition of *kufr*, which she understands as the rejection of the transcendental aims and the ethical and rituals prescriptions of Islam. Note that each of her examples of the worst effects of modernity relate to gender, sex, and sexuality, whether in Muslim or non-Muslim societies. While rampant immorality was most egregious in the West, Jameelah lamented that Muslims themselves helped to create the conditions of *kufr* in their own societies.

Gender, sexuality, and feminism were the central nodes around which these boundaries are drawn. Women's bodies constituted particularly "sticky" objects in Jameelah's writing.[38] That is, Jameelah reserved *her most negative* emotions for women as symbols of modernity's depravity. This stickiness applied to Muslim and non-Muslim women alike. Jameelah assumed a universal set of gendered expectations to which all women—whether Muslim or non-Muslim—ought to conform. For a civilization to thrive, each woman had to privilege caregiving responsibilities within the home, ensure that sexual expression was limited to marriage, and submit to the leadership of her husband. Feminism encouraged women to engage in premarital (or extramarital) sexual activity or, even worse, she thought, in homosexual activity. In Jameelah's catastrophizing worldview, feminism was the worst possible manifestation of this materialism because it privileged individual choice over collective good and material goals over transcendent aspirations.

While she held out the possibility that an Islamic state might facilitate a thriving Muslim society, Jameelah emphasized the nuclear family structure as the core religious and political building block of a resurgent Islam. To her, the one ubiquitous sign of civilizational collapse, whether in Pakistan or the US, was the decline of the family. Whereas Mawdudi and many revivalists were more oriented toward the state and focused on building Islamist organizations, Jameelah's approach reflected the American postwar sensibility that the family was the basis for social stability and the locus of religion in the modern society.[39]

What, then, linked revivalist Muslims across the vast geographies and cultures that separated them? Jameelah understood that political persuasion is as much about feelings as it is about ideas. Affect had the potential to cross transnational boundaries in a way that specific political or legal prescriptions could not. Jameelah's vision depended on the portability of negative affect as the basis for Muslim unity. In this way, her use of anti-modern affect underscores the impact of the "transcultural problematic of modernity" articulated by Islamist thinkers that crossed religious, cultural, and political lines and that hinged on the recognition of a common set of crises: modernity as a kind of pathology; the erosion of morality; and the decline of community.[40] Even when Jameelah was not naming or invoking specific emotions, her polemics were—always—shot through with affect.

In unpacking the role of collective emotion in modern Muslim politics, I want to acknowledge the ways that the politics of emotion have been weaponized against women and against Muslims. As a woman, Jameelah was subjected to tropes that associate femininity with being disproportionately emotional. Charges of excessive emotionality directed toward women, whether as "hysterical," irrational, or silly, have been used to discount women's political critiques, to diminish their capacity to narrate their own experiences, and to cast doubt on their ability to serve as authoritative observers and experts.[41]

The first two decades of the twenty-first century have also generated fraught discourses around Islam and emotion. Muslims have historically been portrayed as emotional actors who are irrationally bound to backward conceptions of politics. These representations play on well-worn colonialist associations of "other" religions as backward and primitive—in contrast to "enlightened" and "rational" religions, namely Protestant Christianity. In the climate of the "War on Terror," practices of surveillance, discrimination, and violence against Muslims were justified in part by the assumption that Muslims were excessively attached to their religion, driven by fits of irrationality and blind rage.[42] Muslim women were thus triply "othered" on account of their gender, religion, and (presumed) racial difference.[43] I argue that the excessive affect that undergirds Jameelah's writings has as much to teach us about a distinctly American religious politics as it does about the global Muslim revivalism.

By exploring the many sources of Jameelah's affective framework, especially the American strains, I underscore that her stark, binary views were not an expression of an irrational, radical Islam that can somehow be extracted or isolated from other aspects of her religious and political trajectory. To do so would reinforce the very binaries that Jameelah sought to uphold and ignore the political and economic conditions through which religious violence is justified. Instead, I examine how Cold War politics—in Pakistan and the US, but also in transnational revivalist networks—shaped her vision.

As a case study, Jameelah's corpus attunes us to the multiple affective threads that shape representations of Muslim women, which became particularly emotionally charged in the twentieth century. Often portrayed as victims of an oppressive, patriarchal religion, Muslim women became symbols of the Islam/West binary.[44] Jameelah made her career about entrenching this opposition and the constellation of big negative emotions around it. Jameelah suffered and struggled throughout her life against the weight of injustices that she discerned keenly as an intellectual and felt viscerally as a human being. She believed that Muslim women *were* victims, but not because they were subject to the patriarchal authoritarianism of Muslim men. Instead, she saw Muslim women as the paradigmatic victims of colonialism and capitalism. As a result, Jameelah sought to cultivate a range of bad feelings around women in order to demarcate how the "West" threatened to corrupt a pristine (imagined) Islam.

An Unconventional Biography

As the reader has probably already gathered, this book is *not* a conventional biography. For a textured account of Jameelah's life, consider *The Convert: A Tale of Exile and Extremism* by Deborah Baker. Baker examines the dynamics of Jameelah's interpersonal relationships, and I leave these dimensions of her story in Baker's capable hands. My focus is more squarely on Jameelah's ambivalent and sometimes fraught position within the global Islamic Revival: as an American, as a convert, as a woman, and as a writer trying to make a name for herself.

Jameelah was something of an enigma. As I discuss below, she left a substantial archive. She correctly predicted that her story would be of interest to future scholars. Yet her impact has only begun to be appreciated in recent years. As scholars have begun to investigate Jameelah's contributions, they have naturally felt compelled to start with the particular piece of the puzzle that relates directly to her expertise. Jameelah was first understood as an important convert, most notably in Marcia Hermansen's 1999 comparative analysis of Muslim conversion narratives. Hermansen makes the astute observation that Jameelah's authority hinged on cultivating her insider status to American culture.[45] Jameelah has also been compared to other towering Muslim figures of the twentieth century, appearing as the sole woman in John Voll's and John Esposito's 2001 *Makers of Contemporary Islam*.[46] More recent studies have examined Jameelah beyond her immediate Muslim context, exploring her lifelong engagement with Judaism and with feminism. Abraham Rubin argues that Jameelah ought to be viewed as a Jewish thinker, not just as a Muslim one.[47] Amina Jamal and Elora Shehabuddin have shown that how Jameelah is a key figure in transnational feminist and Islamist networks that linked the United States to South Asia because her work so clearly is indebted to feminist frameworks—even though she was a fervent anti-feminist.

These prior studies evince why Jameelah's story belongs in multiple conversations. However, these extant accounts largely do not engage how scholars in other fields have interpreted her impact. By bridging these conversations, I reach a different set of conclusions about what Jameelah's story and corpus teach us about contemporary Islam and American religious history. Instead of altogether eschewing her Jewish and American past, I show that Jameelah was a "perpetual convert" whose authority and position in her Muslim milieu depended on preserving an ongoing Jewish identity and American insider status. Jameelah never fully left the American context behind. As such, I consider her affective approach in relation to anti-feminist, conservative voices of the US religious Right. Like many female political and religious figures associated with such movements, such as Phyllis Schlafly (d. 2016), the prominent American Catholic anti-feminist activist, Jameelah used her public platform to decry the state of the modern world and to argue that women's obligations were primarily in the domestic realm. Jameelah contributed to an American religious politics that hinged on generating negative collective emotions toward modernity, with gender and sexuality as the focal point.

Moreover, taking a global approach to American religious history illustrates how actively rousing collective feelings is essential to enhancing the cross-cultural appeal of universalist visions. By expanding the geographic lens to include both the US and Pakistan, I demonstrate the multidirectional vectors that engendered religious revivalism. While she never returned to the US in person, Jameelah's ideas—and the affective framework upon which they were built—resonated through multiple generations of Muslim Americans. Having circulated widely in South Asia, Jameelah's ideas found considerable traction among US Muslims who arrived after the 1965 Immigration and Nationality Act, many of whom had revivalist proclivities. From the late 1960s onward, this important group of American Muslims looked to Jameelah's writings as they navigated the emerging culture wars around gender and sexuality.

My analysis also draws on recent innovations in the methods of critical biography that demonstrate the importance of seemingly idiosyncratic figures for understanding contemporary religion. One touchstone is Sarah Imhoff's self-described "weird biography" of Jesse Sampter, the American Jewish Zionist poet who moved to Palestine in 1919. Imhoff argues that "distinctive embodied experience points to the far wider cultural phenomenon of the complex relationship between the body and religious thought."[48] Within this framework, scholars embrace "imperfections and incongruities" as a key feature, rather than as an exception, of contemporary religious politics.[49] As historian Lois Banner puts it, "A life deeply lived, like any complex historical narrative, moves across space, time, and areas of human involvement both capriciously and predictably, validating certain historical constructions while challenging others."[50] Jameelah's vision illustrates the fragmented, multivalent threads of collective feelings that form the basis for ambitious projects of reform and renewal. Our deeply felt attachments to large-scale communities—religion, nation—emerge out of a bricolage of affects that are often galvanized through unlikely proponents. It is precisely Jameelah's unexpected qualities that drew readers to her work in the first place.

In fact, Jameelah's subversions of the boundaries that she sought to construct and maintain enhanced rather than detracted from her appeal. To name a few: she was an expatriate and convert from Judaism who unwaveringly asserted her Americanness and Jewishness; she was a prominent female author and intellectual who sought to deny those opportunities to other women; and she was a critic of colonialism who deployed colonial tropes and rhetoric to critique her fellow Muslims. Even as she wrote about the antisemitism and social exclusion that she experienced as an American Jew, Jameelah portrayed her childhood communities as inevitably assimilating into whiteness. However, in Pakistan, she was seen as a white American with indisputable access to the privileges of membership in "mainstream" America. Jameelah understood herself as special because of her prescient recognition of the evils of American life—which she had sacrificed for the cause of the umma.

While Jameelah worked tirelessly to present her vision of Islam as coherent, timeless, and unassailable, her story illustrates the messiness that undergirds the quest to maintain distinct religious boundaries. The incongruities of Jameelah's corpus further demonstrate the unpredictable ways that religious communities intersect. Such convergences are often less visible for religious traditions whose relationship has become highly politicized, as they are for contemporary Muslim and Jewish communities. This book argues that modern Jewish converts to Islam—who at first glance seem to be outliers—are essential for understanding "literal" and imagined crossings of religious and cultural boundaries. Through their multivalent religious lives, converts like Jameelah provide a lens into aspirational visions for new religious and political communities.[51] In this respect, she embodies a core dimension of twentieth-century religious history: the transnational religious imagination.

Although Jameelah spent her career asserting the incompatibility of "Islam" and "the West," she was, of course, shaped in turn by both American and Muslim politics. Just as important, Jameelah's writings exemplify the kind of "recombinatory," contingent encounters that have typified much of contemporary Islamic history. Jameelah embodied these incongruities in perhaps exceptional ways, but she should not be dismissed as exceptional. Instead, I contend that remarkable lives such as Jameelah's throw into sharp relief the unpredictable events that create the possibilities for crossing lines of religious and cultural difference.

Archives and Sources

Jameelah was a keen archivist of her own life. She spent hours and hours in the New York Public Library (NYPL), where she made friends with archivists, including Mr. Parr, who helped her locate books by Muslim authors such as Qutb and Mawdudi, and books on religions such as Buddhism. Over time, her research and writing produced her own mass of materials, encompassing hundreds of letters, newspaper and magazine clippings, dozens of drawings and other artwork, bibliographies, interview transcripts, family photographs, and two VHS tapes. Coming full circle, ultimately Jameelah selected the NYPL as the repository for her life's work.

That Jameelah chose an American institution to preserve her legacy attunes us to important dimensions of her self-understanding and her intended audience. The choice of venue is somewhat curious given that Jameelah so vociferously lambasted American institutions for their imperialistic designs and their suppression of marginalized voices and narratives. However, given her positive associations with the place, its staff, and its extensive collections, it is likely that Jameelah saw the library as an exception to this rule. The NYPL gave Jameelah the freedom to read widely and deeply. Largely an autodidact, she used her time there to delve into American intellectual paradigms, as well as into African and Asian scholarship that challenged US academic frameworks. Jameelah deposited the first installment of her archives, consisting of her childhood drawings and a first draft of *Ahmad Khalil*, in the Rare Books and Manuscript Division just before she left for Pakistan in 1962. Over the following decade, she intermittently sent additional materials back to the library. In the 1990s, as she approached the end of her life, Jameelah mailed even larger batches of her letters, unpublished papers, and drawings as gifts to the library. Her expressed intention was to create an archive that would carry on her legacy and facilitate critical research on her work. In 2005, she sent a final set of materials to the NYPL. I would wager that Jameelah also hoped that she would one day become a formidable public intellectual who appealed to the American masses.

Jameelah recognized that her personal story was essential to her stature as a Muslim intellectual. She even compiled a "Chronology of Life History and Articles," which she sent to the NYPL in the late 1990s, for scholars whom she imagined would be interested in her impact on contemporary Islam. She created detailed timelines of her life that included the dates of her first and last menstrual period, her marriage and the births of her children and grandchildren, the death of her daughter Ayesha in 1964, and the dates of her parents' passings, as well as the time that she spent in multiple mental health institutions. She also included the names and dates of the religious institutions that she attended, her childhood art and dance classes, her volunteer activities, the publication dates of her major books, and the appearance of Urdu, Arabic, Indonesian, and Turkish translations, among others.[52]

At the same time, Jameelah was less scrupulous in crafting the overarching *narrative* evinced by the materials in her archive. For example, her files contain an overabundance of letters purportedly exchanged with her parents and sister, spanning from 1945 through her journey by boat to Pakistan in 1962, and then a different set of letters written after her emigration. The letters have been collected in two volumes published in 1989: *A Quest for the Truth: Memoirs of a Childhood* and *Youth in America, 1945–1962: The Story of One Western Convert*. At first glance these letters provide a treasure trove of contemporaneous accounts of her remarkable journey and her subsequent life in Pakistan, detailing her adjustment to a new culture, her struggles as a mother, and her interactions with Mawdudi, his family, and the Jamaat-i-Islami. However, it is highly likely that Jameelah wrote many of these letters retrospectively, even several decades after their supposed dates, particularly the letters that are dated prior to her arrival in Pakistan. In addition to the peculiar fact that these early letters include no replies from her parents, many of the letters include anachronistic references to events that took place *after* the supposed date they were written.[53] The letters also provide a polished narrative, culminating in her climactic conversion and emigration. In other words, they read more like a hagiography than like personal letters home.[54] Jameelah's later letters do appear to be authentic and became the primary way that she sustained her relationship with her parents.[55] Through these letters, Jameelah also requested middlebrow publications, such as *Time*, be sent to her in Pakistan, which then provided her with crucial insider knowledge of current American events.

I take a very different view of the 1960–62 correspondence between Jameelah in New York and Mawdudi in Lahore. Central to my analysis, these letters demonstrate the prominent role that affect played in the two thinkers' respective visions of Islam. Unlike some of the letters purportedly sent to her parents, these letters were actually *exchanged*, and they provide a singular perspective on how personal relationships can shape transnational religious movements as well as how Jameelah navigated for her purposes the challenges and opportunities of Mawdudi's revivalism. As a highly visible figure, Mawdudi likely understood all his correspondence to be for public consumption in some way, and he seemed aware that their exchanges were potentially subject to Pakistani state surveillance and monitoring. But that does not seem to have been his primary motivation for writing back to Jameelah, nor was it her motivation for writing to him. Jameelah, in fact, kept most parts of his letters: the Urdu originals in Mawdudi's handwriting, the English translations typed by his secretary, and the postmarked envelopes. Three decades later, a Saudi publishing house edited and translated their correspondence into English.[56] These translated letters confirm the story that Jameelah told about how she came to live in Pakistan. Note that the published volume omits several less savory details, such as Mawdudi's admonition to Jameelah in saying her lack of linguistic skills would limit her appeal—a prediction that proved to be untrue.

It is unsurprising that Jameelah sought to shape her biography directly. She understood that her ability to reach a broad audience depended largely on how her conversion from Judaism to Islam was narrated and received. As such, I approach both her NYPL archive and correspondence with Mawdudi cautiously, focusing my analysis on the collective emotions that she wanted these archives to generate.

Chapter Outline

This book encompasses two parts. The first section is structured chronologically, examining the transnational religious and political convergences that transformed Jameelah into a Muslim public intellectual and shaped her affective vision. These first three chapters, which focus on the late 1940s to the early 1960s, frame Jameelah as a "perpetual convert" for whom the story of her conversion was an essential and enduring feature of her appeal to transnational Muslim audiences. Chapter 1 traces Jameelah's early childhood and adolescence in American Jewish communities and her experimentation with a variety of religious traditions. I excavate the range of postwar anxieties that shaped Jameelah's anti-modern affect: from her navigation of diverse religious and intellectual spaces in the 1950s to the beginnings of her assessment that modernity posed an existential threat not just to Islam, but also to religion more broadly. The second chapter explores Jameelah's conversion to Islam in the early 1960s as well as how she sought to cultivate her religious and intellectual authority. Through her religious and intellectual journeys, she developed the conviction that religious belonging was primarily emotional and cultivated affective affinities with real and imagined Muslims. The third chapter argues that Jameelah's appeal within Pakistani revivalist circles led by Mawdudi hinged on the expression of shared anti-modern affects. Despite Jameelah's triple disavowal of her Judaism, her whiteness, and her socioeconomic privilege, these were the very elements that made her so appealing to Mawdudi and other revivalists.

The second part of the book analyzes the affective economy of the Islamic Revival through the lens of Jameelah's corpus, exploring the dynamic emotional frameworks that undergirded her effort to build a global Muslim community. Gender and the family became essential emotional nodes for that project. Chapter 4 takes up the affectsphere of suffering that Jameelah cultivated around Palestine. I focus on her novel, *Ahmad Khalil*, which tells the story of a fictional Palestinian family who lost their home in 1948. As I demonstrate, she was decidedly disinterested in the politics of territory, law, and citizenship, instead framing the Israeli occupation of Palestine as the paradigmatic site where families were being destroyed by the dual evils of colonialism and capitalism. Chapter 5 turns to Jameelah's writings on gender. Her project of mobilizing global Islamic revival relied, foremost, on generating shame (and related negative affects) around the status of women in the modern world. The sixth and final chapter traces Jameelah's impact in the United States, where her work found a broad readership through American Muslim publishing networks, especially among the Muslim Students Association. Jameelah's writing combined the universalism of many post-1965 immigrants with a critique of American gender norms. This critique helped to cultivate religious outsiderhood as a moral stance while also enmeshing American Muslims in the emergent culture wars. By identifying these surprising convergences, I demonstrate that Jameelah's embrace of anti-modern affects are part of broader religious conservative reactions to a perceived ascendant liberal modernity.

PART I

The Perpetual Convert

1

A Jewish Youth Adrift in Suburban America

IN 1945, at age eleven, Margaret "Peggy" Marcus drew a vibrant pastel portrait, which she titled *Yemenite Jewish Girl of a Kibbutz in Palestine* (fig. 1.1). She depicted her imagined subject, a young woman who appears to be around her own age, wearing a red-and-white checkered scarf around her head. She grins widely at the viewer, showing her teeth. The girl wears a wide-collared shirt more in the style of postwar suburban New York than Mandatory Palestine. Her smile exudes joy, infused with an optimistic energy about the future that awaits her.

When I first encountered the portrait, I was struck by its distinctiveness. Its exuberance starkly contrasts the negative emotions that I had previously encountered in Jameelah's writings. As a result, I initially dismissed the image as an idiosyncratic childhood art project.

A closer look illustrates enduring features of Jameelah's religious imagination. Most importantly, the portrait attunes us to the out-of-placeness that led Jameelah to convert and that defined her positionality as a Muslim intellectual. During her childhood, when she was known as Peggy, Jameelah persistently felt out of place. She was adrift, floating between her public school and her family's Reform Jewish communities in postwar suburban New York. Peggy also struggled to make friends. Instead, she devoted her time to solitary

FIGURE 1.1. Maryam Jameelah, *Yemenite Jewish Girl of a Kibbutz in Palestine,* 1944. Pastel drawing. Manuscripts and Archives Division, New York Public Library.

activities, drawing imagined others with whom she developed a deep connection. She was far more comfortable forging relationships with distant places and people whom she would never meet.

From a quite young age, Jameelah also developed the conviction that true religious communities were facing existential threats.

The young girl in the portrait exudes the authentic life that Jameelah yearned for. She imagined her subject as a Yemenite Jew, a marginalized group within a minority community that endured persecution to survive through multiple cycles of political upheaval. Peggy imagined her subject living on a kibbutz, a member of an intentional community bound by a zealous commitment to communal solidarity. These features evince Jameelah's intense fascination with maximalist ways of being religious. Moreover, this drawing expresses one of Jameelah's core convictions: authentic religiosity was impossible to realize in the United States. Already at age eleven, she was skeptical of religious pluralism, especially the flattening of ethnic and religious distinctiveness that she observed among her fellow Jews. Instead, she dreamt of life in Palestine where Jewishness was central rather than peripheral.

This chapter argues that Jameelah's vision was indelibly shaped by postwar American Judaism. Her Muslim imagination was refracted through her experiences in suburban Jewish New York and her lifelong debates with American Jewish thinkers. Jameelah's writings are shot through with anguish over the loss of Jewish distinctiveness in the wake of acculturation. The chronicles of her childhood reflect the "ambivalent embrace" of postwar prosperity that many American Jews experienced during this period.[1] By all accounts, including her own, Jameelah's ambivalence morphed into anxiety over the fate of religion in the modern world. She became deeply concerned by what she detected as excessive consumerism in her family and in her synagogue; she was equally preoccupied by the horrors of the Holocaust and the near eradication of Jewish communities just a few years prior. During an era when many American Jews became more optimistic about their rising social and economic status, young Jameelah instead saw only steep moral decline.[2] Indeed, the joy that Jameelah felt in 1946 morphed into a much darker set of emotions that would define her religious imagination.

I approach Jameelah's Muslim and Jewish identities as mutually informing one another—not just in her youth, but as an enduring feature throughout her career. Contrary to her self-presentation as a convert who altogether rejected the social and religious communities of her childhood, her authority as Muslim thinker hinged on the ties that she maintained to American Judaism.[3] Even in her later writings, Jameelah referred back to the American context she had purportedly rejected, clearly remaining invested in the outcomes of those debates that had animated her intellectual and religious journey from an early age. Most importantly, the affective urgency of her work continued to be propelled by deeply American concerns about the relationship between religion, gender, and materialism. Although she would spend the bulk of her career calling for hardening boundaries between faiths, a closer look at her path reveals that she *became* a Muslim intellectual through a confluence of many traditions.

The Jewish roots of Jameelah's global Muslim imagination are also essential for understanding Jameelah's legacy. In particular, I argue that Jameelah's enduring connections to American Judaism help to explain *why* Jameelah's framework appealed to American Muslims in the latter half of the twentieth century. Investigating Jameelah's Islamic influences yields only a partial explanation of why her arguments were compelling to other Muslims. Even more important was her insider knowledge of American culture and her powerful call to preserve religious distinctiveness in the face of secularism and materialism.

In this chapter, I chart the important cultural and religious developments of the 1940s and 1950s that shaped Jameelah's Muslim imagination: the rise of religiously diverse communities in suburban New York; her education in a Reform Jewish congregation and the Ethical Culture movement; the period of spiritual seeking that her family pursued; and her mental health struggles, culminating with a diagnosis of schizophrenia and admittance to an inpatient facility in 1953. By her early twenties, Jameelah had few prospects to fulfill the social roles expected of her as an American Jewish woman. From this marginal position, she began to discern Islam as the one true religion and the path to securing the social belonging that she sought.

All of these biographical threads featured prominently in Jameelah's corpus as it developed over the next two decades. In her books and pamphlets, Jameelah often wrote about episodes from her childhood in postwar suburban New York. These writings generate both distance and proximity from her American Jewish background. I also use these sources to demonstrate how Jameelah used her biography to craft her legitimacy as social critic and Muslim thinker. Above all, Jameelah staked her authority from the position of a Western insider who had chosen Islam. In her own telling, Jameelah's conversion to Islam represented both a rejection of her Jewish identity and a natural discovery of what she had been all along: Muslim. Rather than being a singular event, her conversion to Islam represented a gradual series of spiritual, intellectual, and cultural transformations.

A Comfortable Suburban Life (1934–45)

In 1934, Herbert and Myra Marcus of White Plains, New York, had a baby girl they named Margaret. The Marcuses were third-generation Americans of German origin. When Margaret was in elementary school, they settled in Mamaroneck, an upscale suburb in Westchester County. Single-family houses were beyond their means, so they rented at the Larchmont Acres Apartments at Palmer Avenue and Richbell Road. Peggy and her sister, Betty, attended Central Elementary and Mamaroneck High schools. The family belonged to Reform Jewish congregations. Peggy took music and dance lessons, and she was a Girl Scout from 1943 to 1946. In 1943, the Marcuses enrolled Peggy and Betty in the Sunday school at Temple Israel in New Rochelle, New York, which they attended for two years. Temple Israel had been founded in 1908 by Reform Jews who were mainly of German descent, as were the Marcuses. In the 1920s, the congregation broke ground for a synagogue on Webster Avenue—which was occupied until the late 1960s, when a new building was erected to accommodate the swelling numbers of congregants. Jameelah's suburban environment was facilitated by key demographic shifts, especially the growing numbers of Jewish families who left American cities in the mid-twentieth century. By moving to the suburbs, the Marcuses signaled their desire, shared by many other Jews, to break with the intergenerational ties of urban life and forge new social and religious communities.[4]

By all accounts, Jameelah led a comfortable childhood. Her parents took an active role in her education and extracurricular activities, supporting their daughter in her academic interests by taking her to the Larchmont Public Library and encouraging her to socialize with classmates. A passionate young artist, Peggy painted portraits of many family members and, as we have seen, of imagined subjects that captivated her.

Jameelah attributed her initial fascination with Islam to her early Sunday school classes. In addition to studying Hebrew and the Torah, she recalled being introduced to narratives of Jewish history that sparked a lifelong anxiety about the destructive effects and false promises of modernity:

> I trace the beginning of my interest in Islam when as a child of ten, while attending a Reform Jewish Sunday School, I became fascinated in the historical relationship between the Jews and the Arabs. Despite my fascination with the study of Jewish history, I was extremely unhappy at the Sunday School. At this time, I identified myself strongly with the Jewish people and their horrible fate under the Nazis and I was shocked and pained that none of my fellow classmates took their religion seriously. For instance, during religious services at the synagogue the children would read comic strips hidden in their prayer books and make fun of the rituals.[5]

Here, Jameelah identifies a persistent theme in her career—that modernity posed an existential threat to true religion, which she later singularly identified as Islam. But in her youth, this enduring anxiety over the precarity of religion was shaped by concerns over the survival of Jewish communities in the wake of the Holocaust.

As a child, Jameelah was enmeshed in conversations where the horrific and unimaginable loss of Jewish life felt omnipresent. At mid-century, grief over the murder of six million Jews was woven into the "public life" of American Judaism.[6] While Jameelah's family, having arrived in the nineteenth century, was multiple generations removed from European immigration, she engaged the Holocaust intensely. Jameelah's affective critique of modernity emerged as a child grappling with her community's near annihilation. As historian Hasia Diner shows, American Jewish engagement with the Holocaust in the postwar period "blended a deeply felt anguish over this very particular Jewish tragedy with concerns for humanity writ large."[7]

In calling out her classmates for insufficiently grasping the grave danger Jews faced, Jameelah sought to position herself as a serious truth teller. Out of this affectsphere of grief, loss, and guilt, she constructed the most consistent thread of her writing: the claim that materialism, and its concomitant intentional destruction of religion, was a catastrophe for religious communities—Jewish and Muslim alike. She challenged what she saw as the naive faith that others around her seemed to have in postwar material progress, both in the rising American power abroad and the technological development promised at home, especially in the white suburbs.

By contrast, Peggy Marcus had no time for fun. Her autobiographies portray this "serious" nature as precisely the affective disposition that enabled her to develop a critical lens on US society. In the wake of the mass death of the Holocaust, she was shocked and dismayed at her peers for their apparent indifference to the suffering of Jews and their lack of interest in Palestine. Jameelah presented these early experiences as part of her growing realization that she was largely out of step with American suburbia—even among fellow Jews, whom she chided for having embraced the creature comforts of suburbia while ignoring the ongoing threat to their faith's very existence.

Jameelah also developed a strong disgust toward the emergent ideology of religious pluralism that she encountered in suburban

New York.[8] This new sense of religious nationalism was rooted in the "pluralist" understanding of "tri-faith America," which centered on the celebration of political unity through religious diversity. The movement of Jewish and Catholic families from urban ethnic enclaves into more blended, middle-class suburbs helped to create and instill the tri-faith ideology. Suburban Protestants, Catholics, and Jews embraced religious "diversity" as the cornerstone of liberal democracy. This pluralist vision was typified by towns like Mamaroneck. The real estate section of the *New York Times* even celebrated the benefits of living in religiously diverse Mamaroneck: "Local lore has it that the population is one-third Catholic, one-third Jewish, and one-third Protestant, but no data exist to support this claim. The community's religious institutions, though, are split evenly, with two Catholic churches, two Protestant [churches] and two synagogues."[9] Deep into the late twentieth century, "tri-faith" religious pluralism was seen as embodying the ideal suburban community, a key site for the building of a strong America.

Jameelah also grew up amid the large-scale postwar American religious revival. Suburban communities spurred significant growth in congregational religion, which helped to make religious symbols and narratives more visible in public life. Magazines such as *Time* emphasized the size and scale of religious events, such as Billy Graham's revivals, as evidence of America's religious and national unity.[10] Religious authorities were also increasingly professionalized by large-scale organizations and educational institutions that trained and employed them. Catholic and Jewish communities built parishes and synagogues to accommodate growing numbers of suburban faithful, alongside their Protestant counterparts. This emphasis on patriotic unity across tri-faith America was perhaps the definitive signifier of Cold War America's providential destiny to defeat the "godless" Communist threat.

From these early childhood encounters, Jameelah was enmeshed in a milieu that saw America as a place of exceptional promise for Jews, a site for Jewish flourishing that could serve and benefit Jews around the world. Her childhood world was marked by booming Jewish religiosity and the corresponding perception that being Jewish was becoming a religious rather than ethnic or national identity.[11] In greater New York, there was a wide variety of youth and adult programs to choose from, reflecting the institutionalization of Reform, Conservative, and Orthodox communities in the postwar period.[12] It was a bona fide "Jewish revival" centered on institutional growth and congregational life.[13] These recently arrived suburbanites lacked the close familial ties that had characterized the urban areas they had left behind. As a replacement, they began forming new local networks that were less tethered to ethnic and national pasts. These included synagogues, of course, as well as associations such as the women's Zionist organization Hadassah. As Jameelah entered her adolescence, however, she began to articulate profound concerns about the loss of Jewish distinctiveness, to which we now turn.

Ambivalence in the Wake of Acculturation

Much to Jameelah's chagrin, her parents seemed far less interested in the ritual requirements and transcendental benefits of religion than they were in the social opportunities that Jewish communities afforded. She was particularly troubled that these religious holidays seemed to be a mere pretext for parties, which she described as having minimal ritual observance or spiritual intent: "At home the atmosphere for religious observance was scarcely more congenial. On the Jewish High Holidays instead of attending synagogue I felt it blasphemous that my sister and I were taken out of school to go out on picnics and parties."[14] For Jameelah, postwar American Jews prioritized the community aspects of their religious identity, but had forgotten the original, ultimate purpose of gathering together. Rather than determined by the ritual calendar, contemporary Jews followed a schedule of get-togethers in their suburban neighborhoods. As far as Jameelah could tell, God and transcendental horizons were largely absent in American Judaism.

Jameelah's early writings emphasized how her refusal to conform to the gendered expectations of postwar America left her feeling "out of place." She highlighted her maladjustment as a sign of precocious religious conviction and as a basis for her religious authority: "From the outset of my adolescence until my migration to Pakistan at the age of twenty-eight, I was a hopeless misfit. A young girl as serious-minded as I was, always with a pile of books at the library, who abhorred the cinema, dancing, and 'pop' music, who did not enjoy 'dating' and mixed parties, and took no interest in romance, glamour, cosmetics, jewelry or fashionable clothes, had to pay the full penalty of social ostracism for being 'different.'"[15] While Jameelah acknowledged that her individual proclivities contributed to her acute rejection of postwar American norms, the above passage also implies that any devout Muslim would be extremely uncomfortable in such an environment. She portrayed herself as both a unique observer and a stand-in for all devout practitioners who would find American secular culture disorienting and disquieting. All her examples—dating, movies, dancing—became flashpoints for revivalist-oriented Muslims as they sought to reclaim public space for Islam and to regulate female bodies within those spaces.[16] And though Jameelah recalled feeling out of place on an embodied, intuitive level, as she became more invested in intellectual and spiritual exploration she found that these practices posed more than simply a threat to her individual well-being; they were moral evils that precluded an ethical, God-oriented society. Jameelah moved from feeling that she did not belong as an individual to attributing those feelings to the moral failings of her entire society.

This passage also fit squarely into American Jewish ambivalence—particularly the tension between rising prosperity and religious authenticity—over the community's relationship to dominant cultural forms in postwar America. Jameelah came by her catastrophizing propensities through this broader intellectual and religious trajectory that attributed a lack of spiritual depth to the rampant materialism of postwar American life. Her critiques of American Jewish life echoed a deep unease that she shared with a vocal minority of Jewish thinkers, students, and religious leaders over both the growing material wealth of American Jewish communities and what they saw as the erosion of spirituality. Jameelah's vision also challenged modes of religious and national belonging that were described in Will Herberg's *Protestant-Catholic-Jew*, published in 1955.[17] Herberg argued that the religious boom of postwar America was driven by a "social necessity of 'belonging.'"[18] In other words, being Protestant, Catholic, or Jewish was the primary way that postwar Americans asserted their Americanness. For Jameelah as for Herberg, religion in American had become a superficial shell, lacking the commitment and fervor that characterized a true religion as a "way of life."[19] She lamented that American Jewish communities had abandoned Judaism's core set of truths in favor of acculturating to forms of belonging that Jameelah felt were antithetical to the religion's core.[20] Some Jewish thinkers often expressed their anxieties in similarly "Manichean terms," warning their audiences about the potential catastrophic results should American Jews not achieve the right relationship between religious, national, and class belonging.[21]

For Jameelah, American Jewish communal life had become far too easygoing to be authentically religious. She would have her coreligionists seek transcendental meaning and purpose in their tradition in the wake of such communal tragedy, but instead she saw them becoming enamored with the finer things of the American way of life—to the extent that they had begun to worship those things instead of God. From Jameelah's perspective, being a devout Jew was supposed to be hard. With Jewish community being under threat of annihilation, even children needed to take their roles more seriously. If Jews lacked firsthand experience of suffering or, at the very least, attunement to the suffering of their fellow Jews at the hands of the Nazis, the very foundations of a distinctive Jewish identity were at risk of being lost.[22]

Even worse, Jameelah believed that her parents and their friends had cultivated a religious identity that, though recognizable to other Americans, was unrecognizable to God and to prior generations of Jews. Throughout the stories of her upbringing in American Jewish circles, Jameelah lamented that her fellow American Jews maintained only a superficial shell of their faith: "I have always regarded Reform Judaism with the utmost contempt because in the effort to adjust to modern Western life, it had become nothing more than a collection of empty platitudes devoid of meaning for me. As a result of utter disregard of the sacred Law, its adherents were Jews in name only."[23] In Jameelah's eyes, Reform Judaism had compromised the core of Jewish identity—the "sacred law." Jewish ritual and everyday legal observance was what made Jews different from other groups, and when Reform Jews no longer kept kosher or dressed in a distinct way, Jameelah believed they had given up the essential aspects of being Jewish in the first place. As I explore later in the chapter, Jameelah briefly spent time in Orthodox Jewish communities, whom she saw as being the only Jews in the US who upheld their commitment to traditional religion. For now, I want to establish the range of negative emotions—contempt, shock, indignation—that Jameelah presented as the correct reaction to these obvious affronts to religion.

Jameelah conveyed the same constellation of emotions over the state of contemporary Judaism as she would later generate around Islam. In decrying the state of her childhood faith, Jameelah tapped into much longer Jewish and American traditions of the jeremiad, or a "sustained lament," levied at a community that the author believes has fallen short of standards set down by God.[24] Seeing herself as a prophetic voice, Jameelah felt compelled to warn her Jewish community of the dire consequences they faced if they continued down their current tortuous path. She identified similar issues plaguing both her childhood and chosen religions: "Reformed Judaism not only failed to check the cultural assimilation of the Jews I knew but actively encouraged the process. As a result, they had become Jews by label only. None had any religion worthy of the name . . . even at that early age, I knew that such a watered-down, half-hearted compromise could never hope to retain the loyalty of its members, much less their children. How dismayed I was when I found among the Muslims, the same threat!" Her writing echoed the critiques of Jewish thinkers such as Abraham Joshua Heschel, who were similarly alarmed by what they saw as a widespread embrace of material comfort and a suburban religion devoid of spirituality.[25] Jameelah's writing contributed to what Abraham Rubin calls a wider "elegiac discourse" through which "Jewish communal leaders, activists, and rabbis questioned the viability of authentic Jewish life and the prospects of Jewish survival in their new suburban environment."[26] As we will see, she then focused her laments on her new faith, upbraiding fellow Muslims for similarly failing to embody the pure Islam that Jameelah believed God had mandated for all—over and against a morally corrupt "West."

At the same time, throughout her corpus Jameelah highlighted the fraught and uneasy position of Jews in the postwar pluralist framework of the New York suburbs. She recalled how American Jews continued to experience antisemitism and exclusion from the American mainstream.[27] These stories of experiencing discrimination carried a double critique: against ongoing American forms of discrimination toward religious minorities, and against those American Jews who responded to that discrimination by assimilating into dominant cultural norms. In her writing, Jameelah recounted several instances of mistreatment at the hands of her Christian classmates on account of being Jewish. In one episode, she recalled the exclusion she felt at Christian holiday celebrations that took place at school. These experiences, Jameelah wrote, "convinced me that being Jewish meant being 'different' and not really belonging to the society of which we were supposed to be a part."[28] At the same time, Jameelah castigated her fellow Jews for aspiring to assimilate into white, Christian America at all, because for her that entailed ceding their religious faith to a toxic brew of materialism and nationalism.

Jameelah also grew up during a period of change for Jewish women. Ambivalence toward Jewish upward mobility and suburbanization manifested itself in gendered terms. From a young age, Jameelah was exposed to anxieties over the role of women in sustaining the future of the Jewish community and the American nation. In particular, many Jews wrestled with whether women should be more or less visible in public life and whether their communities had become too "feminized" and "watered down" in the suburbs.[29] Decades earlier, Reform communities had created mixed-gender seating in their synagogues and began to perform bat mitzvahs for Jewish girls. By and large, American Jewish thinkers and religious leaders concurred that women had a special role to play in raising Jewish children and in maintaining the home as a key site for religious observance. At the same time, more affluent Jewish women, who were becoming more highly educated but did not usually seek compensated employment, were afforded circumscribed opportunities to take on more public religious roles—for example, through fundraising for religious and political initiatives—in their children's schools and in the burgeoning suburban synagogues, and serving on synagogue boards. But debates about whether women's activities outside the home facilitated or impeded the growth of robust American Jewish communities continued through the Cold War.

As we will see in subsequent chapters, in Jameelah's work the enhanced visibility of women figured as the primary sign of catastrophic social decline. Her concern over the sexual and social "emancipation" of women was threaded with distinctly American anxieties about the rise of materialism and secularism, as encapsulated by Soviet-style communism. While in the late 1960s and 1970s Jameelah's work would focus on liberal democracy as its own unique threat, in the early 1960s she expressed scorn for communist approaches to what she saw as the "so-called" liberation of women:

> Although I believe that every woman should be educated for the fullest use of her intellectual capacities, I certainly question the advantages of taking women out of the home (particularly those with young children) to compete in business offices and

> factories with men and substituting nurseries and kindergartens for a home upbringing. This is exactly what has happened in Soviet Russia and Communist China where the so-called "emancipation" of women is being deliberately used by the rulers to destroy the family. To a lesser degree, a similar situation exists in my country.[30]

Thus, the specter of communism represented the possible destruction of the family. The above passage, from a letter to Mawdudi, was written one year after Vice President Richard Nixon's and Soviet Premier Nikita Khruschev's 1959 famous kitchen debate in Moscow, in which the two leaders engaged in an impromptu conversation about the benefits of capitalism and communism, staged in a model suburban American kitchen at a technological exposition. Even though cultivating women's "intellectual capacities" had its merits, Jameelah embraced the postwar notion that the family represented the core institution of a religious and moral society. A woman's place within that ideology meant that she belonged at home embracing a domestic life away from the bureaucratic demands of male labor.

Echoing critiques of communism for its overturning of "traditional" gender norms that abounded in postwar America, Jameelah promoted an ideal family based on a male breadwinner who performed wage labor and a full-time housewife who provided the material and emotional labor that went into making the home a site for order, morality, and tranquility.[31] In contrast to Nixon's celebration of consumer comforts, however, Jameelah recognized that the nuclear family as it was enacted in suburban US contexts frequently facilitated the very materialism and individualism that she dedicated her career to fighting. In other words, the threats to morality came from within the system itself. Jameelah's rhetoric smacks of a 1950s paranoia about internal dangers—especially the need to "contain" subversive and perverse groups and mass entertainment that promoted individual freedom and sexual experimentation—in an effort to restore order and control over female bodies.

All of Jameelah's accounts of her alienation in Jewish and American spaces set up an important theme of her entire oeuvre: that the freedom promised by the West was a false one. Jameelah's conversion narrative portrayed postwar America as a place of conformity, replete with social consequences for failure to follow the narrow path set for women of her social, religious, and economic position. She felt crushed under the weight of gender norms and expectations that she could not fulfill properly. Moreover, she believed that these constraints imposed on women led them down a path of moral decline and spiritual emptiness. For Jameelah, the paradigms of individualism and choice rang particularly false given that she found no possible avenue for her to pursue a different future within such constraints. She would have to look elsewhere for a more authentic existence.

Spiritual Seeking, Experimentation, and Combinations (1946–53)

Jameelah often decried her parents' lack of spirituality, but in fact they were also seekers who were drawn to the new forms of liberal religiosity that were emerging in postwar America. In the mid-1940s, Herb and Myra Marcus began to explore other religious options. Secure in their Americanness, they joined the Ethical Culture movement in 1946. Ethical Culture functioned as a complementary program to existing religious communities; its activities were offered on Sundays to avoid conflicting with Shabbat services, and it became popular with many Reform Jews in the New York City area. By Jameelah's own account, she had been deeply invested in the Ethical Culture movement. She regularly attended Sunday school there from ages eleven to fifteen, and had come to "regard all traditional, organized religion with scorn."[32]

Jameelah's experiences with the Ethical Culture movement played a particularly important role in shaping her views on women and gender. Anxieties over gender in the Ethical Culture movement, as articulated by its founder Felix Adler, made a particularly deep impression on Jameelah. Adler saw the rise of women's autonomy and their stepping into new social and economic roles as contributing to the disintegration of moral authority. The resonance between Adler's and Jameelah's views on women—especially the view that the erosion of traditional gender roles represented an existential threat—demonstrates that Jameelah's perspectives on this issue were shaped by multiple, combinatory sources, not just Islamic ones.

As Jameelah approached her twenties in the early 1950s, the Marcus family embarked on an even more expansive period of religious exploration.[33] After four years of belonging to the Ethical Culture movement, Jameelah's parents decided to break with Judaism altogether and became Unitarian Universalists. For her part, Jameelah began to explore forms of "Eastern" religion and spiritual orientations that historian Robert Ellwood calls "alternative altars."[34] For a brief period, she explored the universalist movement of Baha'i, joining an offshoot group known as the Caravan of East and West led by Mirza Ahmad Sohrab (d. 1958). The organization was a branch of the New History Society, founded in 1929 by Sohrab, Lewis Stuyvesant Chandler, and Julia Chandler. Jameelah hoped that Baha'i would combine the interest in religions that she associated with Islam and her attraction to the universalist message of "the oneness of mankind."[35] But she found that, like so many other religious communities, the Baha'i movement did not live up to the promise of its message, and so she left less than a year later, "bitterly disillusioned."

Jameelah was part of a small yet influential group of American Jews who sought meaning in the universalist traditions of Eastern, Asian faiths prior to the countercultural movement of the 1960s. In many ways, she anticipated the Jewish "countercultural ethos" that emerged in the late 1960s, an ethos rooted in the rejection of assimilation and material comfort in favor of a quest for a forgotten authenticity.[36] For example, early and mid-twentieth-century Jews became prominent leaders and authorities in various

Buddhist communities and movements. Many of these movements, such as those associated with Zen Buddhism, focused on making Buddhism palatable for American religious sensibilities by eliminating hierarchical and monastic elements, among others.[37] In exploring many faiths associated with the "exotic" East, Jameelah's experimentations resemble that of other US Muslims, such as Alexander Russell Webb, who came to Islam through both an interest in "Eastern" faiths and a liberal religious outlook founded in experimentation and intellectual discovery.[38] While most American Jews who became Buddhists looked to dissolve boundaries between faiths, Jameelah took the opposite view. She saw Islam as similarly authentic and traditional, and because she located it in the "East," she rejected that brand of universalism. Instead, she sought a distinct, rigid boundary between religions, and believed that Islam offered the only true path. Maintaining Islam's distinctiveness was the only way to ensure its ongoing authenticity.

Jameelah also continued to seek out Jewish communities during this period. She started attending Orthodox services and events because of her conviction that *halakha* represented the only true expression of the Jewish faith. During the same period she also attended Zionist gatherings at a Mizrahi community in nearby White Plains. While she would later claim that her rejection of Zionism was immediate and instinctual, her movement through these communities suggests an ongoing engagement with various forms of Jewish religious politics as she tried out different spaces in her yearslong quest to belong.

In Jameelah's accounts of her journey to Islam, each subsequent foray into another religious community was one important step in the progression toward her eventual discovery that she had been a Muslim all along. This period of spiritual seeking demonstrates that Jameelah's conversion was a process that unfolded over many years, not a singular epiphany.[39] Over time, she aligned her communal affiliation with her inner conviction and her authentic self. The autobiographical accounts of her time with the Ethical Culture and Baha'i movements amplify the image of Jameelah as a sincere seeker of religious truth who participated in an expansive network of communities that ultimately could not satisfy her spiritual needs. In this way, Jameelah fits quite well into histories of other American converts, who described their conversions not as a free choice among all the available options, but rather as an obligation to claim the identity of the religion that was their only true option.[40] As other European and American Muslim conversion narratives of the twentieth century attest, there is rarely a singular moment of conversion, but rather a series of significant moments that converts come to recognize as a process of "recognition."[41]

Breakdown and Confinement (1953–58)

In her timeline that details her major life events, Jameelah labeled 1953–58 as a period of "schizophrenic breakdown." During these years, she underwent psychotherapy sessions with multiple doctors in New York City. As argued in the introduction, I am not attempting to ascertain a medical or psychiatric diagnosis to determine the causes of Jameelah's particular suffering.[42] Her archives attest that doctors and therapists determined her to be mentally ill. By her own account, she also understood herself to be ill.[43]

This period was marked by both profound distress and spiritual transformation, and Jameelah's experiences in psychiatric institutions are significant for understanding the complicated path that Jameelah took in becoming a Muslim. Her breakdown episodes also play a prominent role in her autobiographical and biographical writings. As such, her mental illness was very much part of her public persona, which was constructed differently by Jameelah, by Mawdudi, and, as we will see in chapter 3, by the biographies that accompanied her work. In what follows, I trace the social context that structured Jameelah's experiences with medical institutions during this period—while also engaging her own interpretations of those experiences as being transformative in her journey to becoming Muslim.

In Jameelah's eyes, her suffering was both individual and social. She was forthright with her readers that she suffered from a range of physical and emotional ailments, including depressive episodes that led her to withdraw from, first, her parents and then, later, her spouse and children.[44] She described the toll that her breakdown episodes had on her parents, who were "desperate" to help her, first through psychotherapy and later through her internment in state hospitals. Regardless of the diagnoses or the causes of her distress, Jameelah exhibited what anthropologist Janis Jenkins identifies as a core aspect of mental illness: that of struggle to thrive in the world and to cope with the cascading ensuing struggles with family members and other intimate relationships that arise when a person is unable to thrive.[45]

In the summer of 1952, Jameelah spent two months working as a machinist in a plastics company; she began classes at the University of Rochester that same fall. Jameelah reports that she was sent home in 1953 because she suffered a "nervous breakdown":

> Although I wanted to become a Muslim my family managed to argue me out of it. I was warned that Islam would complicate my life since the faith is not part of the American scene. I was told that Islam would alienate me from my family and isolate me from the community. At that time my faith was not sufficiently strong to withstand these pressures. I became so ill that I had to discontinue college. For a long time, I remained at home under private medical care, steadily growing worse. In desperation my parents had me confined to a hospital, where I stayed for more than two years.[46]

After receiving outpatient psychotherapy, in 1957 Jameelah was admitted to what she described as the "disturbed ward" at Nichols Cottage at New York Psychiatric Hospital in White Plains, a short distance from Mamaroneck; later she was transferred to Hudson River State Hospital in Poughkeepsie, New York. She remained under institutional care at the crumbling facility until her release in 1959.

Schizophrenia was understood to be progressively debilitating—leading to a host of secondary symptoms, such as hallucinations and delusions, that further hampered a patient's ability to function. Schizophrenia, as described in the 1910s by Swiss psychologist Eugen Bleuler, who coined the term, was characterized by a range of symptoms, namely: difficulty making logical associations, having a flat affect, maintaining conflicting or "split" emotions or views, and "autism," which he defined as experiencing separation from reality.[47] Unlike the predecessor diagnosis—"dementia praecox" (1890s–1930 or so), which European psychologists and psychiatrists considered incurable, schizophrenia in its American context was seen as grave but somewhat treatable, though nonetheless life-altering for many patients. In the worst cases, some patients were sterilized for eugenic purposes.

In the 1950s, the term "schizophrenia" encompassed a broad range of symptoms observed by doctors and therapists and was defined variously both across cultural contexts and among clinicians. By the mid-twentieth century, medical literature identified biological processes as the primary cause of schizophrenia, though researchers could not identify the mechanisms through which the disease progressed.[48] As a result of the gravity of the diagnosis, institutionalizing patients diagnosed with schizophrenia became common because they were seen as being unable to function in "normal" social settings.[49] Since there were no definitive laboratory tests that indicated schizophrenia, the severity of an individual case, and the ensuing treatment, were determined by observation of patients' behaviors. Treatments such as drugs, talk therapy, electroconvulsive therapy, and insulin coma therapy were standard; the efficacy of these treatments was assessed primarily by clinical observation and interpretation of patient behaviors. Jameelah received hydrotherapy as well as group and individual psychotherapy. Although her father signed the consent forms for electroconvulsive therapy, Jameelah did not report having received that treatment. Patients earned privileges by exhibiting "normal" behaviors, and Jameelah seemed to comply with those expectations. She reported having freedom of movement within the facility, as well as access to books and materials for writing letters to her family members.

In the period when Jameelah was undergoing treatment, white women were the most likely demographic to be diagnosed—on account of symptoms deriving from the pressures of being a housewife and caregiver. Indeed, doctors and clinicians often recorded disinterest in domestic and caregiving labor in their diagnoses of white women.[50] Psychiatrists and researchers continued into the 1960s to argue that the individual pathologies of women—namely schizophrenia and, increasingly, depression—were responsible for society's broader ills because a weakened nuclear family threatened America's national stability.[51] Members of another group to which Jameelah belonged—who were among the first patients diagnosed with schizophrenia—were "dreamer" intellectuals, who were known for and confined because of their romantic flights of fantasy.[52] These early patients were rarely seen as dangerous; rather, they were considered infantile subjects who needed protection. Jameelah's attachment to distant places and people was possibly viewed as evidence of her detachment from reality and the result of an illogical and delusional attachment to a faith and culture that was foreign and unfamiliar.[53]

Whatever the specific justifications that doctors provided for her diagnosis, the key takeaway is that Jameelah saw her treatments, and her embodied experience of illness, as a crucial episode in her much longer conversion and her development as a thinker. As she explains to her audiences, she vowed that after her recovery, she would "become a Muslim." Jameelah did not shy away from sharing these episodes over the decades of her career. Instead, they became a core part of her conversion narrative, as evidence for how much she had overcome to embrace the true religion. Ultimately, Jameelah interpreted her suffering as further evidence for the moral failings and corruption of the West. She portrays her eventual conversion to Islam as the only way both to heal her internal struggles and to repair the sickness underlying modern civilization itself.[54]

Discovering the Qur'an

During this period of isolation from her family and her community, Jameelah discovered and read the Qur'an for the first time.[55] The text provided her with the comfort that she sought and the conviction that she was, in fact, meant to become a Muslim: "Throughout the darkest days during my years of hospitalization, I kept a paperback edition of Pickthall's translation with me as my constant companion which I read over so many times. I must have worn to pieces half a dozen copies. May Allah abundantly reward Pickthall with the choicest blessings for making the knowledge about the Quran so easily and cheaply available to England and America! Were it not for him, I would not have been able to know and appreciate it."[56] Jameelah described this intense period of reflection on the Qur'an as both invigorating and exhausting. On the one hand, she felt that she had aged several decades, and on the other, the spiritual power of the Qur'an provided Jameelah with the resolve to more deeply explore Islam. The time of her confinement removed her from the expectations of marriage, school, and career, and provided her the space and time to spend with the Qur'an, reading it over and over again even as the book started to fall apart in her hands.[57]

Although she presented herself as a scholar who possessed certain knowledge of religious truth, Jameelah was forthright about the emotional difficulties that she underwent. As much as she presented herself as a scholar who had achieved a "rational" understanding of religious truth, so much of Jameelah's writing comes from this place of embodied, emotional attachment to her new religion. While it is impossible to know which passages most deeply resonated with her readers, the fact that Jameelah continued to write about these episodes decades into her career suggests that the intensity of these encounters helped to forge her expansive religious imagination.

These conversion narratives also had a wide universal message for potential converts—the Islamic message is available in many forms and in unlikely places. Like many American converts, she first experienced the Quranic text in English. Her ability to access the text through the language of English is further evidence for the "blessings" of God and the inevitability of her conversion. Anticipating a role that she would later claim for herself, Jameelah credits Pickthall with performing a great service to the faith in offering the sacred text and its teachings to a wide, English-speaking audience in an unbiased fashion.[58]

As we will see, this notion of making an intentional and intellectual choice to commit herself to Islam was one of her primary bases of appeal to other Muslims. In other words, for Jameelah, any true Muslim would feel emotionally disturbed by living in suburban postwar New York. From this point of view, the mental illness that she suffered was a result of the broader pathology of US society, which could only be remedied by turning to Islam. Upon her release in 1959, Jameelah endeavored to find her place within a Muslim community.

Conclusion

The affective politics of postwar American Judaism are essential for understanding Jameelah's religious imagination and the emotional currents that animated it. The anxiety and ambivalence that undergirded Jewish debates about assimilation and acculturation became a key feature of Jameelah's writings about Islam and Muslims. In particular, Jameelah saw the loss of religious distinctiveness as a core crisis of modernity, brought about by a materialist ethos that was rotting society from within. Most importantly, Jameelah developed a deep conviction that communities who embraced an optimistic, joyful contemporary politics had lost their way. By contrast, authentic religious communities expressed a constellation of negative feelings—anxiety, ambivalence, disgust, and grief—that coalesced into the anti-modern affect that would define Jameelah's vision for building global Muslim solidarity.

As the remaining chapters explore, Jameelah's religious authority continued to be constructed, in part, through her American and

Jewish identities. Her conversion story positioned her as a mediating figure between the two opposing categories that she envisioned and sought to maintain: "Islam" and the "West."[59] Jameelah emphasized that, through her American, Jewish, middle-class identities, she retained an embodied, insider knowledge of American culture. These connections to America were facilitated by her ongoing relationship with her parents, Herb and Myra. While she never returned to the US, Jameelah wrote regularly to her family, often asking for her mother to send magazines and books so that she could stay updated on recent political developments. Myra obliged, making it possible for Jameelah to pursue the middlebrow approach that would become her staple. The Marcuses also came to visit her in Pakistan twice, once each in the 1970s and the 1980s.

As a result of these ongoing American links, the aspects of Jameelah's identity that she most forcefully rejected were the most crucial for establishing her position as a Muslim authority. Her positionality functioned as the starting point through which she claimed the ability to speak for Islam as a distinct, superior faith. At the same time, the continuities of Jameelah's life and corpus demonstrate that we often cannot determine which parts of ourselves resonate most with others and that, try as we might, we often cannot shed aspects of our upbringing that we may come to reject.

2

Discovering Islam in New York City

AS WE saw in the previous chapter, Jameelah's global Muslim imagination was indelibly shaped by her postwar Jewish upbringing and her journey of spiritual experimentation. I now turn to the brief yet consequential period (1958–61) when Jameelah became Muslim and launched her career as a public intellectual.

The vibrant religious, cultural, and intellectual networks of postwar New York City made Jameelah's distinctive trajectory possible. After her release from the hospital in 1958, she began to seek out Muslim communities and resolved to formally convert. The city had a plethora of Muslim institutions, and Jameelah easily found her way into several, namely on college campuses and at the Islamic Mission in Brooklyn. Both kinds of spaces were characterized by their ethnic and racial diversity, as well as their openness to converts. Black Sunni communities played an important yet underappreciated role in generating Islamic revival in the US. The Islamic Mission had a formative impact on Jameelah, expanding the aspirational dimensions of her transnational religious imagination and cultivating her activist orientation to religious practice.

Jameelah's participation in multiple Muslim communities did much more than transform her religious identity. These experiences generated a profound dissonance between her observations of the imperfect religious practices that she observed among her fellow Muslims and the pristine Islam of her imagination. This gap would form the affective center of her writing for decades to come. Just as important, Jameelah came to see herself as possessing special insight into the dangers that such dissonance posed to the survival of Islam.

By charting Jameelah's participation in Muslim spaces, I show how she began to lean into negative collective emotion as the basis for religious solidarity. I argue that this affective impulse amplified tensions around racial difference and religious authority in her vision for Muslim unity. Jameelah believed that she need only *feel* Muslim or Arab in order to authoritatively speak on behalf of a community oppressed by modernity's unrelenting evils. Jameelah made ample use of the malleability of racial and ethnic identities in postwar New York, sometimes emphasizing her whiteness, sometimes rejecting it, all the while never acknowledging or perhaps realizing, that she was doing so. Whereas Muslims and Arabs had to maintain the purity of their inherited culture and religion, she possessed the capacity to appropriate and play with multiple identities.

The romanticization of Arab "others" helped Jameelah to reimagine a place and time in which the recovery of a distinctive religious identity was possible. This utopic imagination placed Jameelah squarely within what Zareena Grewal calls narratives of "American Muslim countercitizenship."[1] Through these multiple affective attachments to timeless people and places, Jameelah created a "moral geography" that set the morally bankrupt West against a pure, authentic East.

Jameelah's sense of her capacities was also honed through intellectual exploration at libraries and universities. Through reading, she began to develop affective attachments to many "others," whom she saw as essential to the project of building Muslim solidarity. At the New York Public Library, Jameelah discovered new cultural worlds and the richness of Islamic thought. The library's extensive collections gave Jameelah access to a wide range of Muslim thinkers, including the revivalist periodicals where she read key thinkers and where she would soon publish her first series of articles. Jameelah fashioned herself an expert in much more than her new religion. She also set about making herself an authority in a wide variety of fields, reading widely in European and American philosophy, feminism, sociology, and Buddhism.[2] While she had dropped out of college, she enrolled in single courses at New York University in comparative religion, which exposed her to academic arguments about Islam, against which she developed many of her core ideas.

In just three years, Jameelah moved through a remarkable number of religious and intellectual spaces in postwar New York City and began to make a name for herself in transnational Muslim publishing networks. Not many American Jewish young adults traversed such a wide array of religious and academic communities. Few self-styled intellectuals gain recognition so quickly. In 1960, her first article appeared in the South African publication *The Muslim Digest* under the name "Margaret Marcus." She came to feel that she was a Muslim intellectual, and other Muslims began to see her that way too.

Through *The Muslim Digest*, Jameelah gained a platform through which she honed her brand as a middlebrow Muslim authority. She aimed to make complex ideas accessible to primarily English-speaking, middle-class audiences. Jameelah selected quotations from scholars such as Mawdudi to distill Islamic law into a set of clear instructions. She explained academic concepts such as modernization theory to demonstrate the complicity of Western scholarship in the colonial enterprise. And she relied on middlebrow sources to provide her readers with insights into American culture and politics, making ample use of periodicals such as *Reader's Digest* and *Time*. Jameelah deftly wove together an astonishing variety of sources to construct an easily digestible declension narrative. Through this bricolage of seemingly disparate sources, she sought to cultivate a coherent set of negative affects—shame, disgust, anxiety—through which her readers could build religious solidarity.

Finding Other Muslims

The first Muslims Jameelah met personally were university students. Indeed, many twentieth-century converts found their way to Islam through meeting Muslim students on college campuses.[3] Through an unnamed Jewish friend who had also become interested in Islam, Jameelah began attending Muslim Students Association (MSA) meetings at Columbia University around 1959–60. It is difficult to estimate the size of this and other organizations started by international Muslim students during this era, but they were likely small, perhaps a few dozen students at each campus. Muslim students became important conduits for the conversion of a small number of both American Jews and white Christians. Similar to Jameelah, these converts largely found their way to Islam through academic study and English translations of Muslim texts,[4] having sought alternative communities of belonging after feeling similarly "out of place."[5] Muslim students were also likely an important channel for Jameelah's discovery of the works of Mawdudi and other contemporary Muslim thinkers, which were translated into English by Muslim students by the 1950s.[6] A decade later, as we will see in chapter 6, Jameelah's work would be reproduced in MSA publications, exported back to the cultural context that she had rejected.

In her recollections of this time, Jameelah sparsely narrated the spiritual transformation that she was undergoing. Instead, she spent far more time lamenting the lax ritual observance that she observed among her fellow Muslims. Jameelah found plenty wrong with the way Muslim students practiced their Islam. She described her shock that many Muslim students did not perform daily religious observances such as prayer and flouted prohibitions around drinking alcohol. To Jameelah, individual piety became a proxy for political orientation. The Muslim students who did not perform their prayers were the same ones who tried to convince her that "Kemal Ataturk was a good Muslim."[7]

Seeking guidance on how to observe the ritual requirements of Islam, Jameelah began to visit local mosques. In January 1961 she visited the Islamic Foundation of New York to learn from Dr. Nuruddin Shoreibah. Dr. Shoreibah taught Jameelah the five daily prayers in Arabic and how to prepare for fasting during Ramadan for the first time.[8] Founded in 1957, the Islamic Foundation of New York (likely the New York Mosque Foundation) was located on 72nd Street and Riverside Drive.[9] The mosque was founded in the wake of the establishment of the United Nations headquarters in New York City, which brought a new influx of Muslim diplomats and other elites to the city.[10] Like its other imams, Dr. Shoreibah was a graduate of Al-Azhar University in Egypt; Jameelah took pride in her connections to a scholar with such a vaunted lineage.

Jameelah's path to Islam was more profoundly shaped by the diverse and growing set of Black Muslim communities in New York City. She formally converted to Islam at the Islamic Mission in Brooklyn on May 24, 1961 by taking the *shahada*, or declaration of faith. She received her "Islamic Certificate of Adoption" from Shaykh Daoud Faisal. Following her conversion, she reported that she had taken the name "Maryam Jameelah," with which she would "henceforth sign all correspondence and writing."[11] Her conversion at the Islamic Mission demonstrates the prominent role of Black Sunni leaders in converting new Muslims and its prominence in New York City's Muslim circles. It is not entirely clear how Jameelah became acquainted with Shaykh Daoud and Mother Khadija. Yet her presence at the State Street Mosque testifies to the couple's broad influence in the city. In 1939 Shaykh Daoud Faisal and his wife Khadija, who were both immigrants from Granada, opened the State Street Mosque, which served as a major Sunni community for diverse groups of newly arrived immigrants and Black workers who moved through New York's port economy, as well as students and diplomats.[12] By the time Jameelah walked through the Islamic Mission's doors, Faisal and his wife Khadija had been leading the mosque community for nearly three decades; Shaykh Daoud had become the most prominent Sunni Muslim leader in postwar New York.[13]

The Islamic Mission was one among many communities that developed new spiritual capacities and alternative constructions of Black selfhood, ancestry, and history.[14] Through them, Jameelah became enmeshed in an international community of Muslims in New York City that embraced a "Black Muslim cosmopolitanism."[15] These communities were crafting a range of religio-racial identities and envisioning new strategies for building a more just society.[16] Movements such as the Moorish Science Temple and the Nation of Islam carved out new possibilities for religious community and racial identity through Islam. The Nation of Islam had a strong presence in the city, having opened Temple No. 7 (the first in New York State) in Harlem in 1946. Brooklyn was another epicenter for Muslim community and practice in the 1940s and 1950s.

Most importantly for Jameelah's trajectory, these Brooklyn-based communities were also steeped in transnational revivalism. The Islamic Mission was a key vector through which Jameelah embraced revivalism as the solution to modernity's problems.[17] The State Street Mosque exposed Jameelah to several key strands of global Muslim thought, including Islamic internationalism and anti-colonialism, that resonated across her corpus. Shaykh Daoud was a staunch critic of white Christianity for its complicity in the transatlantic slave trade and the ongoing legacy of economic inequality and political disenfranchisement that continued to oppress Black people in the US.[18] He also articulated an anti-colonial message and drew parallels between the experiences of colonized peoples across Asia, Africa, and the Americas, which became a central affective node in Jameelah's project.[19] At the Islamic Mission, Jameelah also learned about American Muslim efforts to forge religious solidarity across racial, ethnic, and national differences. The mosque was also part of a multiracial group of Muslim organizations in New York that spanned the world wars and at various times formed umbrella groups to coordinate their activities, the most successful of which was the Federations of Islamic Associations of the United States and Canada in the early 1950s.

Although Jameelah was inspired by her encounters with actual Muslims, she grew increasingly troubled by her observations that American Muslims suffered from the same religious deficiencies as American Jews. Much to her chagrin, she began to suspect that Muslims did not always, or even usually, prioritize the religious over the material in the way that she believed was necessary. That members of the one true religion did not adhere to its tenets amplified Jameelah's sense of impending doom. As one example, she recounted a 1959 conversation that she had with another American Muslim student who was taking courses in Middle Eastern studies:

> When I expressed regret that Arab women were abandoning their traditional dress for the modern she asked me what that had to do with Islam? Couldn't the women believe in Allah and the Holy Prophet just the same wearing a mini skirt? . . . I replied the letter lives in the spirit and the spirit demands its concrete cultural expression in human society if it is to survive and grow. . . . Next to a man's body, his clothes are the nearest things to his soul and have tremendous potentialities for corruption or purification. Every civilization without exception has its definite, physical appearance; the inward is expressed in the outward; the spirit in the tangible reality.[20]

As a convert, Jameelah positioned herself as possessing insight into the true Islam. Too many Muslims born into the faith had lost their connection to visible markers of piety that were essential to the practice of religion. Note here that Jameelah collapsed Arab identity into Islam, such that wearing Arab "traditional" dress was solely an expression of religious, not ethnic identification. Within her moral geography, "Islam" was the only religion that retained a stable core impervious to the changes demanded by the contemporary world. The binary choice between corruption and purification required Muslims to hold fast against encroaching Western materialism. Muslims needed to once again become creators of culture rather than imitators. Clothing was a primary means of accomplishing that aim.

Despite her experiences in a multiracial community at the Islamic Mission, Jameelah continued to idealize Arabs as true Muslims and to measure her fellow Muslims against those romanticized representations. As we saw in the previous chapter, long before Jameelah met actual Muslims, she had dreamed of the lands of the "East"—and especially its Arab, Muslim inhabitants—as authentically religious and morally praiseworthy. Along with Jews, Arab people were one of her most frequent artistic subjects, and in her drawings they were always clad in what Jameelah envisioned as "traditional" dress. As pictured in this pastel drawing, *Scene on a Third-Class Railway Car in Tunisia / 1946 Age 12* (fig. 2.1), men and young boys sit on wooden benches. The man in the foreground wears a bright red fez and a striped, blue robe. The boy who accompanies him is wearing a simple white tunic and trousers. Sitting in the row behind the two figures is a woman wearing a white face veil and a garment that resembles a chador.

No one in the drawing is wearing European clothing, even though men's suits had by then become fairly common in Tunisia.[21] For Jameelah, being authentically religious required a humble, impoverished state. She imagined an authentic Arab community made up of practitioners who eschewed material comforts in favor of spiritual aims—and who represented their ethnic and religious distinctiveness through their modest, simple dress. Being a true Muslim required a visible, symbolic expression of that core identity. Thus, encountering Muslims who did not conform to Jameelah's imagination created a deep well of moral concern, which then translated into the conviction that she needed to carry the mantle of authentic Islam.

Feeling Muslim

As she was formally converting and learning how to perform the basic rituals of her new religion, Jameelah began to *feel like* she had become a real Muslim. One way that she expressed her new identity was to wear long dresses and to cover her hair in a headscarf.

FIGURE 2.1. Maryam Jameelah, *Scene on a Third-Class Railway Car in Tunisia / 1946 Age 12*, 1946. Pastel drawing. Manuscripts and Archives Division, New York Public Library.

These practices signaled her belonging to Islam as a faith, but even more importantly, Jameelah believed that her sartorial choices transformed her into a racial other in the eyes of other Americans. This experience produced an intense set of emotions:

> When I entered my adolescence and learned these facts [of colonization] my first reaction was profound revulsion against such horrors. I wanted to dissociate and disown myself from the civilization responsible for these atrocities. I was overcome with the shame of being Western, of being white. I wished instead that I had been born colored and from then on, I identified myself *emotionally* with the oppressed, colored people of Asia and Africa. During this mental awakening, when I was learning the truth about the West, if a stranger on the street identified me as English, I felt insulted but if another stranger mistook me for a Syrian Arab, I would feel happy and highly complimented.[22]

Although Jameelah sometimes emphasized the "not quite white" of being Jewish in postwar America, here she underscored her whiteness and her Americanness, and the emotions that those identities elicited in her. Feeling revulsion at the collective responsibility of colonialism was incumbent on all white people. For Jameelah, donning "Arab" dress, which she saw as a marker of non-white identity, would help to remove the shame of being white. It is hard to imagine how or why Jameelah would have been mistaken for an Arab, much less a specifically Syrian Arab, in 1950s New York. Moreover, given their complex relationship to whiteness, few Syrian Arabs were likely to recognize themselves in her description.[23] Rather, this episode foregrounds how Jameelah's own understanding of being Muslim was refracted through a romanticization of religious and racial otherness.

Being recognized as non-white made Jameelah feel happy. This expression is significant given that she rarely registered positive emotions, amidst the onslaught of horrors that she regularly cataloged as an astute observer of modernity. Yet the alignment of the "spirit" of a civilization and its public expression was just such an occasion. The public recognition of the performance was equally essential. Indeed, Jameelah's books often included a photograph of her in a full face veil: unmistakably Muslim, signifying her complete rejection of Western culture through her dress. Like many converts, Jameelah was keen to show her zealous commitment to the requirements that she believed Islam made incumbent upon her as a Muslim woman—while also using the paradigmatic symbol of Muslim otherness, the veil, to mark racial difference.

In some ways, Jameelah's description of her attempts to pass as Arab represents a precursor to the lives of contemporary white women such as Jessica Krug and Rachel Dolezal, who have appropriated and claimed Native and Black identities. In the vein of "reverse passing," Jameelah aspired to and performed Arab and Muslim identity over and against an assimilating Jewish one. "Reverse passing" often occurs in settings where racial and ethnic diversity has been commodified or where institutions, such as the courts, take a highly reductive approach to racial diversity.[24] The 1950s, however, did not offer Jameelah incentives, such as educational or employment benefits, for reverse passing. Rather, she sought recognition and acceptance from her fellow Muslims, which she believed hinged on rejecting her whiteness.

While she did not use the term, Jameelah implicitly accused her fellow American Jews of "passing"—that is, being perceived as no different from their Christian neighbors in dress, behavior, and social practices in order to fully enter American society.[25] In turn, this assimilating effort diminished their Jewish distinctiveness. Rejecting this form of passing, Jameelah embraced another, specifically attempting to be perceived as Arab, Syrian, and Muslim, rather than white, American, and Jewish—without seeing that she was herself diminishing her Jewish distinctiveness by assimilating into the Muslim culture as she did.

This passage created an implicit yet unmistakable contrast between Jameelah's racial and religious identities—which were malleable, intentional, achievable—and those of her fellow Muslims. Jameelah presented herself as being denied access to an authentic spiritual faith in postwar America, and yet her journey of experimentation and self-discovery of Islam was made possible by the social conditions of her youth. While all Muslims, including Muslims born into the faith, must make the intentional choice to redouble their commitments to Islam, for many the path to doing so was far more constrained and far less experimental than what Jameelah was able to carve out for herself. And yet she judged them for their choice; she considered them to be marked by the false "crime" of conversion to Western materialism without taking into account how different their experiences were—and how much greater her resources were.[26]

Jameelah's selective appeal to whiteness and Arabness complicated her capacity for affective solidarity with Black Muslim communities, who shared some of her goals and had in fact begun to enact them. She appropriated what Sylvia Chan-Malik calls "affective insurgency"—a positionality that emerged out of Jameelah's religious conviction that the dominant racial and gender politics in the US were fundamentally unjust.[27] Though she never acknowledged these influences, Jameelah drew on an affect of insurgency embodied by Muslim women of color, who practiced Islam as a religion of "againstness" in response to hegemonic structures of race, gender, and class that marginalized them as social others.[28] As Chan-Malik puts it, "Feeling Muslim is to move through the world with the knowledge that both your body and your religious beliefs—the misperceptions of your internal and external states—rouse fear, loathing, and violence in others."[29] Jameelah herself described the strongly negative reactions she got from others, including her family, in response to her conversion; she put forward this reception as evidence that she had embraced the true religion. The fact that she was defying social norms and enduring the consequences of that defiance made Jameelah even more committed to her alternative path as well as to convincing others that they, too, should take a similar stand.

Moreover, she certainly echoed insurgent aspects of Muslimness and "non-liberal" frameworks that focused on women's roles.[30] Chan-Malik shows that the "insurgent domesticity" of Black Muslim women elevated domestic spaces and caregiving practices as "sites of political struggle."[31] As Ula Taylor argues, the Nation of Islam was "unapologetically patriarchal," which appealed to many Black women who wanted to strengthen their families while also garnering respect and agency within the domestic setting.[32] Jameelah similarly amplified the family and the home as affectively potent, and saw Islam as the only path through which aspirational ideals of domesticity could be achieved and a moral civilization restored.[33]

At the same time, Jameelah leveraged whiteness strategically and in ways that undermined her claim to be dismantling the racial hierarchies that harmed her fellow Muslims. Jameelah believed that she need not experience segregation or other structural manifestations of anti-Black racism; she only needed to *feel* that she identified with that oppression to speak on behalf of other Muslims. She elided the shame of her whiteness with the experiences of oppression. Moreover, the ease with which she presented herself as crossing racial and religious boundaries ("English" in one moment, "Syrian Arab" in the next) evinced the mobility that her racial and socioeconomic position afforded her. Jameelah made use of the malleability of racial and ethnic identifications in Muslim and Arab spaces during the 1960s and 1970s, sometimes emphasizing her whiteness and sometimes rejecting it—all the while never acknowledging that she was doing so.

Moreover, Jameelah completely ignored, or was perhaps unaware of, Black Muslim women who advocated for similar gendered norms and practices as those that she sought to enact. Many Black Muslim women of Jameelah's generation found protection and dignity in the face of white supremacy through Muslim community and practice that centered their specific contributions as wives and mothers.[34] With the notable exception of Mother Khadija—whom Jameelah acknowledged only much later as a key influence—she engaged solely with white feminist thinkers to pursue her critique of the West as excessively exploitative of women. The next chapter will explore these claims more fully, but here I want to flag that Jameelah, who converted in a transnational Black Sunni community, did not see fellow US Muslim women as worthy of emulation—or even of mention—for their efforts in advocating for the protection and dignity of women through an Islamic framework.

At the same time, Jameelah was keen to place herself on par with famous male Muslims who had transnational reach, namely Malcolm X. Her affinity for Malcolm X reveals the affective stakes around religion and race that she wanted her story to evoke. In one passage she described Malcolm X as going through the "same experience" as she did:

> Only after I studied and finally embraced Islam did I discover, just as did Malcolm X during the last year of his life, that the fault of the white man was not his race but his ideology. It was only after I settled in Pakistan and met so many westernized Pakistanis that I learned how quickly and easily the brown man can become mentally and culturally indistinguishable from the white and just as ready to commit the same crimes once he has been converted to the white man's materialistic outlook on life.[35]

Much like true religion, Jameelah imagined racial hierarchies and identities to be universal, resonant across cultural and national contexts. She had expected that formerly colonized peoples would be lining up to oppose capitalism's excesses out of "natural" affinity with traditional ways. But she came to believe that even formerly colonized people were just as likely to perpetuate economic exploitation. Her years in Pakistan had shown her what she had only intuitively discerned from the US—that the pernicious threat of materialism was strong enough to wrench the "brown man" from his authentic, indigenous cultural heritage.

While Black Muslim communities had a formative influence on Jameelah's conversion story, these threads were nearly absent in the autobiographical passages in her writing from the 1960s and 1970s. She had not wanted to be bogged down by the particularities of the American Muslim experience; she wanted to be seen as unmoored from her specifically American context, a spokesperson for Islam in a universal sense. Malcolm X was the only American

Muslim figure whom she invoked as speaking to a shared Muslim experience. Though she had sought to insert herself into a global revivalist community rooted in the postcolonial experience, she had not acknowledged the important transnational networks in the US that had informed her religious imagination during the period of her conversion. Instead, the significance of her early encounters with global Islam as mediated through the Islamic Mission had been subordinated to the tradition of revivalism and renewal that she traced solely to figures like Mawdudi and Qutb, who aligned with her imagined moral geography of Islam.[36]

However, it is essential to keep in mind that Jameelah's aspirations to racial otherness had a different set of consequences in a non-American context. As the next chapter explores, Mawdudi and the Jamaat-i-Islami saw value in amplifying her American, middle-class identities, and thus did not want her to shed them. Within the universalist ethos of the Jamaat-i-Islami, the conversion of a white, American woman was viewed as an emotionally compelling piece of evidence of Islam's superiority.[37] In one of the many ironies that Jameelah's journey evokes, her path to prominence amplified rather than diminished the very whiteness she sought to downplay. For all her attempts to portray her conversion as complete and irreversible, the conversion narratives that accompanied her books amplified the significance of her identity as an American woman who discerned the superiority of Islam.[38]

Becoming a Religious Expert

If her reading of Pickthall's translation of the Qur'an represented her spiritual conversion, Jameelah's foray into the fields of comparative religion and Islamic studies represented the moment of her intellectual and political transition. Her gradual conversion also entailed the development of her identity as a public intellectual. There are two main ways that Jameelah sought to establish herself as a religious expert: through her formal and informal study of comparative religions and her self-education in Muslim texts and thinkers. In 1959, her parents wanted her to find a paying job—for which reason she later entered a course to become a typist, one of the few careers available to her after leaving university prematurely. Instead, she spent much of her time poring over religious and philosophical texts and pursuing new educational opportunities.

In the 1950s, the field of comparative religions expanded in both the academy and the public square—understanding religion was seen as vital to the humanities more broadly and especially to the fight against communism.[39] In 1959 Jameelah began taking courses in comparative religion taught by Abraham Katsch at New York University. As chair of the Hebrew Department at NYU, Katsch promoted the study of the Hebrew language in institutions of higher learning. He was also a prominent comparativist and archivist who founded NYU's Library of Hebraica and Judaica, through which he built collections including an important set of Cairo Geniza documents. His book, *Judaism in Islam* (1954), made an enduring impression on Jameelah—a text that she would engage throughout her career as an example of all that was wrong with scholarship on Islam.[40]

Jameelah's experiences at NYU deepened her dissatisfaction with both American Judaism and scholarship on Islam that was being published by American scholars. As she wrote in *Islam and Modernism:*

> My professor was a Rabbi who tried to convince his students—all Jews—that Islam was derived from Judaism. Our textbook took each verse from the Qur'an, painstakingly tracing it to its allegedly Jewish sources. His lectures were liberally illustrated with films and coloured slides in praise of Zionism and the State of Israel. Although his real aim was to prove to his students the superiority of Judaism over Islam, he convinced me of just the opposite. . . . When my professor explained that the divine right of the Jews to Palestine had always been a central theme of Judaism, I was instantly repelled by such a narrow-minded conception of God.[41]

Notably, in reporting that she was "instantly repelled"—that is, emotionally repelled—by her professor's analysis of the Qur'an and history of Israel/Palestine, Jameelah portrayed her instinctual reaction as evidence of her authentic commitment to the universalistic theology of God that she found in Islam *and* as evidence of her intellectual proclivities. At this point in her journey, Jameelah had no intellectual counterarguments to her professor's claims. Crucially, his arguments didn't "feel right" to her.[42] And that feeling would later be borne out by extensive reading and studying in the NYPL. What she possessed instead was the proper *affect* when confronted with ideological frameworks that she thought posed existential threats to the survival of Islam. Foregrounding the discernment that emerged from her emotional response, she urged her readers to see their own affective responses as part of a broader intellectual project behind the revivalist mission.

These formative intellectual experiences seemed to have intensified Jameelah's focus on Palestine, which became a fixture of her religious imagination for her entire life. This fascination with Israel/Palestine grew out of Jameelah's engagement with Islam but crucially also Israeli society became the focal point for many Jewish critics of American largess. Opponents of suburban acculturation often idealized Jewish communities in Israel, which they represented as lacking in material possessions but overflowing with authentic spirituality.[43] In this way, Israel became the foil to the supposed complacency of middle-class American life—a representation that had emotional implications, such as collective guilt and anxiety over the future of Jewish religiosity in America. Jameelah's writings reflect this longing for a spiritually richer place where she could interact with people who had more direct access to an authentic existence. A genuine religious life was impossible in the US; one needed to look elsewhere.

The Zionist currents Jameelah observed in academic and congregational settings resulted in a series of culminating moments when she found she "could no longer consider [her]self a Jew at heart."[44] Through this narration of these academic engagements with Zionism, Jameelah sought to convey that her critique was initially rooted in an intuitive, emotional response that was later confirmed by her immersive study of religious politics. She narrated an increasing conviction that Arabs had suffered "terrible wrong" with the creation of Israel and that most American Jewish communities either supported or turned a blind eye to the dispossession of Palestinians. Palestine thus became Jameelah's locus of religious authenticity, with Palestinian Muslims being the true inheritors of a genuine religious existence. In her eyes, Palestinians possessed all the features of Israeli Jews in the American Jewish imagination: they were hard working, sacrificing, devout. But for Jameelah, it was Arab Muslims who had the rightful claim to pursue God's will in Palestine.

Her assessment of the field of comparative religion set up another problem that Jameelah sought to remedy through her life's work: the lack of Muslim scholars who possessed the platforms to contest Western-centric understandings of their faith. Katsch represented a new set of Jewish experts who began to shape narratives about Jews and Judaism in the postwar period. These rabbis, intellectuals, and scholars turned to academic methods—especially social-scientific ones but also humanistic approaches—to "explain themselves to, and, and as, America."[45] There was no analogous set of Muslim intellectuals in the US that Jameelah could find who did this kind of visible work. And in their absence, Jameelah expressed alarm over how Muslims were being unfairly and inaccurately portrayed. The religious identity of the scholar mattered very much to Jameelah; only a Muslim could offer a true accounting of Islam and a Muslim "way of life."

In Jameelah's eyes, the danger posed to Islam by Orientalism was that its methods had seeped into Muslim intellectual and religious spaces on account of its institutional and political support, as well as its ability to disguise its true intentions—that is, to undermine the foundations of Islam from the inside and to transform it, through the guise of comparative religion and interreligious dialogue, into a shell of its true and robust character:

> The primary goal of modern Orientalism is to incite Muslim-named scholars through this pseudo-scientific "research" to dare assert that our Holy Quran and Hadith is either of composite origin and not even revealed to the Holy Prophet or that the Holy Quran, like the Bible and the scriptures of other religions, has undergone change and modification with the passage of time! If this proves to be impossible . . . if under the influence of Orientalism, Muslim-named scholars could come to regard the Holy Quran as merely a book like any other book full of errors or that at best its specific injunctions were intended only for a particular time and place, God forbid, it would *automatically* lose all of its authority and eventually cease to command any obedience or even respect.[46]

For Jameelah, scholarship was never a disinterested enterprise; it was a political one. This through line, first articulated over a decade prior to the publication of Edward Said's 1979 *Orientalism*, revealed the high stakes that Jameelah wanted her readers to grasp regarding the power relations that structured Western scholarship of Islam. According to her narrative, European scholars had an interest in distorting Muslim sacred texts because such misrepresentations undermined the appeal of Islam and thus portended Muslims losing their attachment to their religion. Such a development was a religious crisis with immense political implications. Losing members of the umma meant that Muslims would lack the strength to combat the threats of cultural imperialism and capitalist excess. Jameelah was not the first to make this connection, of course, but she did raise the alarm about the erosion of scriptural authority in particularly affective terms.

Echoing her critique of Reform Jews for abandoning what she saw as the core of Judaism and taking up the example of nineteenth-century biblical criticism, Jameelah predicted a similar collapse of religious authority and tradition among Muslims should they start enrolling in American and European graduate programs in the hopes of understanding their faith better. Not only was the

Orientalist enterprise morally corrupt, she claimed, but it was dubious on scholarly grounds as well, a kind of "pseudo" enterprise that disputed basic facts about the origins of Islam.

In describing herself as an expert in comparative religion and the academic study of Islam, Jameelah sought to position herself as a credible critic of the modern academic enterprise—and as an alternative to fellow Muslim scholars who purported to be faithful Muslims and rigorous scholars but who (Jameelah argued) were attempting to undermine the faith. Case in point were Muslim scholars such as Pakistani scholar Fazlur Rahman (d. 1988), who Jameelah declared in 1965 "is so utterly incapable of producing any work of the slightest originality, creativity or independent thinking, what can be expected of his less intelligent followers?"[47] At the time, Rahman was director of the Islamic Research Institute in Rawalpindi, Pakistan, and would go on to become a renowned professor of Islamic thought and Quranic studies at the University of Chicago. Such critiques were one strategy in Jameelah's wider effort to establish herself as an expert in modern Islamic thought in her own right, and as an autodidact and outsider who revealed that formal academic institutions had distorted the "real" history of Islam and Muslims.

Eager for more knowledge of her new faith, Jameelah expanded her intellectual expertise and deepened her commitment to Islam between 1959 and her departure for Pakistan in 1962. Jameelah attributed the practice of reading to her rediscovery of religion as more than an individual, private concern—indeed, it was a whole "way of life." She made a "second home" for herself at the Oriental Division of the NYPL, where she spent "much of her leisure time reading books about Islam." A librarian, Mr. Parr, helped her discover Muslim thinkers and texts. She described how she "became an avid reader of all books and periodicals in English [she] could find on Islamic subjects."[48] In her own telling, fifteen years later, those days spent at the NYPL were formational in her becoming a Muslim. Similarly, many European and American Muslim converts discovered their Islam through reading.[49] Jameelah exemplified this strain of conversion, describing in *Why I Embraced Islam* (1975) how she found the "true meaning" of the Qur'an during one of her many hours in the public library:

> It was then that I learned that a proper and detailed understanding of Holy Quran is not possible without some knowledge of the relevant Hadith, for how can the Holy Text correctly be interpreted except by the Prophet to whom it was revealed? . . . The teachings of the Holy Quran, made even more explicitly by Hadith, were thoroughly compatible with my temperament. When I embraced Islam, my parents, relatives and their friends regarded me almost as a fanatic, because I could think and talk of nothing else. To them, religion is a purely private concern which at the most perhaps could be cultivated like an amateur hobby. But as soon as I read Holy Quran, I knew that Islam was no hobby but life itself![50]

Her emphasis on having embraced the true meaning and interpretation of the Qur'an and hadith in the public library, as opposed to in a Muslim institution of learning, echoes the message that she is a scholar in her own right, having found for herself the pure and original interpretation of the Qur'an in the Prophet Muhammad's own words and deeds. While her family and friends saw her as an "irrational fanatic," or indulging a new fad, Jameelah presents her intellectual journey as culminating in a rational recognition of her true self in the sacred sources of Islam.

At the library she found the works of prominent converts to Islam, whom she later used to affirm her role of cultural mediator. She was especially inspired by Muhammad Asad (d. 1992), the Austrian Jewish convert whose memoirs *The Road to Mecca* and *The Crossroads of Islam* spurred her interest in Islam. Asad's account of his own conversion and descriptions of traveling through Saudi Arabia and Pakistan gave Jameelah a window into a possible life that promised the reconciliation of her identity as a Muslim who did not belong in postwar America but in a cultural context where she would presumably find recognition. By invoking Asad, who also left his country of origin for a more authentically Muslim place, Jameelah rendered her own eventual departure from the United States more legible. Jameelah also found in Asad a possible model for her to emulate as a fellow former Jew. Asad showed that a whole career could be made as a liminal observer who moved between two separate entities—"Islam" and "the West"—while claiming the credibility and authenticity of a true Muslim. Jameelah sought to create for herself a similar position from which she could influence and critique other Muslim intellectuals.[51]

Jameelah thus used her discovery of Asad's story to mark her transition from a critic of postwar American Judaism to a critic of Muslims who capitulated to the same allure of Western materialism and nationalism. She was fascinated by Asad's critique of the West as spiritually inauthentic and by his descriptions of how much Muslims had lost their greatness under the onslaught of modernity. As we have seen, Jameelah was staunchly critical of her parents and their friends for giving up their religious distinctiveness as they blended into tri-faith America. In Asad's memoirs, she discovered that Muslims were also giving up those essential practices that marked them as distinctively Muslim. Writing to Mawdudi in 1961, Jameelah expressed disdain for Muslim figures who wore "Western clothing" and were "clean-shaven." She wrote that, of such a man, she "cannot help but consider his faith defective because in his dress, he is advertising to the world that he is ashamed by his identity. Have you read *Islam at the Crossroads* by Muhammad Asad which takes up this subject at length?"[52] By invoking Asad, Jameelah positioned herself as an arbiter of culture and religion with the ability to select the religious and cultural features that mattered in the bifurcation between a Muslim "way of life" and a Western one. As such, dress was very important in marking the distinction between the two opposing entities; it was also an exterior practice that exposed a person's moral and religious interior self.

Like many other Jewish and American converts to "Eastern" faiths, Jameelah believed that tapping into the timeless wisdom of traditional cultures would help solve the woes plaguing Western modernity. In this way, while Jameelah was critical of "Orientalism" in its academic sense, she enthusiastically embraced elements of Orientalism in its cultural manifestations as an alternative to a stagnant, empty American culture. Historian Marc Baer describes a similar logic at work in the writings of Hugo Marcus (no relation, as far as I know, to Jameelah's family), a Jewish convert to Islam in Weimar Germany. Marcus believed that the deep social and economic crises of his society required a religious renewal that could be accomplished through mass conversions of Germans to Islam, in order to address their political and cultural challenges.[53] The slogan "Islam is the Solution" is most closely associated with the rise of Islamism in Arab contexts, and it is certainly an idea that Jameelah herself endorsed. But the concept of Islam as offering a panacea to the ills of the modern world more broadly was also widely resonant for European and American converts who were inspired by the wisdom of the East. Jameelah's story also resonates with the experiences of Jewish converts to Buddhism, who were drawn to faiths outside of Judaism because they were turned off by their parents' materialism and sought an alternative religion that could solve problems such as poverty and racism.[54] Whether drawn to Islam or to Buddhism, Jameelah's and other Jewish convert trajectories of the twentieth century speak to the creative combinatory, transnational threads that characterize modern religious lives. In one of many ironies of Jameelah's journey, it was precisely this kind of religious, cultural, and religious complexity that she would soon be keen to flatten among her fellow Muslims.

Between *Reader's Digest* and *The Muslim Digest*

Jameelah's literary sources and publishing venues further reflected these combinatory threads. Although she did not earn a college degree, Jameelah was a dedicated autodidact who loved reading and wanted to write books that appealed to a broad audience. She grew up in a liberal religious context in which reading was imbued with moral significance.[55] Additionally, books on religious topics were highly desired in postwar publishing venues. Major publishers added books about religion to their lists and promoted reading as a ritual act that produced good citizens. Middlebrow novels, film, serials, and literature also had a significant impact on how American Jews saw themselves in relation to their fellow Americans and, in turn, how Americans saw them. These publications transformed Judaism into a "middle-class, mainstream religion" and amplified the religious dimensions of Jewish identity.[56]

Jameelah was particularly drawn to the middlebrow approach of *Reader's Digest*. She was an avid reader of the magazine in her youth; her parents continued to send her copies long after she left the US. Seeking to cultivate "consumer-citizens," *Reader's Digest* offered American readers a digestible account of global events.[57] Along with other middlebrow publications, the magazine constructed an uplifting affective framework to make sense of Cold War politics, imparting interpretations that made readers feel good about themselves and about America's place within the world.[58] *Reader's Digest* was the second best-selling magazine of the twentieth century, behind only *TV Guide* in subscriptions. Rather than construct a feel-good narrative about the place of Muslims in the contemporary world, Jameelah offered up a middlebrow narrative of decline, replete with negative emotions such as shame, disgust, and sadness.

For Jameelah, as for other Muslim intellectuals of the twentieth century, the written word was also essential to building a resurgent umma. Reading publics were central to the project of reviving Islam as embraced and articulated by a range of twentieth-century South Asian Muslim communities, who competed for readers, devotees, and practitioners through mass-produced texts.[59] Even before she formally converted, Jameelah's first published work appeared in *The Muslim Digest*. Published under the auspices of the World Federation of Islamic Missions—a missionary organization founded by the scholar and preacher Maulana Mohammad Abdul Aleem Siddiqui al-Qaderi (1895–1954)—*The*

Muslim Digest was a prominent revivalist publication based in South Africa. It appealed to English-speaking Muslims in the UK and the US, as part of global revivalist publishing networks that linked South Asia with South Africa.[60] Early in her spiritual and intellectual journey, Jameelah identified it as a place to publish her own writings. It is quite possible that she discovered the publication in the New York Public Library, which maintained an active subscription and circulated the periodical in the 1950s, though it is less clear how she went about submitting her first article. *The Muslim Digest* featured short, accessible pieces reporting on current events, describing the activities of global Muslim scholars and intellectuals, and emphasizing the importance of Muslim rituals such as fasting for Ramadan. It is also how Mawdudi recognized Jameelah in the first place when she wrote to him, because she had published in the same venue that he had.

Jameelah published her first article in *The Muslim Digest* in March 1960. The piece, a critical review of Wilfred Cantwell Smith's *Islam in Modern History*, appeared under the name Margaret Marcus in the annual Ramadan issue. Through the article, Jameelah commenced a lifelong, one-sided argument with the renowned scholar of Islamic studies and religious studies. (Smith would later found McGill University's Institute of Islamic Studies and become director of Harvard University's Center for the Study of World Religions.) Smith functioned as Jameelah's prime example of Western scholarship and the danger it posed to Muslims and Islam. In the piece, she took issue with Smith's concerns about corruption and political conflict within the newly created state of Pakistan, offering that "Islam is more than a religious faith. It is a complete civilization, which in both theory and practice is antithetical to Hindu culture. . . . In order for Islamic civilization to find full freedom of expression, there had to be a Pakistan."[61] As we will explore in the next chapter, in this and other early articles, Jameelah articulated key points that resonated with Mawdudi's vision and that caught his attention: Islam was a distinct system that was irreducible and incompatible with other world systems, including other religions; it encompassed all of social life, including politics and government; and Muslims had to cultivate an activist religious identity in order to live out their obligations as Muslims.

At stake in this piece was who had the authority to speak on behalf of Islam. Jameelah believed that Smith was a disingenuous thinker, a charge that she brought against many non-Muslim scholars. Any claim to objectivity with respect to Muslims was in fact (according to Jameelah) nothing more than another Orientalist intent on dismantling true Islam. In other words, she believed it was impossible for an outsider to accurately convey her new faith's core truths. Curiously, Jameelah did not extend this prohibition to her own pronouncements on religions to which she did not belong, such as Christianity, and nor did she hesitate to cast judgment on Muslims before she became a Muslim. Nevertheless, the identity of the scholar made all the difference for Jameelah. She resolutely argued that Muslims ought to be given the opportunity to represent the truth of their own faith on their own terms. The prominence of non-Muslims such as Smith in academic positions and centers, which gave them an outsized platform and financial resources in representing Islam to the broader world, deeply troubled Jameelah because it smacked of colonialist designs to control Muslim education and its youth.

This middlebrow approach was also compelling in the context of the expansion and democratization of Muslim publishing in the twentieth century. European colonial governance had fragmented and displaced local educational institutions, created new schools that marginalized traditional Muslim authorities and the Islamic sciences, and encouraged new pathways for elite status through the English language and the introduction of European models of higher education. Meanwhile, increased literacy, cheaper publishing technologies, and a cosmopolitan literary culture enabled new authors and intellectuals to emerge, including prominent revivalists such as Mawdudi and Sayyid Qutb—who also followed unconventional educational and professional paths and were deeply engaged in comparative political and religious thought. Their landmark interpretative works—Qutb's *In the Shade of the Qur'an* (1951–65) and Mawdudi's monthly periodical *Tarjuman al-Qur'an* (1942–72)—are among the most widely read and cited Islamic texts of the twentieth century.

As she established her writing career, Jameelah became part of a small, disparate, yet influential group of female revivalist thinkers. Writing and publishing was a primary path for Muslim women thinkers to contribute to the revivalist project, but these contributions have not been extensively studied. Instead, scholars have largely explored the role of women in mobilizing local communities toward ritual practices of self-cultivation and the study of Islamic texts—but have paid less attention to the essential role of female intellectuals in shaping the narratives and categories through which Islamic revivalism became a global movement.[62]

Revivalist female authors helped to frame women's bodies, female sexuality, and the nuclear family as the key sites for nurturing Islamic piety and for the emergence of a new kind of Muslim politics.[63] Through the written word, female authors aligned with revivalism have called for the end to the oppressive structures of modernity to make way for a just Islamic society to emerge. Jameelah was one of the earliest authors to achieve this kind of reach, articulating an essential connection between building strong and robust nuclear families and the broader aim of challenging other forms of oppression from colonialism, capitalism, and secularism.

Perhaps because she felt so out of place wherever she lived, Jameelah was always trying to forge affective attachments to strangers.[64] Rather than building relationships with actual people, Jameelah was much more captivated by the possibility of constituting an imagined Muslim public that was laser-focused on mitigating the destructive forces of Western hegemony. Jameelah imagined that she and other Muslims who shared in this opposition to modernity fused into a potentially powerful counterpublic, a vanguard of opposition and resistance to the hegemony of Western modernity.[65]

Conclusion

Jameelah's conversion story offered a compelling narrative to show how feeling Muslim—how feeling, specifically, the anti-modern affect that infused her writings—could overcome the vastly different experiences of marginalization, political disenfranchisement, and economic inequality in the umma. In claiming that she *felt* oppressed, Jameelah's work offered a possible ground through which attachment could be cultivated around the shared feeling of being subjugated by the modern world, even if Muslims had highly disparate experiences of that oppression. Such passages provided an affective road map for other Muslims—suggesting that, whatever racial and national differences divided them, Muslims around the world could feel affinity with one another in their shared rejection of modernity.

Tracing the lives of figures like Jameelah further illuminates the conditions under which transnational religious networks take shape. On the one hand, Jameelah's path to becoming Muslim and a public intellectual was highly unusual. On the other, this period of experimentation and exploration reveals Jameelah to be a paradigmatic American religious figure. Rather than an edge case, Jameelah embodied religious "recombination" in action. She moved into unexpected places and forged relationships with unexpected allies (and opponents) that blurred the boundaries of identities, traditions, and communities. These recombinations and even contradictions are not unique to Jameelah nor to converts.[66] Rather, they point to the contingent identities and attachments that structure modern religiosity. Such unpredictable choices, made by individuals in real time, generate new religious and political possibilities.

Jameelah's journey also demonstrates the crucial role of publishing and translation in the formation of global Muslim publics. Extant scholarship on Islam in America typically identifies the opening of immigration from Asia in the 1960s as the starting point for a broader Muslim presence in the US. Jameelah's story suggests an earlier, different process by which Islamic thought circulated in the US through publishing networks and community spaces that facilitated engagement with revivalist thought. Mawdudi's work in English translation was widely available to Jameelah in varied institutions, namely the Islamic Mission and the New York Public Library. She easily found other publishing venues that expanded upon his vision, such as *The Muslim Digest*. These same distribution and transnational apparatuses would become essential for the dissemination of Jameelah's work and to establishing her as a Muslim authority figure. The next chapter turns to her emigration to Pakistan and the start of her career as a revivalist figure with transnational reach.

3

Generating a Shared Emotional Vocabulary Around Modernity

AS SHE was exploring Muslim communities in New York City, Jameelah also began to write letters to the authors whose work she had encountered at the New York Public Library including Sayyid Qutb and Said Ramadan, among others. Astonishingly, at least one of them wrote back: Abul A'la Mawdudi, the Pakistani scholar and leader of the prominent revivalist organization Jamaat-i-Islami. It was the beginning of a life-changing relationship. Over the following months, he would eventually persuade her to relocate to Pakistan. Through their letters, Jameelah came to see a move to Pakistan as the chance that she had been waiting for—the opportunity to thrive as a Muslim woman. In his first letter to Jameelah, Mawdudi validated her feeling of being out of place: "You seem to be just like an equatorial sapling implanted into the Arctic Zone and you had to face the inevitable. Every person can best grow and shine in a favorable atmosphere. In a hostile climate one is apt to lose or dubbed to have lost one's mental balance and all one's capabilities are likely to wither away. Similar are the reasons for your being still unmarried. Your society can't like the type of women that you are. All your merits are considered as defects there."[1] When I first encountered these letters, I was curious about why Mawdudi responded to Jameelah in the first place. Their interaction seemed perplexing. Why would one of the most famous

Muslim figures of the twentieth century write back to a young American woman who had contacted him out of nowhere? Even more curiously, Mawdudi replied with a generous response. He validated Jameelah's alienation, offering reassurance that her despair was the product of a much larger historical pattern, and not a personal failing on her part. The answers to these questions lie in the shared emotions and interpersonal interactions that often structure transnational solidarity.

This chapter argues that Jameelah's appeal to Mawdudi, and to other revivalists, was primarily affective rather than ideological. A combination of the emotional resonance of Jameelah's story and her expression of "right" feelings made her a compelling revivalist figure. Indeed, a shared emotional vocabulary is what enabled Mawdudi and Jameelah to bridge the cultural differences and the geographic distance that separated them. Mawdudi saw Jameelah as a true Muslim precisely *because* her affective and embodied experience of living in Western society—discomfort, anxiety, and malaise—revealed the clarity and prescience of her vision. Mawdudi thus recognized Jameelah's struggles not as markers of weakness or societal maladjustment but, instead, as signs of religious fortitude and moral strength.

The affinity that Mawdudi and Jameelah cultivated through their letters reveals the matrix of collective emotions at the heart of the global Islamic Revival. They show that Mawdudi understood Jameelah's predicament as a proxy for the broader embattlement of Islam and marginalization of religion in the modern world. The story of her alienation and subsequent conversion amplified the absolute incompatibility of Islam and Western society. Her sufferings proved that the American and European "way of life" posed a mortal threat to Islam as a faith and as a political project.

I use two main sources to explore how Jameelah established herself within global Muslim revivalist networks. First, I delve into the series of letters exchanged by Mawdudi and Jameelah from 1960 to 1962. These letters shaped Jameelah's trajectory in several key ways. One, the exchange catalyzed Jameelah's decision to leave the

United States for Pakistan. Mawdudi first made the offer for her to move to Lahore in February 1961. Their final letters concern her decision and logistical planning to move to Pakistan, which she did in early 1962. Two, the letters provide key insight into Mawdudi's perception of Jameelah and her potential contributions to the Jamaat-i-Islami, namely as an inspirational model for other young Muslims to prioritize their Muslim identity over other identities. Through this correspondence, Jameelah tested out many of the ideas that would become the hallmarks of her corpus. Mawdudi functioned as a crucial audience of one, endorsing her critiques of American materialism and confirming that her negative feelings toward the US were a sign of her profound commitment to Islam.

After delving into the letters, I analyze the conversion narratives that accompanied each of Jameelah's subsequent books and pamphlets. These short biographies of Jameelah, which were typically authored by Jamaat-i-Islami leaders, leveraged her personal story as a means of establishing her credibility as a Muslim intellectual. Told and retold at the start of her publications, these conversion narratives amplified Jameelah's Americanness and Jewishness, thus linking her legitimacy to the nation and religion that she had renounced. I argue that Jameelah's story functioned as a "usable past," as a story that differentiated her from other revivalists and allowed her to break through as a woman in that male-dominated milieu. As a result, Jameelah remained a convert who was always in the process of conversion.

An Unlikely Correspondence

From late 1960 until May 1962, Mawdudi and Jameelah exchanged two dozen letters, ranging in length from just a couple of paragraphs to several thousand words (figs. 3.1 and 3.2). The letters are remarkable, not just for how significantly they shaped Jameelah's life trajectory, but also because they reveal the exceedingly unlikely personal convergence of two individuals: Margaret Marcus, a suburban, upper-middle-class Jewish twentysomething who was

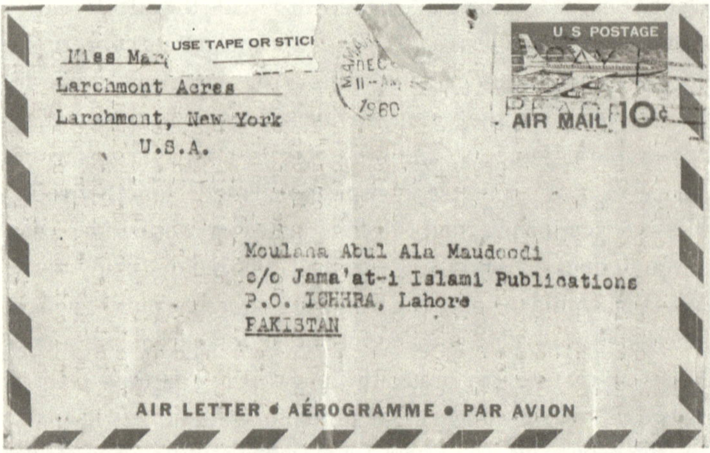

FIGURE 3.1. Postmarked envelope addressed from Maryam Jameelah to Abul A'la Mawdudi, 1960. Manuscripts and Archives Division, New York Public Library.

undergoing a yearslong conversion to Islam after dropping out of university; and Abul A'la Mawdudi, one of the most highly visible and influential transnational Muslim intellectuals and the leader of a powerful political movement—whose influence on Muslim politics extended to the United States, the United Kingdom, and South Africa as well as throughout South Asia and the Arab world.

The earliest documented letter that Jameelah wrote to Mawdudi in Pakistan is dated December 5, 1960. In it she introduced herself and described her desire to become Muslim. Mawdudi penned most of his letters in his native Urdu, though he wrote some sections in English. As Mawdudi explained to Jameelah, his secretary managed correspondence with her and others, and translated the Urdu letters into English.

From the beginning of their correspondence Mawdudi affirmed her choice to reject the religion and culture of her birth and to embark on a most unconventional path. Mawdudi expressed delight and confusion that Jameelah's ideas so closely tracked his

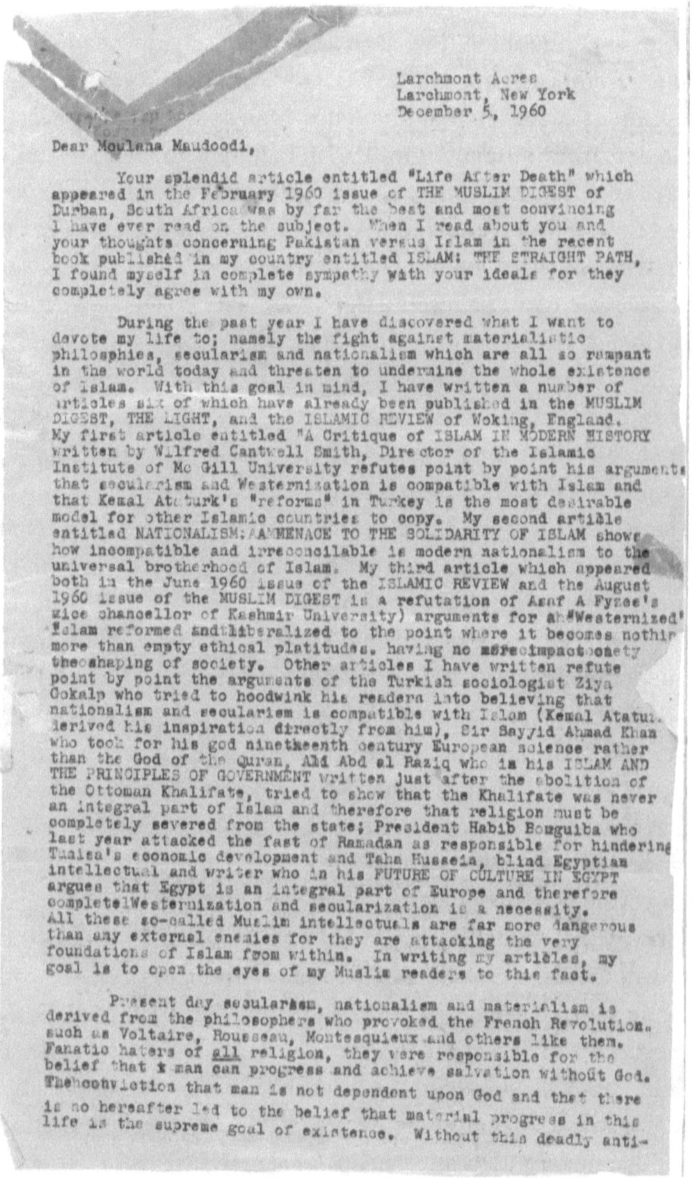

Larchmont Acres
Larchmont, New York
December 5, 1960

Dear Moulana Maudoodi,

Your splendid article entitled "Life After Death" which appeared in the February 1960 issue of THE MUSLIM DIGEST of Durban, South Africa was by far the best and most convincing I have ever read on the subject. When I read about you and your thoughts concerning Pakistan versus Islam in the recent book published in my country entitled ISLAM: THE STRAIGHT PATH, I found myself in complete sympathy with your ideals for they completely agree with my own.

During the past year I have discovered what I want to devote my life to; namely the fight against materialistic philosphies, secularism and nationalism which are all so rampant in the world today and threaten to undermine the whole existence of Islam. With this goal in mind, I have written a number of articles six of which have already been published in the MUSLIM DIGEST, THE LIGHT, and the ISLAMIC REVIEW of Woking, England. My first article entitled "A Critique of ISLAM IN MODERN HISTORY written by Wilfred Cantwell Smith, Director of the Islamic Institute of Mc Gill University refutes point by point his arguments that secularism and Westernization is compatible with Islam and that Kemal Ataturk's "reforms" in Turkey is the most desirable model for other Islamic countries to copy. My second artiàle entitled NATIONALISM: A MENACE TO THE SOLIDARITY OF ISLAM shows how incompatible and irreconcilable is modern nationalism to the universal brotherhood of Islam. My third article which appeared both in the June 1960 issue of the ISLAMIC REVIEW and the August 1960 issue of the MUSLIM DIGEST is a refutation of Asaf A Fyzee's (vice chancellor of Kashmir University) arguments for a "Westernized" Islam reformed and liberalized to the point where it becomes nothing more than empty ethical platitudes. having no more impact on the shaping of society. Other articles I have written refute point by point the arguments of the Turkish sociologist Ziya Gokalp who tried to hoodwink his readers into believing that nationalism and secularism is compatible with Islam (Kemal Ataturk derived his inspiration directly from him), Sir Sayyid Ahmad Khan who took for his god ninetheenth century European science rather than the God of the Quran, Ali Abd el Raziq who in his ISLAM AND THE PRINCIPLES OF GOVERNMENT written just after the abolition of the Ottoman Khalifate, tried to show that the Khalifate was never an integral part of Islam and therefore that religion must be completely severed from the state; President Habib Bourguiba who last year attacked the fast of Ramadan as responsible for hindering Tunisia's economic development and Taha Hussein, blind Egyptian intellectual and writer who in his FUTURE OF CULTURE IN EGYPT argues that Egypt is an integral part of Europe and therefore completelWesternization and secularization is a necessity. All these so-called Muslim intellectuals are far more dangerous than any external enemies for they are attacking the very foundations of Islam from within. In writing my articles, my goal is to open the eyes of my Muslim readers to this fact.

Present day secularism, nationalism and materialism is derived from the philosophers who provoked the French Revolution. such as Voltaire, Rousseau, Montesquieux and others like them. Fanatic haters of all religion, they were responsible for the belief that man can progress and achieve salvation without God. The conviction that man is not dependent upon God and that there is no hereafter led to the belief that material progress in this life is the supreme goal of existence. Without this deadly anti-

FIGURE 3.2. Letter from Maryam Jameelah to Abul A'la Mawdudi, December 5, 1960. Manuscripts and Archives Division, New York Public Library.

own, telling her, "And now I cannot help expressing my pleasant surprise at one thing. I want to know precisely how and why a young American girl could arrive at such a clear and genuine conception of Islam." In that first letter, Mawdudi invited Jameelah and her family to spend Ramadan in Lahore with his own family. He relayed that, though she had not yet formally converted, he was "certain that you are already a Muslim. . . . I find you quite on the threshold of Islam and only one firm step forward will bring you into the fold of the believers. I think this final step will be a natural and logical culmination of your ideas."

In February 1961, Mawdudi mused that she could either "gather a group of sympathizers and co-workers" in the United States or move to Pakistan, and "find yourself amidst many like-minded people barring the language difference. God-willing you will receive here all moral as well as material support and encouragement. Moreover, there is every likelihood that you may find a virtuous young Muslim to be your life-companion." He believed that migration to Pakistan would enable Jameelah to fulfill this foundational aspect of being a Muslim woman.

Jameelah's and Mawdudi's letters focused on three main topics: Jameelah's conversion and concurrent struggles living as a Muslim in the US; the decline of gender roles and other "traditional" practices among both Muslims and non-Muslims; and the existential dangers of nationalism, colonialism, and materialism. Typically, Jameelah raised an issue that she found emotionally troubling or outrageous—usually both. Then she inquired as to whether Mawdudi was aware of the issue, and whether he concurred with her outrage. The two assumed a pattern in which Jameelah posed questions and Mawdudi, in his position as the political and religious authority, provided the definitive answers. Their exchange demonstrated the intertwining of ideological and affective affinities that undergirded this transnational revivalist vision.

The letters reveal that Jameelah did not really understand the extent of Mawdudi's global stature, a point that further underscores the unlikeness of this interaction. Mawdudi, too, had taken an unconventional path to becoming a political leader and Muslim intellectual. Born in 1903 to a prominent Muslim family based in Lahore, he did not initially become educated as a religious scholar. Only later did Mawdudi dive into the Islamic sciences, enmeshing himself in the study of the Qur'an, *fiqh* (Islamic law), and theology. Instead, in the 1930s he became a journalist, a role that gave him insight into the strategic value of the press as well as insight into the British colonial system and the rise of Indian nationalism. Mawdudi became a major player in anti-colonial Indian politics; he wrote on what he saw as the intentional exclusion of Muslims through the elimination of Urdu from Indian educational curricula.[2] He created the Jamaat-i-Islami in 1941 to oppose the Muslim nationalist movement and to establish a vanguard of committed cadres that would promote the Islamization of politics. The organization gained popularity as an alternative to the Muslim League, which had been founded in 1906 in Dhaka (Dacca), British India. When the nation-state of Pakistan was founded in 1947, a branch of the Jamaat-i-Islami remained in India and Mawdudi emigrated to West Pakistan and established in Lahore a political party of the same name, which worked to instill Islamic principles and laws into the new government.[3] Other Jamaat-i-Islami branches were established in neighboring countries such as Afghanistan and East Pakistan (later Bangladesh).

By 1960, Mawdudi had become a prolific and famed writer of wide-ranging books and pamphlets on Islam and the state, Islamic jurisprudence, Quranic interpretation, and the status of women. Through a series of books written in the late 1930s through the early 1950s, Mawdudi's "conservative anti-colonialism" stressed the vital importance of creating an Islam that could withstand the significant challenges posed by nationalism, communism, and materialism.[4] As Humeira Iqtidar explains, Mawdudi "viewed society as a means to individual ethical perfection and his primary concern was with the moral laxity that flowed from the assumption that society could be fundamentally reorganized and 'man-made laws' could replace divine ones."[5]

One of Mawdudi's key contributions to Islamic politics during this period was his concept of *hakimiyya*, or God's sovereignty. As Muhammad Qasim Zaman that the term was "in the air" in colonial India as part of Muslim responses to the drastically increased role of the state in the lives of both Hindus and Muslims under British rule; it was also in the thought of Young Ottoman activists and encapsulated a wide range of meanings.[6] Yet Mawdudi's specific formulation was especially salient and enduring. Starting in the late 1930s, he began to write and lecture about God as the supreme lawgiver, declaring that sovereignty rested with God alone. Muslims who did not recognize *hakimiyya* were committing idolatry, which, as Zaman emphasizes, is "the most heinous of sins in a monotheist's universe."[7] Consonant with his conviction that Islam was a complete way of life that encompassed politics, Mawdudi articulated a clear, simple formulation of the concept, predicated on the binary division of believer/unbeliever. This vision, advanced during a time of immense anxiety about the future of minority Muslim communities against the backdrop of Indian nationalism, helped catapult Mawdudi into a formidable political and religious position. Mawdudi's vision for how to realize *hakimiyya* created an opening for the Jamaat-i-Islami's entry into Pakistani electoral politics after the creation of Pakistan in 1947. The Jamaat-i-Islami grew into a formidable organizational force that openly challenged Pakistan's ruling government to more fully integrate Islamic legal concepts and procedures into governmental institutions. In the process, in splitting into Indian and Pakistani branches, the organization also began to take a more pragmatic rather than ideologically pure approach to politics.

Mawdudi saw modernity as an unrelenting slog, an uphill climb that necessitated sacrifice and difficulty. He argued that Muslims had relinquished the political sphere to secular forces such as materialism and colonialism and now needed to restore divine principles into the governmental structure. By the 1950s, various Pakistani intellectuals and religious scholars, Sufis and modernists, deployed *hakimiyya* in their religious politics; the concept also found purchase among Arab Islamists. Mawdudi's term became a rallying cry for movements engaged in Islamic politics in South Asia and beyond. Sayyid Qutb took up Mawdudi's formulation of *hakimiyya* in his own work, which in turn had a wide influence on the Muslim Brotherhood in Egypt and beyond.

When Jameelah first wrote to him, Mawdudi's reputation as a global Muslim figure had been well established. In addition to his intellectual work, Mawdudi was actively involved in fostering grassroots support for his cause. As he reported to Jameelah, he received a constant stream of invitations to speak at universities, seminaries, and political organizations.[8] This international prominence also contributed to the perception that he and the Jamaat-i-Islami posed a significant challenge to the ruling government. In a letter dated May 19, 1961, Mawdudi wrote to Jameelah about the political constraints under which he operated in Pakistan and his efforts to build transnational religious networks. "It is," he wrote, "a hard, unremitting struggle all the way." At the time, he told her, he was preparing for a trip to Africa to assist Jamaat-i-Islami missionary efforts there. The organization's publishing networks were an important vector for this global prominence; through monthly Urdu publications such as the *Tarjuman al-Qur'an* as well as English-language periodicals such as *The Criterion*, the Jamaat-i-Islam cultivated reading publics across South Asia as well as audiences in the Anglo-American diaspora. As we saw in the previous chapter, Jameelah's discovery of Mawdudi's and other Islamist thinkers' work testifies to the success of these revivalist publishing efforts.

Cultivating Affective Affinity

Jameelah's and Mawdudi's letters demonstrate the essential role that affect played in her ability to cultivate relationships within Muslim communities outside the US. The affinity of the two interlocutors reveals the shared affective vocabulary, a "matrix" of collective emotion, that structured transnational Islamic revivalism in the mid-twentieth century. A rather wide gulf separated the two writers in the early 1960s in terms of age, family life, culture, professional status, and educational background. Indeed, Jameelah appeared to be only marginally aware of the gap in resources, social capital, and influence that separated her and Mawdudi.

At the same time, their letters exposed complicated power dynamics between the pair. As she described herself to Mawdudi, Jameelah believed that "as a woman she had no 'market value.'"[9] These hierarchies denoted the possibilities and constraints that Jameelah's relationship with Mawdudi created for her. Jameelah very much needed Mawdudi more than he needed her. Mawdudi's connections to Muslim organizations, intellectuals, and activists were unparalleled during this period. Though he was under political repression from the Pakistani government, Mawdudi was in high demand around the globe and had several major trips planned—for example, a month-long tour of Africa, or a 1961 trip to Saudi Arabia to help to establish the Islamic university in Jeddah. This makes a stark comparison with a young American woman who, though from a well-off family, had limited options as an unmarried, marginally employed college dropout who was deep into a life-altering spiritual journey.

Letters, on the other hand, facilitated the building of a relationship that was largely unmediated by others. By writing letters, Jameelah had the opportunity to share her ideas directly with the Muslim leader, which would not have been possible face to face. One-on-one, in-person audiences with Mawdudi were restricted by both the Pakistani government and his own Jamaat-i-Islami comrades; moreover, both parties shared convictions about gender segregation and preserving boundaries around interactions between men and women who were not related or part of the same household.

As such, Mawdudi was a crucial sounding board, confirming that she had interpreted his ideas correctly and affirming that her observations of the US would resonate with like-minded Muslims. He also sometimes corrected her when she presented what he saw as erroneous or misleading assessments about Muslim politics and pushed her to read more widely. Mawdudi had enmeshed himself in the project of comparing cultures and religions—through wide-ranging sources, from Kant to the *Encyclopaedia Britannica*—in his quest to determine definitively that Islam was the superior system. Jameelah embraced this eclectic approach; as we have seen, she delved into a broad range of academic approaches and sources.

Mawdudi also provided significant encouragement for Jameelah to take her ideas into the public sphere and that propelled her to dive deeper into the affective dimensions of her writing. In addition to affirming her ideas and emotions, Mawdudi offered to publish her essays and her novel, *Ahmad Khalil*. He encouraged her to send him new materials that could be printed by the "Islamic Publications" press in Lahore and to translate and publish "extracts of her essays and letters, omitting, of course, intimate personal details," in the *Tarjuman al-Quran*. And Mawdudi made good on his promises once Jameelah came to Pakistan, publishing nearly a dozen books and many more pamphlets under Jamaat-i-Islami imprints, and distributing them around the world.

In light of Mawdudi's political and religious status, it is worth dwelling on why he responded to Jameelah in the first place. Several explanations are plausible. First, Mawdudi regularly corresponded with leaders, activists, and scholars around the world.[10] These contacts helped to build global support for his political and religious project. Some of his correspondents were other well-known political figures while others were more obscure—suggesting that Mawdudi did not always have a specific goal when choosing to respond to a letter. Secondly, under the repressive conditions of the regime of President Ayub Khan, the Jamaat-i-Islami had shifted its strategy from the formal political process to redoubling its publishing apparatus, as well as enhancing social services in rural areas. Given that Mawdudi found himself confined to his home more often than previously, he likely had additional time to pursue correspondence and build new supporters as part of accomplishing his broad vision for renewing Islam across society.[11]

Specifically, Jameelah's conversion story resonated with a core aspect of Mawdudi's conviction that being Muslim entailed "an intentional, active commitment to the religion."[12] For Mawdudi, Muslims who merely relied on their inherited faith were insufficiently prepared for the challenges posed by colonialism and nationalism. The Jamaat-i-Islami's membership policy stressed that intentional embrace of Islam was far more important than accident of birth. To join, Muslims needed to declare their intention and commitment by reciting the *kalima tayyiba*, or the declaration of faith. Any Muslim or non-Muslim who demonstrated and declared their commitment, from any region or nation or ethnic background, could join the Jamaat-i-Islami. Jameelah embodied the intentionality and commitment that Mawdudi sought to cultivate in his networks. As a result, she could serve as an exemplar to others: as someone who had chosen Islam and persevered in her choice through difficult circumstances.

Jameelah's story and work were of considerable use for Mawdudi in his efforts to build a broader coalition of young Muslims, in Pakistan and beyond, willing to choose the path of Islam as articulated by the Jamaat-i-Islami. As Mawdudi relayed to Jameelah on June 20, 1961, "I think they will serve as an eye-opener to the Muslim youth . . . here is a young woman born into a 'reformed' Jewish home in modern America who has been struggling for the Truth and who is striving to practice it when she has found it out at last. I hope your example will teach them a lesson." Jameelah's conversion as a white American made her story potentially even more powerful. His repeated marveling about her youth and her gender suggests that he read into her story an innocent, simple narrative of a suffering girl who found respite and belonging in Islam: "I read about your circumstances with great interest and attention. While reading them, I realized how someone of a decent nature, if pure of prejudice and willing to understand the truth can find the right path."[13] Mawdudi saw in her an innate attraction to Islam that he hoped others would find inspirational and worthy of emulation.

Mawdudi was also willing to overlook obvious limitations in Jameelah's linguistic capabilities because her story was so compelling to his cause:

> For the book you want to write about Islam's renaissance, you need to be familiar with Urdu, Persian, Arabic, and Turkish as authentic sources are in these languages alone, and on this topic in English, not only is there very little content but whatever there is has very defective, even distracting, information. However, if you read English books with an extremely critical eye and alertness then maybe to a certain extent you can succeed in your aim. In this endeavor, you can receive my assistance whenever you wish.[14]

Her youthful discovery of Islam outside a Muslim-majority context likely represented to Mawdudi a pure embrace of the true religion. In marveling at how she "could get at such a clear and true conception of Islam" he seemed not to consider the possibility that she arrived at those conclusions by reading his own work—and that of thinkers who were inspired by him, such as Qutb—and was simply echoing his own ideas back to him.[15] While Jameelah was keen to present her conversion as an intellectual enterprise, Mawdudi seemed less interested in that narrative than in preserving her story as an example of Islam's innate superiority, one that could be made plain to anyone living in what he saw as a context hostile to religiosity writ large.

Embodied Intellectual Aspirations

A shared emotional vocabulary was essential to establishing affinity between these two unlikely correspondents. In his first letter, Mawdudi asked that Jameelah share how she came to be interested in Islam. Jameelah responded with an account of her isolation and alienation from her peers, while acknowledging that she benefited from her parents' "tolerance" and support for her conversion. Mawdudi reassured her: "I quite understand your feeling of loneliness for lack of an Islamic society. No doubt this is the most acute agony for a Muslim in a non-Muslim country. But it might give you some consolation to know in the present world, every true Muslim is sharing these pangs of loneliness with you, though it may be to a lesser degree or in a somewhat different way." Jameelah's inability to thrive in her suburban milieu underscored for Mawdudi the incompatibility of Islam and the West and the emotional predicament of Muslims in modernity. Mawdudi's belief in the incommensurability of the two sides of the binary meant that Jameelah's personal trajectory "contained nothing unexpected." Without "mental and moral" support Muslims could not live according to the ideals and norms of Islam, which resulted in frayed nerves and the loss of one's senses. Jameelah's anguished journey reflected the struggle between two conflicting world systems.

Mawdudi understood Jameelah's mental illness as a social problem rather than an individual affliction. His assessment provided a powerful counterpoint to her diagnoses and treatment up until that point. Rather than a medical diagnosis, Mawdudi offered a historical and social explanation for her suffering. He relayed to Jameelah that her mental and emotional breakdown was an understandable, if not inevitable, outcome of living in Western society. It was actually the result of the depth of her anxiety, and her despair was evidence of her elevated status as already being a "true Muslim." Her family and doctors had offered diagnoses, pathologies, and treatments in response to her condition—whereas, for Mawdudi, her confinement represented the culmination of her struggles to become a Muslim in an environment incapable of sustaining her spiritually. It would therefore be "unnatural" if Jameelah had not undergone significant struggles as she underwent her process of conversion.

These letters also attest to the embodied experiences of illness that undergirded Jameelah's and Mawdudi's respective intellectual enterprises. Both writers reported illnesses and ailments to one another and how those experiences fueled their determination to meet their common religious goals. On occasion Mawdudi was delayed in replying to her, for which reason he would offer explanations, such as that he suffered from stomach trouble. He shared his medical test results and even reported on stays in the hospital. In turn, Jameelah was quite open about her ongoing emotional struggles due to her inability to find a community where she belonged.

Such exchanges are far from incidental; rather, they provide an essential window into how even the lives of religious actors with a highly politicized and ideological visions are shaped by their embodied experiences.[16] The intimacy of their letters underscores how shared affects structure the possibilities for transnational religious affinity. Both Mawdudi's and Jameelah's published writings drew rigid moral and political boundaries and condemned others for not living up to ideological purity. And yet, they reveal how the pair saw each other as fellow travelers who were dealing with the emotional impact of their illnesses. These limitations impaired their mobility, but also provided additional motivation to challenge the political and religious injustices that they observed all around them.

The central role of affect in these letters further demonstrates the rich emotional landscape underpinning the writing of two thinkers who are commonly associated with the "ideologization of Islam" in the twentieth century, which is generally associated with two components. First, this orientation reduces Islam to a core, universal set of religious principles and practices that all Muslims should equally follow, regardless of their individual milieu; and second, it politicizes Muslim identity by calling for the Islamization of society. As their letters attest, Jameelah and Mawdudi did affirm these shared ideological positions, but expended far less ink on them. Instead, their affinity was grounded in a mutual affective urgency around the disaster of modernity—and the desire to bring Muslims to a renewed state of being. For Mawdudi, Jameelah's personal struggles were not the private anguish of an alienated suburban girl, but rather the collective emotional state of a Muslim people who had been denied the proper moral conditions under which Islam could thrive. In other words, being a "real" Muslim required much more than declaring one's commitment or observing ritual requirements. It also entailed a proper affective orientation to modernity.

Gender and the Catastrophe of Modernity

In her early letters, Jameelah expected that she would need to educate Mawdudi about the dire state of women in the United States. On March 8, 1961, she attached an article from *Look* magazine about new fashions "which to me are so repulsive that I refuse to conform and would rather be struck dead than seen wearing it. American and European fashion designers appear to do all they can to make the modern Western woman look like a street-walker. Even professional prostitutes do not go to the extremes of these so-called 'respectable' women."[17] The feeling of repulsion was, for Jameelah, the requisite affective response to ordinary American women donning clothes that were "designed exclusively for commercialized sex."

The stakes around dress could not have been higher; Jameelah conveyed to Mawdudi that the so-called "emancipation of women" was in fact their degradation as sex objects to be bought and sold. Jameelah's assessment mirrored Mawdudi's analysis that the core flaw of Western gender practices was the market-based logic upon which they were established. Whether or not they were selling sex, women who dressed in clothing that Jameelah considered to be too revealing were subject to the same capitalist forces as a sex worker. When Jameelah likened women who embarked on professional careers to prostitutes, she compared women who had become part of the labor force for professional and financial reasons with women who were, for her, the ultimate symbol of licentiousness and immorality. The visibility of women in public was evidence for their degradation and fall from the spiritual heights available to them as wives and mothers. By invoking this comparison, Jameelah sought to amplify the moral threat of materialism not just to Islam and Muslims but also more broadly to ethical injunctions around sexuality, sex, and reproduction in American society. If women did not focus their sexual energies within the confines of marriage and for the purpose of reproduction, society was on the precipice of destruction. The entire fate of civilization rested on the proper enactment of female sexual mores.

In response to Jameelah's inside reporting and her assessment of the situation in the United States, Mawdudi again flagged shared emotions as the basis for their affinity. In fact, he told her the situation was the same across Arab societies:

> The pictures of American feminine dress sent by you are no news for me. We usually see European and American women in Lahore in a similar fashion. I have seen Arab women in Cairo, Beirut and Damascus moving about in this very same kind of dress. I simply cannot imagine how a woman with any sense of decency could thus attire herself even in her own home before her nearest relatives, not to speak of going out like that. I am very much pleased that you *despise* this form of dress.[18]

Jameelah's account provided nothing that Mawdudi did not already know. More important was that Jameelah articulated the appropriate (and intense) affective response that he would expect from a "real" Muslim. She likely felt gratified that he confirmed the righteousness of her view, that women's clothing choices made their sexuality an object of desire for all men to partake of. The correspondents directed the same set of emotional valences—scorn, disgust—at both Muslim and Western women.

While Jameelah framed women's dress as particularly threatening to Islam, all kinds of communities during the 1960s expressed anxieties over mass consumer culture and its potentially corrosive effects.[19] In the 1960s, fashion became implicated in protracted political debates concerning mass consumption, personal freedom, gender roles, and ethnic, national, and religious identities that were by no means limited to Muslim thinkers. Media outlets, politicians, and intellectuals in liberal democracies, socialist republics, and secular authoritarian regimes all weighed in on whether these new fashion trends portended the collapse of morality and threatened social survival. Items such as jeans and the mini skirt became mass produced on a global scale and were adopted by growing urban populations across the world. In postcolonial African and Asian nations, mass female fashion also prompted debates about the extent of foreign influence and how to retain cultural authenticity in its wake.

The strong negative, even punitive emotions that Jameelah and Mawdudi expressed—and argued that true Muslims also shared—were reserved for women who defied divinely sanctioned expectations for female morality. The emotions invoked by Mawdudi and Jameelah—which include scorn, disgust, and resentment toward women who flouted these norms—generate fear for the survival of Islam. The intensity of affects that revolve around women, family, and sexuality in Jameelah's work comes from the conviction that modern women are "out of place" in their departure from divinely sanctioned Islamic norms.[20] What Mawdudi saw was the potential for her to inspire others to also mistrust modernity—essentially, to feel badly—all in the name of loving Islam and pursuing justice in accordance with his vision.

Mawdudi and Jameelah agreed that the status of women generally was mired by a state of "degradation" that represented an affront not just to Islam but also to a "natural" morality. As Mawdudi conveyed:

> The social role which the Western woman is being made to play, is not in reality "emancipation," but perversion and enslavement and as a result of false and misleading propaganda, women are trying to "dewomanize" themselves. They think it is degrading to fill their natural place in life and to perform the tasks assigned to them by nature. Instead they seek honor in manly pursuits. Western civilization has proven to be very cruel to its womanhood. On the one hand, it wants woman to bear the burden of

> nature single-handedly and on the other hand this civilization calls her out to perform the multifarious duties of a man. Thus she has been squarely placed between two grindstones.[21]

Here, Mawdudi reiterated the ideological inversion that formed the basis for his critique of Western materialism. Mawdudi's 1940 treatise on purdah (*Purdah and the Status of Woman in Islam*) contained his most trenchant critique of European and American notions of equality and freedom, as well as his framework for restoring proper gender relations—through a strict program of segregation and seclusion of women from public life. In other words, gender, women, and the family were the site where Mawdudi articulated some of his most influential ideas.

Crucially for our purposes, this work was also where he marshaled strong negative emotions directed at Muslims who flouted God's intended gender roles. Mawdudi flipped the colonial script on liberal democracies of the mid-twentieth century that claimed to be the preserve of freedom, prosperity, and liberation. Not only were Western women subject to a "false propaganda" that posited their emancipation through entering the workforce ("manly," "multifarious duties"), they were also expected to continue to perform their "natural" duties as a woman, enforcing on them a double burden. This confined Western women to a state of "enslavement" in which they occupied the "perverse" condition of no longer being fully women because they had assumed male qualities and roles. This rhetoric cast a wide net of scorn and disgust on a much larger category of women: "Western" women writ large and Muslim women who assumed European and American styles of dress. Both types of women thus contributed to the perversion of "natural" gender roles, a publicly visible reminder of how Muslims had abdicated their essential responsibility for upholding divinely sanctioned wisdom about the proper place of women.

I will explore Jameelah's views on gender in greater depth in chapter 5. Here, I want to emphasize the catastrophic and existential threats that Mawdudi and Jameelah detected in what women who embraced modern roles and values—both Muslim and non-Muslim—were doing. Because they threatened the fabric of the social order by occupying roles not divinely sanctioned to them, such women represented a distinct kind of "enemy within" that Mawdudi and Jameelah targeted with scorn and disgust. The dangers posed by women who broke with traditional norms opened up both affective and ideological space through which Mawdudi and Jameelah found cross-cultural understanding. Their exchange illuminates the broad generalizations that both thinkers made about each other's respective societies—reaching the same conclusions from different cultural positions.

Recall that while Jameelah and Mawdudi shared a catastrophic religious and political imagination, at this point in her life Jameelah occupied a very different cultural context than Mawdudi did. Though she had begun to read more widely, imagining life outside the US, she was still primarily enmeshed in the American milieu of her youth. And though Mawdudi had read widely across European philosophy and literature, he had never traveled to Europe; in addition, his origins in the Indian subcontinent meant he had much more experience with British norms than American ones. Yet they shared strong affective reactions to what they both saw as unacceptable, even evil, transformations to female sexuality, mobility, and gender roles in one another's societies. They both understood the world as being in a state of moral collapse and civilizational decline, a common cause that lent additional *affective urgency* to their exchange.

As Jameelah put it, Mawdudi offered her a vision of Islam in its "pristine purity," uncorrupted by modernity. Jameelah became convinced that a pristine Islam was the only religion strong enough to thrive within a world in which the traditional sexual order seemed to be crumbling all around. The fact that Jameelah saw "purity" as the essential marker of "true" religion suggests the affective potency of gender across religious and cultural lines. The catastrophic urgency that Jameelah felt around preserving "traditional" forms of sexuality was fostered first in the postwar anxieties around the nuclear family in the United States.[22] In her correspondence with Mawdudi, she recognized that a similar affective urgency undergirding Muslim religious and political debates resonated with her. This shared affect of despair and anxiety around gender and sexuality underscores what Roxanne Euben terms the "transcultural problematic of modernity"—in which intellectuals from across religious, cultural, and political lines recognize a similar set of crises: modernity as a kind of pathology, the problem of authority, the erosion of morality, and the decline of community.[23] Euben argues that mid-century Muslim thinkers such as Qutb and Mawdudi identified a rot and decay in modernity that transcended their particular national circumstances. Indeed, as I argued in the previous two chapters, Jameelah took inspiration from other US intellectuals who bemoaned rampant individualism and consumerism at the expense of an authentic religious identity and community. While Euben does not theorize anxiety as a category in her comparative political theory, she identifies it as a common thread across Islamist and Western critiques of modernity in the twentieth century. Despair and anxiety can both lead to political paralysis, yet these affects can also be generative. Jameelah effectively channeled them into a revivalist Islamic vision that she believed could be universalized to any cultural context.

Gender and sexuality, particularly as they concerned women, were the privileged sites for the battle between opposing forces: tradition/modernity, good/evil, continuity/change. Both figures saw the dangers of female sexuality in the highest possible affective terms. Put another way, gender and sexuality intensified and crystallized the anti-modern affect shared between Mawdudi and Jameelah by strengthening boundaries between the "us" who scorned those who would objectify women and the "them" who transgressed God-given gender norms by engaging in the consumption of female bodies. The negative collective emotions that Jameelah directed against women, such as disgust, shame, and scorn, are intended to generate collective solidarity around the ills of modernity. For Jameelah, these affects constitute the necessary condition toward building Muslim solidarity.

The exchange between Mawdudi and Jameelah demonstrates the central role of gender and women in transcultural critiques of the modern world. In their letters, Jameelah and Mawdudi were not just concerned about Muslim women—they were concerned about the redemption of *all* women, who were subject to the eroding effects of materialism and consumerism. Women and gender generated the common affective framework through which their distinct cultural milieus became mutually recognizable. The negative affects that Mawdudi and Jameelah shared about the state of gendered practices in the mid-twentieth century carried the weight of a catastrophic imaginary, as well as vast aspirations to shape the world into a "pristine" version of Islam uncorrupted by materialism.

The Politics of Exclusion

Jameelah and Mawdudi's correspondence also evinced an affective politics of exclusion within the umma. Differentiating "real" Muslims from those who undermined the cause of revivalism became a key point of convergence for Mawdudi and Jameelah that then became a centerpiece of her life's work. In her later letters, Jameelah conveyed to Mawdudi her profound disappointment in Muslim students in the US, who she believed were too at ease with the comforts of life in New York and too eager to return to their home countries, where she imagined they would spread the evils of materialism and nationalism. Mawdudi agreed, asserting that such students held "deep prejudice against Islam and its heritage." These Muslims harbored "resentment" among "the common people" and spoke for only a tiny minority. Mawdudi wrote, "These persons, after returning to their native lands, live like foreigners. They do not mix with others and others do not mix within them." A Muslim who enjoyed living in America betrayed their faith by pursuing materialist rather than spiritual ends. Only those committed to reviving the faith endured the "fire" of the ordeals and struggles that such a cause required. Thus, while Mawdudi and Jameelah agreed that fulfilling the ritual requirements of Islam and upholding its essential beliefs were essential, they underscored that feeling too "at ease" in Western culture was cause for immediate suspicion.

Mawdudi and Jameelah seemed to revel in their mutual disdain for anyone who would betray their faith by pursuing material ends. One aspect linked all the various evils that the pair identified in their correspondence—including nationalism, colonialism, and communism: the absence of transcendent and spiritual underpinnings. The compulsive repetition of Mawdudi's and Jameelah's letters underscores this primary place of feeling, and the intensifying work of affect, in contemporary religious politics. In her letters, Jameelah confirmed and crystallized the compulsion later found in her work: fear, anger, and scorn for these enemies and those beyond the pale of the umma.[24] As their exchange continued, Jameelah offered additional examples of these enemies working against the revivalist cause, and in return Mawdudi provided affirmation of her observations that these so-called Muslims, whether MSA members in New York City or Arab leaders such as Habib Bourguiba, the secular authoritarian leader of Tunisia, failed to live up to the standards of Islam: "Islam engenders within us a spiritual refinement and an aesthetic taste which enables us to shun ugliness and to do everything beautifully. Atheism and materialism, on the other hand, pervert human tastes and make men adore and glorify ugliness. That is why under the spell of present materialistic civilization . . . degeneration has set in."[25] In this drawing of stark boundaries, the term "Muslim" functions as an identity marker that entails political commitments and actions. Jameelah and Mawdudi concurred that being a Muslim by birth is equally insufficient. Rather, a person must actively claim the identity of Muslim for themselves and adopt the ideological stances and embody the bad feelings that both authors promoted. By these standards, only a select group of Muslims was working toward a strong and unified umma; most other Muslims were outside the true faith.

Identifying enemies from within the umma became an enduring feature of Jameelah's life's work. In constructing the binary of Islam/the West, Jameelah inverted the affective matrix by casting both Westerners and their Muslim supporters as enemies of civilization who were driven by a blind hedonism that threatened to send society catapulting toward destruction. As Donovan Schaefer argues, categories of social difference, such as race and religion, often function as "a set of compulsions that drive bodies to generate and police the boundaries of their social worlds. Economies of hate distribute the heady thrill that comes from walling people off."[26] This "walling people off" aligns with Brannon Ingram's analysis of dynamics within Deobandi networks during the twentieth century. For Ingram, "affective language . . . helps to articulate how difference works in a way that cannot be reduced to mere belief. It is this unstated, even emotional bond . . . that makes the network cohere internally and differentiates it externally."[27] Jameelah adopted an ideological and conceptual framework that was more or less already in place, articulated by Mawdudi, Qutb, and others. Her writing contributed the generative, affective work of separating Muslims who rightly felt badly about modernity from those who did not. In the process, she helped to consolidate and build revivalist publics around collective emotion.

Throughout their letters, Mawdudi reinforced that Jameelah's affective response was exactly what a revivalist politics required. When asked repeatedly by Jameelah about what she ought to *do*, Mawdudi responded by encouraging her to continue learning and writing; he also exhorted her on how to *feel*: distressed, agitated, and alienated by the "wilderness of materialism." This exchange thus underscores how affect can serve as an end in itself.[28] Of course, there were other goals that the two articulated, such as establishing Jameelah's literary career, recruiting Muslim students in America to the cause, and finding her a suitable Muslim husband. But as the rest of the book explores, Jameelah would embrace the affective potential of critique for the entirety of her career.

Hijra to Pakistan

As their correspondence continued, Mawdudi expressed particular concern about how a person with such views could fulfill her obligations as a Muslim woman living in a hostile environment. Jameelah soon began to seriously consider Mawdudi's invitation to emigrate. In a letter on April 12, 1961, she reiterated her disillusionment with other Muslims in New York. In contrast, Jameelah promised that she would "devote [her] life to the struggle against philosophy-secularism and nationalism which are still so rampant in the world today and threaten not only the survival of Islam but the whole human race." The final letters between them mainly concern plans for Jameelah's transition to her new life. As she made her preparations, Mawdudi adopted a paternal approach with her, counseling her on the best course of action to improve her emotional health and to foster her literary pursuits. In their earlier correspondence, he proposed that she and her family visit together for the month of Ramadan, but as their letters continued, he began to advocate for a more permanent departure from the United States. Throughout 1961, he reiterated his offer, telling Jameelah that, while he was unable to pay for her passage from the United States, once she arrived in Lahore he would provide for all her financial needs and assist with finding her a spouse, who would presumably take up that responsibility in his stead.

Jameelah hesitated to accept the invitation, largely because, as she wrote in a March 22, 1962 letter, she "could not muster the courage to cut irrevocably all the ties from my family and my past and confidently step into the unknown." Yet she also had come to terms with her situation, which she saw as an increasingly dire predicament: "I am a hopeless misfit. I just cannot live in this society. Since I have no employment record worth mentioning, no commercial abilities or interests, no specialized training or professional skills, and no college diploma—all of this on top of the stigma of having spent more than two years from March 1957 to April 1959 in mental hospitals—I have no hope of finding any productive, useful, or honest livelihood congenial to my temperament."[29] She confided in Mawdudi that she could no longer live in "peace and harmony" with her family because she "would feel intensely unhappy and frustrated living their kind of life which never transcends mundane pleasure and appears to me so superficial, empty and meaningless." Jameelah shared that her parents had provided her with essential financial support in the past, but they were now moving out of their Mamaroneck apartment and planning to travel the world in their retirement. Without them, Jameelah worried, she "could not live here for a single day as a free citizen. I would far rather be dead than a living death in such humiliation and misery. I frankly confess that if it were not for faith in Islam, I would have committed suicide long ago." To her, staying in the US was a form of confinement and imprisonment; migration to Pakistan would not only enable her survival but also liberate her from the "humiliation and misery" that stemmed from her alienation.

In an April 18, 1962 letter responding to Jameelah's confirmed intent to immigrate to Pakistan, Mawdudi laid out the practical details of her arrival in Lahore, which he hoped would occur before his planned trip to Africa in July. Addressing her concerns about leaving behind her parents, Mawdudi wrote, "In any case I am prepared to welcome you forever as a member of my family. I am inviting you to share my hospitality in the spirit with which the early Muslim inhabitants of Medina extended their invitation to their harassed and persecuted brethren in Mecca, and I wish you to respond with a similar spirit of *Hijrah* (migration), convinced that the bonds of faith are firmer and stronger than relationship of flesh and blood."[30] Casting Jameelah's experience as akin to the experiences of the first Muslims, Mawdudi, perhaps unwittingly, played to her aspirations to contribute to the broad arc of Islamic history. Like the early Muslims, Jameelah would discover a new community—and, in the process, the resolution of her long struggles. The resulting affective bonds of the umma would also compensate for the loss of her familial ties to her parents and sister.

While the affective space of letter-writing portended aspirational, mutual affinity, the imminent arrival of Jameelah in Lahore precipitated a shift in Mawdudi's tone. He began to emphasize the culture shock that she would experience, including the hot weather and lack of air conditioning, unfamiliar food, and social expectations for female members of his household. Mawdudi particularly wanted to impress on Jameelah that she had a lot of work to do if she wanted to actualize the belonging she so desired that had eluded her in America. He expected that the language barrier would be frustrating for her, and that it would take many months to learn enough Urdu to communicate properly. In these later letters, Mawdudi became preoccupied with her well-being and with the many possible challenges that taking on a new member of a household would bring to his family and wider social circles.

Indeed, while Jameelah seemed to Mawdudi to grasp the main principles of Islam in a "remarkably clear way" for an American woman, he was less certain about her ability to conform to the specific expectations placed on Pakistani wives and mothers. He fretted about her marriage prospects and the timing of a potential union, suggesting that her status as a single woman would also generate ambivalence in his household and possibly raise eyebrows among his Jamaat cadres. While he wanted her marriage selection to be at her "discretion," he also expressed his intention to find her a "suitable" marriage partner who was as dedicated to the cause of Islamic revival as she was. Jameelah's unmarried status had clearly troubled Mawdudi; he referenced the "problem" repeatedly in their correspondence, and it became a core justification for inviting her to move to Pakistan. Additionally, Mawdudi emphasized her need to acquire the skills necessary to become a good wife, for which she required: "practical training on how a Pakistani Muslim wife runs her home and manages her household affairs. If at all you think of leading a married life, this knowledge will be indispensable. You would not be tied to a westernized man but naturally want to be married to a youth who lives as a good Pakistani Muslim. For such a marital relationship to achieve success, it is essential to learn the etiquette of Muslim families here."[31] Mawdudi volunteered his wife, Mahmudah Begum, for the task of instructing her in these essential practices, without which he imagined Jameelah would never fully realize her potential as a Muslim and as a woman. He appeared to have recognized that, though Jameelah had adopted modest dress and embraced gender separation, she lacked the skills and expertise that Pakistani women possessed. Her role as a writer also sat in tension with Mawdudi's and Jameelah's insistence that women be relegated to the domestic sphere. At the same time, Mawdudi could have seen Jameelah as an exception to those rules, much like his wife and daughters. Begum had a more public presence than Jamaat-i-Islami ideology purportedly allowed, and at various points she did not strictly follow Mawdudi's prescriptions for other women.[32] And though Jameelah's conversion to Islam, her status as a white American, and her education and class position provided her with the option to pursue an unconventional life in Pakistan, Mawdudi was keen to remind her he would ensure that certain gendered expectations were enforced.

As their correspondence ended, Mawdudi seemed to anticipate that affective and ideological affinity might not fully bridge their cultural differences. These final letters, while detailing Jameelah's physical removal from the "West" that she had come to despise, indicate the substantive challenges that Jameelah would encounter once she actually moved into Mawdudi's household and began the difficult period of adjustment.

It is not entirely clear what purpose Mawdudi intended her to serve. Jameelah would fit uneasily into the household dynamics; she spoke no Urdu and had negligible knowledge of local customs and norms—she wanted only to write. Jameelah also would be arriving during a fraught political moment. Mawdudi had only recently been released from a stint in prison for his oppositional views, and the 1962 lifting of the ban on political parties meant that the Jamaat-i-Islami could operate more freely.

Jameelah arrived in Lahore in May 1962. She stayed in the Mawdudi house for only a couple of months and then went to live with friends of the Mawdudi family, Hakim Rai Naimat Ali Khan and Khurshid Bibi, in a rural village known as Pattoki. After just a few months with this older couple she was again admitted to a mental institution, this time at the Lahore Government Mental Hospital, where she was interned for five months. When she left the hospital in late summer 1963, she married Muhammad Yusuf Khan—with whom she had five children born in quick succession. She continued to suffer from what she described as "anxious episodes" that prevented her from devoting much time to caring for her family or tending to household tasks. Similar to the generative years after her confinement in the US, the years that followed became the most prolific period of Jameelah's career.

A Usable Past

As Jameelah established herself as an intellectual in Pakistan, her work was widely disseminated by the Jamaat-i-Islami, and then translated into languages such as Urdu, Arabic, Indonesian, and Turkish. In addition, her books and pamphlets were sent to student organizations, women's groups, and professional societies in Pakistan and beyond. Jameelah's work found purchase in revivalist, literate publics constituted by print media that published, circulated, and translated a wide array of works promoting Mawdudi's political and religious vision. Jameelah also responded to written interview requests from revivalist-oriented organizations and university groups well into the 1990s.[33] As a woman, Jameelah could not be mobile like male cadres associated with the Jamaat-i-Islami. Under the understanding of purdah—gender separation—that she promulgated, women were not supposed to appear in mixed-gender settings, and their presence in public spaces more generally was also frowned upon. Through her typewriter, Jameelah waged her battle for the existential survival of Muslims from her domestic quarters. While she typically did not give speeches in public, she provided long-form replies to organizations that requested them and replied to interview questions in writing. These questionnaires further facilitated her contact with transnational audiences.

Most of Jameelah's books and pamphlets were accompanied by short biographies that narrated her journey from New York to Pakistan. The biographies typically listed Jamaat-i-Islami leader Umar Faruq Khan as their author and sought to bolster Jameelah's legitimacy as a writer and Muslim authority figure in her own right. These accounts of Jameelah's early years uniformly emphasized her upbringing in a middle-class, secular, Jewish, American milieu. The second edition of her pamphlet *Westernization Versus Muslims* contained a typical passage that underscored just how American Jameelah was: "Maryam Jameelah was born in 1934 in New York at the height of the Great Depression—a fourth-generation American of Jewish-German origin. She was reared in Westchester, one of the most prosperous and populated suburbs of New York and received a thoroughly secular education at the local public schools. . . . As she entered adolescence, she became intensely serious-minded, scorning all frivolities, which is very rare of an otherwise attractive young girl."[34] Her family's immigration history, as Jews of German descent who had been in the US for decades, positioned her as indisputably American. Jamaat-i-Islami conversion narratives foregrounded her deliberate choice to reject the material benefits of her youth—a choice made possible by her exceptional ability to discern Islam as the path to salvation. In all other respects, Jameelah possessed the intelligence and beauty of a desirable American woman who had the opportunity to live a comfortable, frictionless life of prosperity. These passages also aimed to play up her embodied knowledge of US cultural norms through the privileged access to normative Americanness that middle-class status conveyed.

These brief biographies thus portrayed Jameelah as a convert who was always in the process of conversion. Despite Jameelah's intentional rejection of the faith and culture of her youth, these biographies demonstrate that her conversion did not result in an irrevocable break with American culture. On the contrary, these accounts highlighted the indelible connection Jameelah maintained with her homeland. This connection enabled her to report back to her readers on the many moral failings of the US and in turn, to extol the superiority of Islam. Jameelah is depicted as having access to the inner workings of US society through her formative experiences in affluent suburban neighborhoods, consumer culture, public schools and libraries, and synagogues.

With some slight variations, these biographical narratives emphasized similar aspects of Jameelah's identity: her background as an affluent American Jewish woman; her familiarity with, and subsequent rejection of, American materialism and spiritual bankruptcy; her intentional embrace of Islam; her connections with prominent revivalists, namely Mawdudi; her "hatred" of materialism; and her ongoing literary output after becoming a mother in the late 1960s. These texts changed little over the course of her career. Taken together, they reinforced the transformation of Jameelah from an American teenager to an impassioned defender of Islam who devoted her life to galvanizing other Muslims behind the project of global Muslim unity.

This American past distinguished her from other Muslim thinkers in the Jamaat-i-Islami's transnational presses, setting her up as a critic with unique insight into the cultural and religious practices that she wanted her audiences to firmly reject. Such accounts generated an "exit narrative" that outlines her reasons for leaving Judaism and at the same time sustains her ongoing connection to the life she purportedly left behind.[35] Jameelah and her Jamaat-i-Islami publishers consistently invoked this conversion narrative in their aim to establish her as a scholar with a unique and compelling perspective.

The conversion narratives that framed Jameelah's writings implicitly highlighted tensions that made her exceptional, noting that, "most unusual for a woman after marriage, she continued all her intellectual interests and literary activities; in fact, her most important writings were done during and between pregnancies. She observes Purdah strictly."[36] Though she did observe purdah, she was not a woman who saw domestic tasks as the basis for her spiritual fulfillment. In reality, though she wrote about how such tasks were essential for women to fulfill their obligations to God, Jameelah largely left her domestic responsibilities to others.[37] Just as she had resisted the early expectations on her to marry a Jewish man and start a family in the American suburbs, so too did she seek to circumvent the expectations for female labor in Pakistan. It is unlikely that she did much in the way of childcare or household tasks such as cleaning or cooking; like many of the second-wave feminists she condemned, she was unfulfilled by domestic labor. Also like those feminists, she much preferred sitting at her typewriter surrounded by books, newspapers, and pamphlets—many sent to her from New York, enabling her to keep her finger on the pulse of American culture. That she was able to do so is testimony to this exceptional place that she occupied within her family and within Jamaat-i-Islami circles writ large—an exception that made it difficult for other women to follow her example.

These biographical and autobiographical texts thus disrupted the very binaries that Jameelah aimed to reinforce. Her status as a critic of "the West" required her to retain proximity to the very practices and norms she deemed to be dire threats to Muslim communities. In doing so, Jameelah and the Jamaat-i-Islami presented her as a mobile, public intellectual who was new to her faith and yet had privileged access to its truths through her affective appropriations of racial and religious alterity. This repeated calling of attention to her past identities heightened the ambivalence around religious boundaries. Taken together, these accounts amplified anxiety around the binaries that Jameelah both created and subverted. She served as her reader's guide through treacherous cultural waters and emerged as the authority on how to navigate them as a true, committed Muslim.

Conclusion

When Jameelah arrived in Pakistan in 1962, she was very eager to live out her new faith in ways that she imagined were only possible in a Muslim-majority society. She took with her a deeply seated conviction, forged through her period of intellectual and religious discovery, that modernity was poised to crush the Muslim umma. Jameelah believed she had a special role to play in rectifying the horrific wrongs her coreligionists endured in postcolonial Pakistan, even though she had no firsthand experience with their suffering. Nevertheless, Jameelah was determined to convince others of her vision of Islam. Critique, she hoped, would be the first step toward building a global Muslim community that would not merely withstand the multitude of threats that faced it but also, eventually, thrive. Forged in postwar America, her appraisal of the modern world as spiritually vacuous resonated strongly with the views of other revivalist thinkers, even those who came from quite different religious and political contexts.

Through the converging religious and political threads of her early life, Jameelah came to promote what she saw as the three core elements of Islam. First, Jameelah came out of her conversion convinced that it was imperative for Muslims to elevate their religious identity above all other social and communal attachments. Second, for Jameelah, Islam was an unchanging set of principles and ritual practices. Though lax and unfaithful Muslims, along with Western imperialists, sought to change these essential features, Jameelah believed that Islam alone retained its spiritual authenticity and was thus primed for recovery and renewal. And third, like many revivalist thinkers, Jameelah became convinced that religion was the ultimate basis for moral authority and political order. To Jameelah, religious renewal started with individual changes in daily life, but she believed that this individual transformation could only take place within societies that had enough committed Muslims to normalize such practices. And so, since she could not conceive of a thriving Muslim community in the country of her birth, she chose to leave it behind.

By writing prolifically and urgently, Jameelah found a place in global revivalist networks. But the unease and the anxiety that animated her turn away from Judaism never found resolution, and, in fact, that tension was highly generative for her approach to unifying the umma. Moreover, her self-understanding as a diagnostician of the West's many ills required her to retain proximity to the pathology's main source—America. As a perpetual convert, Jameelah positioned herself in the complicated and interlocking global politics of alterity, namely around her race, gender, and class identities. Calling attention to this constellation of hierarchies underscores the ways that Jameelah subverted the very binaries that she vehemently defended. In fact, her appeal depended on the affective reverberation that these subversions inspired among her transnational readers.

The ironic subversions that Jameelah embodied, alongside her embrace of right feelings, solidified her position as a key figure in the Jamaat-i-Islami during the 1960s and 1970s. From her new platform, she was able to reach a much broader audience. Yet Jameelah offered more than ideology for her fellow Muslims to engage in revivalist politics; foremost, she provided a collective emotional framework through which revivalist-oriented Muslim could express their feelings about the challenges they faced. She proved that these anti-modern affects could be felt and marshaled across Islamic contexts. Collective emotion thus offered a potent way to galvanize transnational publics around the project of Muslim unity.

PART II

The Affective Economy of Islamic Revival

4

The Affectsphere of Suffering

FROM A young age, Jameelah was enthralled with Palestine as a place that held the promise of liberation from capitalist modernity. She also came to believe that its people suffered the most under the weight of imperialism. In this chapter, I explore how Jameelah used another genre—the novel—to make her readers embrace anti-modern affects. Jameelah's novel, *Ahmad Khalil: The Biography of a Palestinian Arab Refugee*, was something of a lifelong endeavor for her. She began the project as a teenager, finished her first draft in 1961; the novel was first published in 1968 in Lahore. *Ahmad Khalil* was subsequently published in 1977 in India, and in 1986 it was also translated into Indonesian under the title *Along the Gaza Strip*. Over the course of the late twentieth century, Jameelah sent multiple versions of the manuscript, as well as accompanying draft materials and drawings, to the New York Public Library.

As we have seen, Jameelah was prolific, and she identified both the novel and its accompanying drawings as the defining products of her creative output. In her preface to the 1968 edition, she reflected, "This, my only attempt at fiction, is unique among all my other books that aim for the head, in that it seeks to capture the reader's heart. I have written my other books as an intellectual while I have created this story as an artist."[1] Explicitly drawing on the 1958 Zionist novel *Exodus* as her inspiration for *Ahmad Khalil*, she turned to the novel for the "romantic jolt" that it offered.[2]

Jameelah's writing and artwork demonstrate the central role of grief in revivalist efforts to build Palestinian solidarity. The titular character, Ahmad Khalil, undergoes a life of hardship, and the book follows his family's exile from Palestine and their struggles as refugees. Jameelah's drawings of Ahmad Khalil convey the profound sadness that defined her approach to generating solidarity around Palestine. The drawings are all in charcoal, like the image here, which shows Ahmad Khalil feeding his younger brother in a Gaza refugee camp (fig. 4.1).[3]

Jameelah wanted to convey the everyday horror of struggling to survive as the world collapses around you. She did not consider it a given that all Muslims would have strong emotional attachments to Palestine. Rather, she believed that such attachments needed to be generated and nurtured through art and literature.[4]

This chapter explores Jameelah's complex affectsphere of Palestinian suffering, ranging from intimacy to sadness to outrage. I use the term "affectsphere" to describe the political work that this intentional bundling of emotions around the Palestinian people and the land of Palestine does for Jameelah's project of building Muslim solidarity.[5] I also show that Jameelah's depictions of Palestine were grounded in her anxieties about the fate of the family in the modern world. She was decidedly disinterested in the politics of territory, law, citizenship, and nation-building. Instead, Palestine provided a conceptual geography for her binary views of religion, gender, and materialism. As a result, she portrayed Palestine as the paradigmatic site where families were destroyed by a variety of modern threats.[6]

Cumulatively, Jameelah's archive of her novel reflects a distinctive and instructive intertwining of American Jewish imaginings with Muslim postcolonial politics. Jameelah wrote *Ahmad Khalil* from the perspective and emotional arc that she knew best—American Jewish Zionism—in the service of Palestinian liberation. Jameelah's emphasis on the family as the locus of her religious politics stemmed in large part from her idiosyncratic, varied source material, which was enmeshed in American middlebrow

FIGURE 4.1. Maryam Jameelah, *Ahmad Khalil Feeding His Younger Brother, Khalifa, in the Refugee Camp in Gaza,* October 1969. Charcoal drawing. Manuscripts and Archives Division, New York Public Library.

culture. The affective energies that Jameelah poured into the Palestinian cause largely emerged from her study of several bodies of middlebrow literature: articles and sermons by American Jewish intellectuals and rabbis; US periodicals such as *Time* and *National*

Geographic; books and pamphlets by Muslim revivalists; and news stories and opinion pieces in the English-language Pakistani press. This bricolage of sources reveals the many threads out of which Jameelah sought to mobilize support for Palestinian liberation.

The 1967 Six-Day War marked a turning point from this more capacious vision, which Jameelah had primarily expressed through sadness and grief, into a hardened affect that was grounded in outrage and anger.[7] Far from an inevitable turn to "blind rage," this shift in her affectsphere was shaped by contingent historical events and her attempts to make sense of them. In *Ahmad Khalil*, Jameelah portrayed Muslims and Jews as having *both* been crushed under the weight of modernity, but in her later work, Muslims alone bore its brunt. This affective shift corresponded to a changing emphasis on the mechanisms through which to address collective Muslim suffering—away from an empathetic caring for family members toward a new openness to violence.

Before delving into *Ahmad Khalil*, I want to clarify the way that I am using the terms "Zionism" and "antisemitism." Political Zionism refers to the nineteenth-century nationalist ideology that supported the creation of a Jewish state somewhere in the territory of Palestine. As a movement, Zionism emerged out of a variety of historical factors, including the rise of violent antisemitism, the failure of Emancipation to create equality for Jews in Europe, and British colonial machinations in the region. The term "Zionism" also has a religious manifestation, encompassing the historical significance of the Land of Israel as a special place and homeland for Jews.[8] As Jameelah herself notes, not all Jews identify as Zionists, and those who do articulate a range of political and religious visions.[9] I map Jameelah's lifelong engagement with Zionism as an "emotional state" or what I referred to earlier as an "affectsphere."[10]

I also chart the ways in which affect structured Jameelah's critiques of Zionism. Jameelah was influenced by prominent American Jews who opposed the creation of the State of Israel in the early twentieth century. This stance was sometimes accompanied by concern for the political rights of Palestinians.[11] As early as the 1940s, Jameelah argued that political Zionism diminished her childhood religion's universalistic past by aligning Jews with anti-religious forces, namely materialism and imperialism. Once she became Muslim, her writings were also informed by (and soon contributed to) transnational Muslim networks that called for restoring the political rights, economic livelihoods, and religious flourishing of Palestinians. In particular, this critique of Zionism centered on the extraction of economic resources, the effacement of Arab culture, and the mass displacement of Palestinians after 1948.[12]

Finally, this chapter explores affective strains of anti-Jewishness and antisemitism in Jameelah's writing. Anti-Jewishness refers to the long history of narratives that denigrate Jews on account of their religion.[13] Antisemitism, in its modern manifestations of hatred and prejudice, denigrates Jews as a racialized group.[14] In nineteenth-century Europe, antisemitism cast Jews as a race with inherited, immutable characteristics that posed a grave danger to modern society. Jameelah's stories about her childhood catalogued persistent American antisemitic prejudice in the 1940s, such as the teasing of classmates and prejudiced remarks by teachers, even as public critiques of antisemitism were becoming more prominent and barriers to Jewish employment and education were gradually being removed.[15] Beginning in the late-1960s, Jameelah's writing began to include anti-Jewish and antisemitic narratives, specifically a strain of anti-Jewishness, or the "essential Jew," that emerged after 1948 and was "qualitatively distinct" from earlier Christian expressions.[16] Through these essentialized representations, Jameelah linked the actions of the State of Israel to the "historical rebellious conduct" of Jews against Muslim religious and political authority.[17]

Tracking Jameelah's corpus on Palestine demonstrates how affective attachments are made and unmade in unpredictable, and sometimes dramatic ways. Grappling with US Jewish support for Israel, Jameelah's affective lens illustrates the simultaneous proximity and distance that she maintained with her American Jewish past. Whereas she had previously attended to the complexities of being Jewish, she later relied more heavily on generalizations about Jews and Judaism that sat in tension with, and sometimes outright contradicted, her prior arguments about Zionism as the product of modern politics. Rather than attempting to resolve these contradictions, I tease out the complicated, illustrative affective tensions that Jameelah's archive created around Israel/Palestine as a site for global Muslim and Jewish solidarity.

Imagining Palestine Through *Ahmad Khalil*

Ahmad Khalil narrates the fictional story of a Palestinian family displaced by the Nakba (catastrophe), in which 700,000 Palestinian people were forced from their homes, most never to return, after the creation of Israel in 1948. The story of Ahmad Khalil begins during his childhood in the early 1940s, when his family struggles to carve out a difficult rural existence in Iraq al-Manshiyya, a village in southern Palestine. Ahmad Khalil is the son of Malak Wahab, a Sudanese man, and his Palestinian bride, Khadijah, who are both deeply devout Muslims and hard workers with deep attachments to their family and their land. Early in the novel, tragedy strikes the family on multiple fronts. The family's neighbors have begun to sell their land to Jewish settlers. As the farms and businesses of his Jewish neighbors thrive, Malak Wahab struggles to make ends meet—his family lacks adequate food and their clothes become threadbare. In one scene, Ahmad Khalil and his cousins experience these disparities viscerally:

> They gaped as a hiking troupe of Jewish children of all ages with knapsacks on their backs, dressed alike in shorts and scanty blouses exposing their sturdy, tanned arms and legs filed past them. They were munching fruit and chocolate bars out of paper bags as they walked. Some of the younger children, their mouths smeared with chocolate, greeted them with cheerful shouts and friendly waving and one tiny chubby-faced girl with

> golden curls and blue eyes licking an ice-cream cone, looked up and smiled. The Arab children did not smile back. For a moment they listened to their laughter and unintelligible chatter until Ahmad Khalil picked up a rock and threw it at them.[18]

Jameelah depicts the Jewish children as enjoying a prosperous life, replete with snacks of ice cream, fruit, and chocolate, which fortified their strong bodies and produced their carefree cheeriness. Rather than eking out an existence through hard work, these children enjoy ample leisure. Moreover, their revealing attire renders their health and prosperity manifestly visible to Ahmad and his cousins.

The Jewish children symbolize what Jameelah saw as the naive adoption of materialism by Jews (and Arabs, as we will see later in the chapter). The kids exude the collective emotions of those who have benefitted from modernity—optimism, joy, confidence. Their golden curls and blue eyes convey whiteness—one among many places in the novel where Jameelah wrestles with and applies her understanding of American racial hierarchies to the Palestinian context. They smile widely at whomever they meet, laughing as they hike, signaling their ease in a place that rightfully belonged to Ahmad, his family, and his Arab neighbors. As a young boy, Ahmad does not fully understand the broader dynamics at work in the interaction, but he instinctually rejects the comfortable way of life that he discerns comes at the expense of his family's survival. After he hurls the rock at the Jewish children his cousins join in—until they notice that a sheep about to give birth is in need of their care, so they "give up the game."

This scene portends the growing tension between two communities that struggle to live peacefully beside one another. Malak Wahab returns each night to report the violence breaking out between Arabs and Jews, telling Ahmad to prepare for an all-out war to defend their land and their faith. Soon after, Ahmad Khalil and his mother contract typhus. Khadija, who had recently given birth to a second son named Khalifa, does not survive.[19] Ahmad's youth is further upended when he is sent to work in Beersheba, against his will, as a servant to his great-uncle, Mustafa Effendi, a prominent merchant. Ahmad's separation from his family and village is a painful episode poignantly foreshadowing the perpetual loss of both that he will suffer for the rest of his life.[20]

After several years, Ahmad returns to his father following the collapse of his great-uncle's wealth in the wake of the creation of the State of Israel. Following horrific hand-to-hand combat between Arab and Jewish fighters, Ahmad, Malak, and Khalifa flee, eventually finding safety in a refugee camp in Gaza. Ahmad contracts pneumonia, marking his second extended illness of the novel. Ahmad passes the days by reading and studying. He eventually returns to his village to marry Asma, his first cousin and childhood friend. But even the wedding is marred by tragedy because the inhabitants of their village, including the rest of his family, are expelled by the Israeli military. Soon after, Malak, Ahmad and Asma, Khalifa, and a cousin, Rashid, take a boat to Mecca with several hundred hajjis bound for the annual pilgrimage. They settle in Medina, finding work in the city gardens and as groundskeepers of a mosque. Ahmad and Asma adopt a blind orphan, Abd al-Raziq, who has a deep spiritual connection to the Qur'an and begins to memorize the entire text. But they cannot escape the traumas of the Nakba and their lives in Medina are overtaken by struggles with illnesses, disabilities, psychological distress, homesickness, and poverty.

Despite their best efforts to preserve a humble and pious life, the wheels of modernity continue to grind on the family of Ahmad Khalil. The final section of the novel focuses on the contrasting paths of Ahmad's and Asma's two sons, Ismail and Abd al-Raziq. Ismail, descendent of their cursed bloodline, goes to work at the Coca-Cola factory in Jeddah. Seduced by the pleasures of the city, he rarely returns to Medina to see his parents. Their adopted son, Abd al-Raziq, also leaves Medina, but for a much higher purpose: he accepts an offer to study the Islamic sciences at the prestigious Al-Azhar University in Cairo.

The divergent paths of the two brothers come to a head when Ahmad Khalil is diagnosed with a fatal lung disease. Ismail pays for his father to get state-of-the-art treatment at a modern hospital. Ahmad Khalil is horrified by the sterile environment and the disorienting experience of anesthesia and surgery. In a vision, Ahmad sees Abraham, Moses, and Jesus; he interprets the dream as a sign that he is in Hell because Jesus would never be found in such a horrible place. As Ahmad's health declines further, he learns that Ismail has accepted a position as an executive at ARAMCO, the American oil company based in Saudi Arabia, and has married an Orthodox Christian woman. These two developments—employment by a multinational corporation and marriage to a non-Muslim—represent Ismail's complete break from his family and from the model that Ahmad Khalil set for him. Ismail rushes away from his father's bedside, leaving Ahmad coughing and struggling to breathe, furious that his son has abandoned his faith and his family. Opening his eyes a final time, Ahmad sees Abd al-Raziq, who has become a star student at Al Azhar—though he has also been surveilled and silenced by Egyptian president Gamel abd al-Nasser's persecution of Muslim scholars. As he approaches death at the end of the novel, Ahmad cries out to Abd al-Raziq to recite the final surah of the Qur'an.

In 1968, Jameelah wrote that she intended for her novel to serve the cause of Islamic revival. She dedicated the book to "those workers for Islamic revival, especially from occupied Palestine, who are determined to transform the Arab Muslims and their brethren-in-Faith throughout the world, from what they are now into what they ought to be." In a letter to Mawdudi she wrote how the first draft of her novel "emphasizes the evils of Western materialism in the guise of Zionist imperialistic aims and [in] the concluding chapters, the harmful effects of the oil industry in Saudi Arabia." The novel was Jameelah's attempt to map the affective terrain of the anti-colonial writings that she immersed herself in as a teenager and to work out those links between materialism and colonialism that became central to her religious politics over the late twentieth century.

Although Jameelah worried about novels as a Western and therefore un-Islamic genre, she believed that the form of the novel had an affective potential that other kinds of writing did not. She envisioned *her novel* as a story that would "rise above mere polemics and propaganda" by creating characters that were "not shallow stereotypes."[21] At the same time, she worried that "a novel without romance or love interest appeals to few Western readers while it is difficult for the Muslim to appreciate an art form not indigenous to his culture." As always, Jameelah foregrounded sexuality as the key site of difference between Islam and the "West." She also reminded her readers of her unique capacity as an American Jew to mark the boundary between these civilizations—but at the same time to transgress these borders as needed for the higher purpose of unifying Muslims through the story of Ahmad Khalil. The affective payoff outweighed any possible risk, she thought, of amplifying a genre.

Ahmad Khalil was a lifelong project for Jameelah. She began the first draft in 1948, at age fourteen, and continued to supplement it with new drawings and literary scenes for decades after its initial publication in 1968. The various versions of the manuscript and accompanying drawings created over many decades demonstrate the formative place of affective attachments in her transnational religious imagination. As with her biographies, the prefaces and explanatory notes in the archive illustrate the affective lens through which she saw the character of Ahmad Khalil and his significance in the epic drama between good and evil that she saw unfolding in Palestine. In the 1961 typescript, which she deposited at the New York Public Library just before leaving for Pakistan, she admitted that, though the novel "may seem exaggerated in a narrow, superficial sense, I am convinced that, in the wider context, I have depicted an essentially accurate picture of what is taking place." An accurate depiction of events was not the primary goal, which was instead affective: "This book is not for enjoyment. It is not meant to be pretty. Indeed for most readers in Muslim countries it will be extremely painful and embarrassing, for the truth hurts."[22]

As with all of her writing, generating anti-modern affects was the intended outcome.

Abul A'la Mawdudi saw the story's affective potential and enthusiastically encouraged her to publish it. The Jamaat-i-Islami imprint run by her husband published the first edition in 1968, but without any of the drawings. A subsequent edition was distributed in 1977 from Lucknow, India, by the Academy of Islamic Research and Publications, a press run by the Nadwatul Ulama (or Nadwa), the educational institution that was then under the leadership of Abu'l 'Ali (d. 1999). Nadwi had been part of the Jamaat-i-Islami's intellectual networks in the 1950s and was a key conduit for amplifying Mawdudi's message to Arab publics. However, Nadwi had distanced himself from Mawdudi by the 1970s.[23] The fact that the Nadwa endorsed Jameelah's novel both suggests that her influence reached beyond the Jamaat-i-Islami and underscores how revivalist leaders increasingly saw Palestine as a key site for the reinvigoration of Muslim politics.

By portraying the pain of Ahmad Khalil and his family, Jameelah hoped to harness affective attachments to the Nakba in the service of unifying the global umma. In a preface to a version of the manuscript deposited with the NYPL in 1979, in the wake of the Iranian Revolution, she reflected on the role of this fictional character in generating her own "emotional attachments to Islam."[24] She continued to add to the story of Ahmad Khalil in the 1990s and to reflect on her emotional identification with the story. In the preface to the 1991 typescript version, she wrote, "The novel can be considered my fictional biography in its deepest emotional sense, in that its chief characters, 'Ahmad Khalil' and 'Khalifa' are none else but the author."[25] While she added scenes that depicted the lives of Ahmad's children and made some corrections, the characters' commitment to a vanishing religious tradition, just like her own, remained steadfast.

By contrast, she lamented that many "Palestinians in exile have nothing in common with Ahmad Khalil, Khalifa and Rashid" because their imagined way of life as pious peasants living out a traditional existence had been obliterated by "cosmopolitan Arabs." Criticizing twentieth-century Palestinian authors—though not by name—for becoming too secular and too Marxist, she believed that *Ahmad Khalil* rightly portrayed the struggle for Palestinian liberation in "spiritual and religious terms," in contrast to renderings of the Palestinian peasant as the symbol of nationalist resistance to occupation.[26] As with her jeremiads against other Muslims (and against her fellow Jews), Jameelah saw Palestinian nationalists as failing to live up to the traditional, authentic way of life that she believed their ancestors embodied. By the 1990s, for Jameelah, Palestine had gone the way of so many Muslim societies, following a familiar narrative of the small number of the righteous fighting the good fight against materialism.

Illustrating Palestinian Suffering

In addition to the published novel and its many versions, Jameelah created numerous unpublished drawings for the book. Drawing in pastels and charcoal, she worked on these illustrations from 1946 to 1989 and eventually bequeathed most of them to the NYPL. For all of Jameelah's railing against academic Orientalist approaches, her art reflects a yearning for an exotic East that she saw as the reservoir of authentic religious practice and traditional culture—and that was absolutely separate and demarcated from "the West." As we saw in chapters 1 and 2, Jameelah's earliest drawings reflect a buoyant, youthful optimism, as she imagined the lives of young Muslims and Jews in distant lands. As she entered adulthood and for the rest of her life, Jameelah created charcoal drawings of Palestinian refugees that evoked grief over the horrors that modernity inflicted on her fellow Muslims.

A series of small pencil sketches labeled *Everyday Life in Iraq al-Manshiya Before It Was Destroyed by the Israelis in 1948*, which Jameelah drew in November 1989, depicts an imaginary Palestinian village in isolation from the modern world (fig. 4.2). One man leads a camel loaded down with earthenware pots. Another man

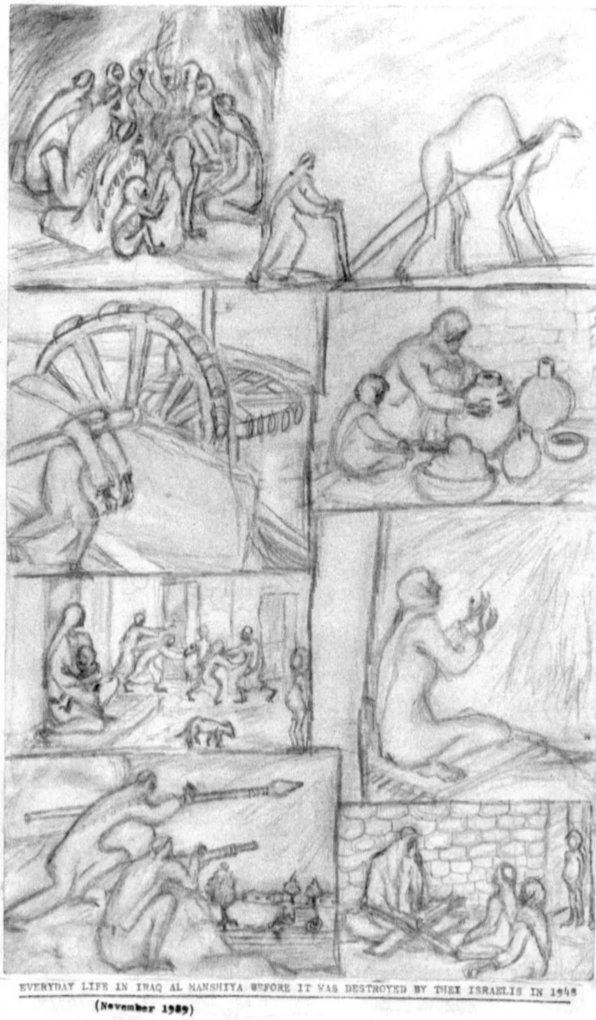

FIGURE 4.2. Maryam Jameelah, *Everyday Life in Iraq al-Manshiya Before It Was Destroyed by the Israelis in 1948*, November 1989. Charcoal drawing. Manuscripts and Archives Division, New York Public Library.

grinds grain by hand, while in another frame a woman weaves on a hand loom. People wear long robes and many of the children are naked—to demonstrate the depths of their impoverished state.

Jameelah's drawings of Palestine evoke a timeless quality that nonetheless marks them as impoverished victims of modernity. Modern objects are largely absent from Jameelah's drawings. In terms of geography and the built environment, the homes and streets that Ahmad Khalil and his family inhabit are not recognizable as a particular landscape or place in Palestine. The only consistent marker of modernity in Jameelah's drawings are the machine guns that Israelis and Palestinians carry, signifying the violent destruction of colonialism and the necessity of resistance. One of the first images of this kind depicts a woman holding an infant son in one arm with a machine gun slung over her other shoulder. The woman's eyes display sadness and determination to protect her son. The other images focus on men who take up arms to protect their homes—and the Israeli soldiers with whom they engage in battle.

Through her art, Jameelah sought to make the plight of Palestinians a central node in the affective economy of revival. In a handwritten page at the beginning of the folio that she assembled of her childhood drawings and donated to the New York Public Library, Jameelah explained that her drawings had been inspired by Per-Olow Anderson's *They Are Human Too,* a photographic essay published in 1957 that documented the plight of Palestinians in a refugee camp in the Gaza Strip.[27] Anderson was a renowned Swedish photographer who documented the experiences of displaced Palestinians in UN refugee camps, portraying the daily lives of families as they adjusted to the reality of statelessness. In the book's introduction, Anderson wrote that while "human suffering is nothing new to me . . . none of my experiences was more shocking to me than my introduction to the plight of the more than one million Palestinian Arab refugees."[28]

From Anderson's images, Jameelah came to see the power of focusing on individual protagonists' experiences to portray communal suffering. Anderson was particularly keen to capture the depth of emotion in his subjects' eyes. He depicted tears welling up, the creases of wrinkles, the hints of mischief in the eyes of children, and the creeping boredom and restlessness in the eyes of adults. Many of his subjects wear threadbare clothes and sit outside makeshift mud huts, with barbed wire in front of them. *They Are Human Too* marks Palestine as a modern place by showing train cars, barbed wire, and a child wearing an Iowa Buckeyes shirt. Altogether, Anderson's portraits underscore Palestinians' daily struggles to survive as well as their hope, dignity, and resilience.

Jameelah's drawings also reflect her consumption of *National Geographic*, which she referenced in several pieces of her writing and in the descriptions that accompanied her drawings and scrapbooks. Her drawings evoke similar representations of "other" cultures—for example through her reliance on portraiture, which the magazine used to create an affective relationship between readers and distant lands and cultures. Intended for middle-class European and American consumers, *National Geographic* was the epitome of a "middle highbrow" publication in postwar America.[29] The magazine's images of Palestinians portrayed their subjects as exotic and idealized, both on the cusp of modern progress and the inheritors of a timeless, authentic culture rooted in the biblical past.

In her drawings these embodied effects of modernity are also visible on the bodies of Israeli soldiers. Though Israelis are discussed in the dialogue of the novel as usurpers intent on taking Palestinian land through violence, Jameelah drew Israeli soldiers in much the same style as she drew Ahmad Khalil and his family. She labeled one of the earliest images that accompanied the novel manuscript as *Yaakov, a Survivor of the Nazi Concentration Camp, of the Jewish Settlement of Negba in a Moment of Reflection (Soon After World War II)* (fig. 4.3).

Yaakov wears a hat and a button-down shirt with pockets on the front. His face is very close to the foreground and his eyes are depicted with the same deep inset as Ahmad Khalil's. Yaakov gazes into the distance with his hand resting on his chin. The numbers "94321" are inscribed on his arm, marking him as a Holocaust

FIGURE 4.3. Maryam Jameelah, *Yaakov, a Survivor of the Nazi Concentration Camp, of the Jewish Settlement of Negba in a Moment of Reflection (Soon After World War II)*, October 1988. Charcoal drawing. Manuscripts and Archives Division, New York Public Library.

survivor. Like Palestinians, Jews who were fighting on behalf of Israel had suffered under the weight of modernity's evils. But—as Jameelah's novel seeks to convey—now they inflict those same harms on others. As the story progresses Yaakov and the other soldiers will commit acts of atrocity against Palestinians, such as mowing down families with machine guns. Her images underscore the human costs of colonialism and the lack of international support for Palestinian refugees who struggled to provide the necessities for their children. The central losses of the novel, and the most poignant scenes that Jameelah depicted, are the anguishing deaths of family members to famine and disease wrought by the experience of displacement. Displacement by war and capitalism was a Palestinian burden, but not uniquely so. By calling attention to Holocaust survivors, Jameelah also portrays intersecting tragedies of modernity.

A Muslim *Exodus*

Ahmad Khalil is both a portrayal of how to be a pious Muslim in a hostile modern world and a critique of Zionism. In the preface to the 1968 edition, Jameelah wrote that the novel stemmed from her early chafing at the State of Israel's outsized role in American Jewish religion and politics—claiming that, from as early as age twelve, she believed that this alignment diluted and undermined Judaism's universalistic aspirations. *Ahmad Khalil* was not only Jameelah's way of documenting the State of Israel's destructive physical, psychological, and religious impact on Arabs and Muslims; it also came out of what she experienced as the negative affective and emotional consequences for American Jewish communities.

Just as she found Islam in books, Jameelah became enmeshed in Zionism through literature. She explicitly drew on two iconic novels: *Thieves in the Night* by Arthur Koestler, published in 1946, and *Exodus* by Leon Uris, published in 1958:

> I conceived this story when only a child of twelve and started recording it in writing at the age of fourteen. [M]y native New York was deeply involved as the centre of Zionist propaganda. . . . Paradoxically, the more propaganda against the Arabs I read in books, magazine articles, newspaper reports or heard over the radio, the more sympathetic I grew towards

> these people and their plight. In particular, two Zionist novels, both of which gained enormous popularity in America against which I reacted violently, acted as a stimulus for the creation of this story—THIEVES IN THE NIGHT by Arthur Koestler (1946) and EXODUS by Leon Uris (1958).[30]

Both novels used fiction as the medium for a political message focused on the restoration of the Jewish right to the land of Palestine and connected the creation of the State of Israel to the survival of democracy, capitalism, and freedom.[31] In *Thieves in the Night,* a novel that received mixed reviews, Koestler takes readers into the world of Jewish underground fighters who planted bombs to disrupt life in Palestinian towns. Exceeding *Thieves of the Night*'s reach by leaps and bounds, *Exodus* was an international bestseller that sold twenty million copies in twenty years and became the basis for the 1960 blockbuster film starring Paul Newman.[32] Historians credit the work with inspiring widespread sympathy for the state of Israel by creating a legible narrative of a confusing and morally fraught conflict in the aftermath of the devastating losses of the Holocaust and World War II.[33]

At the same time, the two novels created negative and enduring stereotypes of Palestinians and Arabs in Cold War America. While Jews were portrayed as brave, determined, and trustworthy inheritors of the Holy Land, Arabs were represented as deceitful, incompetent, and hopelessly backward. In *Exodus,* the backwardness of Arab villagers and townspeople alike justified the creation of the State of Israel to modernize the economy while restoring the Holy Land as a moral place.

Palestinian literary accounts of the Nakba did not figure into her narrative because, by Jameelah's own telling, she wrote the book prior to "becoming personally acquainted with Arabs and Muslims. . . . [M]y only source of knowledge was the meagre literature available in English on the subject at my school and local public libraries written by Western travelers, orientalists or Christian missionaries hostile to the Islamic cause and friendly to

Zionism. Since I had no firsthand experience with the hardships and injustice depicted on the following pages, factual errors and literary flaws are inevitable."[34] Similar to its inspiration *Exodus,* the Palestine of *Ahmad Khalil* is the product of Jameelah's religious imagination, which was itself forged through a complex set of cultural and historical influences.

Broader American representations of the Holy Land also undergirded the epic stakes of *Ahmad Khalil,* as a morality tale about the potential destruction of Islam writ large. *Exodus,* along with other biblical epics such as *The Ten Commandments,* marked a growing recognition of Israel as locus of political concern for white Christian Americans in the context of American exceptionalism, and a way of seeing international politics as intertwined with biblical destiny and the victory of good over evil.[35] Popular culture, especially fiction and film, helped to prime American Jews and Americans more broadly to take a more active and interventionist approach toward supporting Zionism.

Jameelah also transposed postwar American racial dynamics onto Ahmad Khalil's story. Ahmad Khalil's own grandmother described him as a "mongrel" in appearance. This constellation of ethnic and racial markers collapses into an Islamic identity that Jameelah claimed as the "Other" in opposition to what she presented as a middle-class, white existence of her youth.[36] Abraham Rubin argues that Jameelah's childhood fascination with African Americans, Native Americans, and ethnic others "evolved into the adult Jameelah's identification with Subaltern Islam. . . . Blackness, America's ultimate marker of racial otherness is conflated with Muslim identity and difference."[37] Ahmad Khalil inhabits multiple markers of otherness that Jameelah portrayed as evidence for his authentic religiosity and the kind of religiosity to which Jameelah aspired. Ultimately, the story of Ahmad Khalil is that of the primacy of religious identity over other attachments.

In addition to the broader backdrop of American culture, the project of *Ahmad Khalil* grew out of Jameelah's participation in organizations that sought to foster ties between Americans and

Arabs during the 1950s. According to Jameelah's "Chronology of Life and Published Articles," her drawings of Arab subjects were displayed at the New York headquarters for the American Friends of the Middle East from November 10 to 20, 1960. The AFME was an anti-Zionist, pro-Arab organization founded in 1951 by a group of prominent journalists, literary figures, politicians, and activists. It organized academic lectures, facilitated Arab American student exchanges, and published and distributed literature about Arab culture and society in order to combat negative Orientalist stereotypes, foster cultural exchange between Christians and Muslims, and compete with Zionist organizations that were far better politically connected.[38]

Jameelah's own involvement with the AFME helped to solidify her intuition that Muslims and Arabs, as well as their supporters—with powerful forces amassing against them in the postwar period—were on the losing side of modernity and that publishing was a central tool for challenging those forces. In the conclusion to his study, published fifty years after its events, historian Hugh Wilford wondered, "Where was the Arabist *Exodus*, the wildly successful novel about the founding of Israel?"[39] Jameelah wanted *Ahmad Khalil* to be just that—though, of course, the English-language version. She aimed to produce a novel that could engender the mass affective attachments in Muslims to the Palestinian cause that *Exodus* did for American Jews in relation to the State of Israel. On the scale of epic proportions, Jameelah urged her readers to feel how hard the Palestinians fought for their land and for their families—and the devastating, multigenerational consequences of that struggle.

A Family's Suffering

The affective center of the novel is Ahmad Khalil and his anguish as a father and husband who cannot prevent his family's suffering. Much of the novel depicts the deep affection that Ahmad feels for his family and the care and comfort that he provides for his younger sibling, cousins, and later, his children: "Ahmad Khalil felt closest to his cousin when they ate together. Abdul Aziz was preoccupied pushing the biggest chunks of meat towards him while he did the same . . . and the warm intimacy filled Ahmad Khalil with an indescribable happiness as they squatted against the wall."[40] This scene illustrates the anti-materialism that anchors the novel. Ahmad Khalil and his family lack adequate food and yet their want of sustenance also provides the context through which to embody an Islamic way of life, each cousin selflessly offering their meagre food to the other despite being hungry himself.

Despite Jameelah's intention to represent fully fleshed-out human beings, Ahmad Khalil does not evolve or change much over the course of the novel. He retains his humble, pious, and steadfast commitment to God and Islam from his childhood until his death. "He is the victim, not only of the injustices inflicted by the Nakba but equally as much by his westernized Muslim brethren who have been corrupted. . . . In the 46-year span of his life, he is hit with the hardest blows Fate can deal, but Ahmad Khalil is not crushed! He is the constant victim of injustice of every sort but he is not a bitter or angry person. He is kind, gentle, deeply pious and devoid of any trace of cynicism."[41] Through the character of Ahmad Khalil, Jameelah constructs two binaries that reflect her understanding of good and evil: between Palestinians and Jews, and then between traditionalists and modernists. The Palestinian/good/traditionalist camp to which he belongs is obviously morally superior, but it loses political and religious ground over the course of the narrative, even to members of Ahmad Khalil's own family—personified by the figure of Ismail, who stands in for the Muslims who have betrayed their religion for material gain.

Ahmad Khalil is an attempt to foreground transnational Muslim solidarity through affective attachments to Palestine, over and against other kinds of identity—namely Pan-Arabism, nationalism, and Third World solidarity. In Jameelah's telling, Ahmad Khalil and his family were entirely motivated by religious aims and goals. This portrayal reflected her aspiration that religion transcend other possible foundations for Palestinian identity. Rashid Khalidi labels the post-1948 period as one in which Palestinian identity seemed to have "disappeared" to outside observers as its leaders grappled with the destruction of their homeland wrought by the creation of the State of Israel.[42] The post-1948 moment led to a fracturing of Palestinian political institutions and movements. This period also solidified 1948 as the key moment for the consolidation of a unified identity among Palestinians rooted in the shared experience of exile and displacement.

Within this context, the novel portrays Palestinian struggle as a model for all modern Muslims in their struggles against colonialism and capitalism. In particular, the novel takes up the trope of resistance in the wake of hegemonic oppression.[43] Ahmad Khalil continuously sacrifices his physical and emotional well-being for the sake of his family and for the cause of Islam. He refuses to work for corporations and seeks out residence in the symbolic heart of Islam, Saudi Arabia. While the threat of war fades in the Gulf, Ahmad Khalil discerns that the threat of capitalism is even more all-encompassing. No Muslim is safe from the imperial designs of Coca-Cola and ARAMCO, which have infiltrated even the sacred center of the one true faith, corrupting its younger generations with the promise of wealth and carefree days. Ahmad Khalil valiantly and unfailingly resists these twin evils threatening to destroy Islam—and with it the only hope for renewing and reviving civilization. In this way, he can claim moral triumph in the face of defeat.

However, moral triumph is the only victory available to Ahmad Khalil. In the end, two sons remain frozen in their opposing roles as religious scholar and corporate executive, playing their parts in a wider cosmic battle, the outcome of which is far from certain. While postwar Zionist epics such as *Exodus* culminate in a hopeful future, a pessimistic tone pervades the end of *Ahmad Khalil*, whose eponymous hero dies without fulfilling the Palestinian dream of return. Even more importantly, he is unable to stop the forces of materialism and authoritarianism from "destroying" his sons' lives, nor to soothe the pain of his brother, Khalifa. In fact, by the end, the worst possible outcome—one of his sons becoming a tool of capitalist greed—exemplifies the overwhelming challenges that Muslims face. Even a man as pious and as committed to his family as Ahmad Khalil cannot stop the tides of capitalism and colonialism—the twin evils that work by destroying Muslims, one family at a time.

Through *Ahmad Khalil,* Jameelah aimed to generate a potent, dynamic mix of negative emotions centered on the catastrophe of modernity. Ahmad Khalil and his family become stateless, and the Palestinian people lose their sovereignty and their land. Though these are devastating losses, they are not the central loss of the book compared to the many catastrophes wrought by bullets, disease, famine, rape, economic exploitation, and expulsion. Jameelah's focus throughout is on the destruction these forces have on an extended family unit. Because she saw the family as the foundational institution of Islam, Jameelah's emphasis on the family reflected her desire to frame Palestinian liberation as a religious rather than a national or ethnic struggle. She hated nationalism, and as a result, the prospect of Palestinian statehood did not figure prominently into her imaginary. The core losses of *Ahmad Khalil* are those associated with the death of close personal family members, their ongoing trauma and emotional anguish, and the loss of relatives to the seduction of material wealth.

Ahmad Khalil's suffering stands in for the entire umma embodied in collective grief. His suffering is what makes him a redemptive character, one that is intended to spark affinity with readers. *Ahmad Khalil* narrates the many threats that modernity poses to the nuclear, patriarchal familial unit that Jameelah saw as the foundation for a thriving Muslim society. In this way, *Ahmad Khalil* implies that the potential redemption of the Palestinian people, and implicitly of Muslims more generally, would be the restoration of patriarchal, masculine agency over the fate of a man's family.

A Dynamic Affectsphere

The 1967 Six-Day War precipitated a significant disruption in Jameelah's affective framework. Fought between June 5 and June 10—by Israel and multiple Arab countries, including Egypt,

Jordan, Syria, Lebanon, and Iraq—it resulted in a decisive Israeli victory. Israel became the occupying power in the Sinai Peninsula, the Golan Heights, the Gaza Strip, and the West Bank, including East Jerusalem. As her effort to make sense of dramatic world events in real time, she penned *Islam Versus the Ahl al-Kitab* (Islam versus the People of the Book) in 1967. The work captures the unpredictable realignments of global religious politics following the Six-Day War, and Jameelah's attempt to forge affective Muslim solidarity in response to them. While Jameelah's earlier writings generated collective grief around Jewish and Muslim suffering, after the war her writing evoked outrage that was increasingly directed at Jews and Judaism itself.

Islam Versus Ahl al-Kitab is shot through with an American middlebrow perspective that was Jameelah's cultural touchstone. To demonstrate how American public opinion was being swayed against support for the Arab cause, she pulled from a *Time* magazine editorial published on June 23, 1967, that claimed, "Israel . . . is hated by the Arabs in part because it is a successful modern, Western state."[44] According to Jameelah, this portrayal of Arabs as backward was buttressed by shifting racialized attitudes toward Jews in the United States, in which American Christians aligned with Jews, who were now understood to share a white racial identity.[45] For Jameelah, these racialized realignments explained why Christians were so *emotionally* committed to Israel. Here, Jameelah portrayed the 1967 defeat as one event in a series of rapidly evolving aberrations that required a new kind of affective response on the part of Muslims: the rising political power of a Jewish state; fuller inclusion of Jews into American society; and an unprecedented Christian-Jewish coalition.[46]

The articles that Jameelah selected further emphasized the religious attachments and stakes in the conflict. Such questions supplanted issues such as Palestinian leadership, sovereignty, or citizenship—or, for that matter, Palestinian interpretations of the war and its significance. A case in point is a *New York Post* article that Jameelah received from her aunt that reported on

Muhammad Abdul Rauf's appearance at the United Synagogue of America on November 17, 1967. Abdul Rauf (d. 2003), whose writings on the family I will take up in the final chapter, was serving at the time as imam at the Islamic Center of New York City. He was an Egyptian immigrant, trained at Al-Azhar, and had immigrated in the early 1960s to the US, where he became a prominent Muslim intellectual and author. As quoted by Jameelah, he told the largely Jewish audience, "There is no use being in isolation. When you come together you realize you are human beings." In response, Rabbi Henry Siegman, a leader in the United Synagogue, affirmed that, "the bitterness that has marked the modern encounter between Arab and Jew must not be allowed to obscure the fact that Judaism and Islam enjoy an affinity. If there is ever to occur a genuine reconciliation between Arab and Jew, as surely there must and will [be], then the basis of this reconciliation must be the shared religious values and the legacy of a cultural symbiosis unique in history."[47] Jameelah relayed to her audience that, while important voices in the American Jewish and Muslim communities saw this "shocking event" as an opportunity to forge a "hopeful beginning of reconciliation," she took the opposite view. For her, the realignment of religious and racial politics that 1967 meant that Muslims needed to forge an oppositional stance in relation to the People of the Book, not reach across religious lines in the hope of building new relationships. The deep sadness that she previously expressed began to vanish.

In addition to her engagement with American responses to the war, Jameelah relied on opinion and news analysis published in Pakistan, but for a different purpose—to demonstrate and rally unified Muslim support for the Palestinian cause. *The Pakistan Times*, the English daily paper that was Jameelah's chosen news source, advocated for the Palestinian cause through a framework of Third World solidarity. Headlines and news features about the war spotlighted Asian and African countries who supported the United Arab Republic against what was described as Israeli expansionism. On June 7, 1967, the paper reported a "massive rally in

Lahore" where students, political leaders, and provincial leaders called on the Pakistani government to support the "Arab Mujahideen."[48] In addition to the Third World solidarity expressed by Pakistani literary culture and print media in that moment, Jameelah's writing reflected the central importance of Palestine in various expressions of Muslim solidarity. Although Jameelah believed that Muslims had to engage in defensive struggle against Zionism *as Muslims*, she was also enmeshed in arguments that the occupation of Palestine was part of a broader struggle to liberate colonized peoples.

Jameelah's understanding of the 1967 conflict as necessitating religious resistance also reflected expressions of self-blame among her fellow revivalist intellectuals, aimed at fellow Muslims. In this vein, she laid blame at the feet of her coreligionists who had been swayed by "foreign" ideologies such as nationalism and socialism, as well as the failed promises of pan-Arabism.[49] Similarly, she enhanced the religious, maximalist rhetoric around the Palestinian cause, matching the high stakes rhetoric that Christian and Jewish communities marshaled in their support of Israeli's military campaigns. The war increased the legitimacy of Islamist organizations such as the Muslim Brotherhood in Egypt. Having supported Palestinian resistance since before 1948, the group promoted Muslim revival as a "third way" between socialism and free-market capitalism.[50] For her part, Jameelah praised the Brotherhood for its steadfast commitment to the Palestinian cause and for its early framing of Zionism as a form of colonial oppression.

These religious interpretations were amplified by the annexation of Jerusalem. She wrote, "the conquering of Jerusalem and the desecration of the *Bait al-Muqaddas* and the threat of further aggression . . . raises the question as to whether or not any basis exists for a reconciliation and peaceful existence between Muslim and Jew on the foundation of Islamic teachings."[51] Concern about the fate of sacred spaces such as the Al-Aqsa Mosque and the Dome of the Rock, as well as the dismantling of Arab civil society organizations and ongoing property confiscations, intensified

Jameelah's and other Muslim revivalists' claims that the risk to Muslims in Israel and Palestine was existential. At stake was the integrity of Islam and the capacity of Muslims to visit and honor the places that were central to their identities as Muslims.

A Hardened Affect

While *Islam Versus the Ahl al-Kitab* contains vestiges of Jameelah's earlier humanistic impulses, the text also contains multiple references to the trope of the "essential Jew." First emerging in reaction to twentieth-century colonization of Palestine and particularly resonant after 1948, this discourse centered on the idea that Jews had repeatedly worked against Muslim interests since the time of the Prophet Muhammad. The trope also emphasized certain enduring features of Jews over time. Although Jameelah praised Judaism's absolute monotheism (in its similarity with Islam), she also asserted that Jews were inherently bound by a national, tribal identity that made them reject the message of the Prophet Muhammad: "It was their [Arabian Jews'] nationalist pride which made an unlettered Prophet from among the Arabs utterly unacceptable to them as their guide, even though the Arabs were their nearest kin."[52] This narrative was distinct from Christian traditions of antisemitism and anti-Judaism, which more often trafficked in fantasies of demonic activities and accusations of blood libel. As Taji-Farouki puts it, this newer narrative portrayed the "the establishment of Israel on the Islamic land of Palestine and the policies of the Jewish state [as] an explicit reenactment of the Jews' historical rebellious conduct."[53] In this vein, Jameelah invoked Quranic passages to interpret current events in Israel and Palestine in light of Jewish actions as described in the Qur'an.[54]

Feeling her way through a political and religious crisis, Jameelah put forward a confounding array of claims about Jews and Judaism in *Islam Versus Ahl al-Kitab*. She argued that Zionism, understood as support for a Jewish state and homeland, was a substantive, integral part of Judaism from the beginning, but also claimed that Zionism was a recent imperial design. Similarly, she argued that Zionism was ascendent in American Jewish communities in her childhood (in the 1930s and 1940s) and yet that Zionism had really only become dominant among American Jews in the 1960s. Jameelah peppered her contradictory analysis with historical examples from the ancient Israelites to the intellectual life of Maimonides to the Holocaust, which she used to underscore her key pedagogical point that Judaism was once a legitimate and vibrant faith that in modernity had been co-opted by the destructive forces of nationalism. Alongside the grief that she expressed for Muslims, she also conveyed sadness over what she saw as the loss of her childhood religion to materialism.

In other passages, however, Jameelah portrayed Jews as exceptionally materialist and, thus, exceptionally violent toward Muslims. Referring to Jews as "notorious money-lenders" and "merciless usurers," Jameelah invoked the antisemitic *Protocols of the Elders of Zion*, quoting from a Pakistani edition: *The Jewish Conspiracy and the Muslim World with the Complete Text of the Protocols of the Learned Elders of Zion*, edited by Misbahul Islam Faruqi, published in Lahore in 1967. This infamous text, which originated in Russia in the 1880s, expounded racist narratives about a Jewish conspiracy to take over the globe. First translated into Arabic in the 1920s, by the 1940s it circulated in some Arab and South Asian Muslim intellectual circles through multiple translations.[55] Scholars have identified its influence through the appearance of new conspiratorial elements in Muslim and Arab writings on Jews, which posited the collusion of Zionists with Western imperialism to explain why Arab armies failed so spectacularly in defending Islamic lands.[56] Jameelah excerpted passages from the *Protocols*, to claim that "Jews have always collaborated with the enemies of the Muslims and whenever a calamity struck in Islamic history, Jews have been responsible directly or indirectly, overtly or covertly."[57] Jameelah also cited a series of op-eds from *The Pakistan Times* published in June 1967. In one piece, "The Zionist Conspiracy," author Abdul Majid argued that Jews were on a "scriptural mission" to "eliminate" Arabs—even though Jews had enjoyed protections under Muslim rule, in contrast to Christian efforts to expel Jews from their territories.[58] Taking up this thread, Jameelah claimed that although Christians started the missionary and colonial enterprise, they represented less of a danger to the "Muslim world" than Jews, whose settlements in Palestine, Jameelah told her readers, were far more threatening to the survival of Muslims writ large. Just as "the Hindus of India will tolerate only Hindus, 'Israel' is for Jews only. Wherever Zionism rules, all non-Jews—Christians and Muslims alike are driven out *en masse* by force."[59] Rather than be content with "cultural extermination," as she claimed that other imperial ideologies were, Zionism was bent on the "physical annihilation" of Muslims because they were Muslims.

Amid this perception that Islam faced an urgent existential threat, Jameelah foregrounded a narrowed affectsphere around Jews and Judaism that reflected a new openness to violence. Reclaiming Palestine required a unified religious response under the banner of jihad: "jihad must be waged under the banner of Islam for the glory of Allah alone. The Arabs must be persuaded that they can never hope to achieve the liberation of Palestine under such meaningless slogans as nationalism or socialism."[60] For Jameelah, invoking jihad would necessarily activate Muslim ethical constraints around warfare and buttress the moral foundation of Palestinian resistance. She stipulated that sharia required a formal declaration of war—in contrast to the skirmishes that had defined Israel's conflicts with Arab nations and Palestinian resistance groups prior to 1967. Islamic law would also restrict civilian casualties; limit the devastation of crops and livestock; rein in the use of biological, chemical, and nuclear weapons; prevent sexual assault and rape; and ensure humane treatment of prisoners of war.

Following Qutb, Jameelah argued that religious struggle was not simply necessary but required in Palestine.[61] Engaging in jihad would free fellow Muslims from the shackles of *jāhiliyya*—or state of ignorance—to which they were subjected.[62] Qutb buttressed these anti-colonial claims with antisemitic language that portrayed Jews as inherently evil and responsible for the rise of modernity and its destructive effects.[63] Citing Qutb throughout her post-1967 writings, Jameelah presented jihad as a strategy to realize Muslim unity, bring about a more just world, and attain rewards in the next life. In this way, Jameelah's invoked jihad in the context of transnational ideological and affective frameworks that competed for Muslims' attention and loyalty. As a concept in the textual corpus of Islam—including the Qur'an, hadith, exegesis of sacred texts, jurisprudence, and Sufism—"jihad" is a rich and multivalent term that Jameelah presented here as a means to establish the primacy of religious identity over and against secular nationalist and socialist movements that advocated for Palestinian sovereignty and rights.[64] Roxanne Euben astutely notes that "in the context of what is seen as pervasive *jāhiliyya, jihad* in pursuit of divine sovereignty on earth is neither an expression of blind rage nor simply a response to an other-worldly imperative."[65] Instead, Jameelah's openness to violence emerged out of a much longer affective strategy to galvanize Muslim solidarity around the existential threats that she believed modernity posed to a just Islamic community.

At the same time, by the mid-1970s, Jameelah's writing evoked a kind of brittleness, a "terminal" quality. Even as Jameelah grappled with exceptions and historical contingencies that she herself openly acknowledged, she increasingly reverted to stereotypical tropes because of the potent affective work that such representations could accomplish.[66] As Schaefer argues, "embedded in our bodies are machines surging for the production of both exclusionary, violent affects and inclusive, compassionate affects."[67] What makes *Islam Versus Ahl al-Kitab* so confounding and at times so incoherent, is that the text "surges" with both kinds of compulsive affects—compassionate and violent—in response to a changing, volatile political environment. Her book reflected Jameelah's deep desire to alleviate the pain of her fellow Muslims and to restore justice on their behalf. At the same time, she channeled exclusionary impulses that solidified boundaries between Muslims and Jews, thus hardening many of the religious and ideological borders that she had once experienced as far more porous. As those exclusionary affects became more dominant, the shared grief of Jews and Muslims that she expressed in earlier writings became a less prominent thread. Within this narrowed affectsphere, the political conditions that were necessary for interreligious challenges to modernity's threats became impossible.

Conclusion

Exploring Jameelah's religious imagination helps to illuminate the transnational affective economies that were generated around Palestine and Israel by twentieth-century revivalists. First, her writings demonstrate how religious affects are shaped in real time, and in response to unpredictable political realignments. Enthusiasm for Zionism increased across Jewish communities in the immediate years after the conflict. American Jewish intellectuals, rabbis, and students began to worry less about the problem of "dual loyalty" as they embraced support for Israel as a kind of ethnic nationalism, a celebration of their origins and distinctive identity that was compatible with their Americanness. As a result, immigration to Israel surged.[68] Although Jameelah understood herself to be writing for Muslim audiences, she was also grappling with significant changes in American Jewish attachments to Israel from a Jewish perspective, which then shaped her understanding of how Muslims ought to respond to these changing affective attachments. Jameelah's path from sadness to outrage, from advocating humanitarian care to supporting violence, was a winding and unpredictable one. Her imagined Palestine was constructed through a vast array of influences—postwar humanitarian photography, coffee-table books, middlebrow Zionist novels, Muslim revivalist thought—that articulated vastly different religious and political aspirations.

Second, excavating the transnational webs of Jameelah's engagement with Palestine and Israel illustrates the potency of an affective economy that hinges on anxieties over distinctiveness, the desire to restore pride, and the framing of catastrophic stakes around those anxieties. She staked out Palestine in terms of survival—not just for Palestinians, but for Muslims writ large—and she believed that Islam was potentially collapsing under the weight of assimilation to Western modernity. Jameelah was most drawn into the specific Muslim bundling of these three elements, but this constellation of negative affects is by no means unique to Muslims or Islam.

Jameelah's framing actually echoes the worldview of some radical Jews, who also persuasively harnessed some of the same negative affects, such as Meir Kahane (d. 1990), the founder of the Jewish Defense League. We should note that Kahane and Jameelah were born just a couple of years apart; they were both firmly middlebrow authors; they castigated Jewish liberals for what they saw as rampant hypocrisy and materialism; they were obsessed with preserving religious pride; and they saw religious identity primarily in political terms.[69] As the 1960s drew to a close, both thinkers embraced violence as a means to preserve the survival of their respective communities. As far as I am aware, Jameelah never engaged Kahane or his work, and obviously would have rejected his political positions. Their political distance from one another is all the more reason to highlight how similarly they each leveraged these affective threads. The brief comparison underscores, in other words, that these negative affects resonated widely across twentieth-century religious communities. Although we might otherwise wish to ignore authors like Jameelah and Kahane, their successful marshaling of negative affects helps to explain precisely how Jewish-Muslim discourse became much more hardened around Israel/Palestine in the closing decades of the twentieth century.

For Jameelah, the case for Palestinian solidarity was moral and religious, and as such had to be forged through the family. Through her writings and art, Jameelah desired her readers to "wake up" to the horrors of modernity. She staked out Palestine in terms of survival—not just for Palestinians but for Muslims writ large—because she believed that Islam was potentially collapsing under the weight of assimilation to Western modernity. Notably, Ahmad Khalil never joins an organization or a movement. Instead, Ahmad Khalil's unwavering focus rests with his family, even as they are dispersed around the world in exile. Although he cannot stop colonialism from wrecking his mind and body, or capitalism from corrupting his own son, he represents the model Muslim who maintains the utmost purity of his motivations and intentions. In this way, Jameelah's imagined Ahmad Khalil is an exemplary member of the revivalist vanguard that she longed for: suffering, righteous, and fully awakened to the horrors of modernity.

5

Leveraging Shame to Build Global Muslim Solidarity

AS THE last chapter explored, Jameelah's novel about Palestine centered on the affectsphere of grief and sadness. Here, I focus on how she harnessed a different set of affects—shame and pride—around gender and the family.[1] Female authors like Jameelah played a key role in centering the family as the site to revive Islam. Jameelah was a key figure in this effort to make women's bodies and female sexuality into core issues of global Muslim politics.[2] In order to restore the pride and dignity of the umma, she thought that it was essential for Muslims to acknowledge their own failings. Jameelah believed that modern Muslims had failed in three main areas: maintaining gender separation and restricting female mobility; regulating sexuality to prevent the exploitation of women; and preserving the patriarchal family as a space of Islamic purity.

This chapter focuses on books and articles that Jameelah published in the 1970s at the height of her career. Her writings about gender, women, and the family illustrate how, as a recent convert and émigré, Jameelah continued to grapple with the Islam she imagined, on the one hand, and the messiness of religion on the ground in Pakistan on the other. This gap reveals that many of Jameelah's observations and recommendations fail, in fact, to capture the complexity of women's lived experiences. Unlike many other female revivalist thinkers and leaders, Jameelah preferred not to engage with women's interior spiritual lives nor was she interested in helping them to navigate the daily challenges that they faced.

For this reason, extant scholarship on gender and the Islamic revival, which as largely focused on the educational initiatives and ritual practices embraced and led by Muslim women, sheds only partial light on Jameelah's vision. In her groundbreaking work *The Politics of Piety*, Saba Mahmood foregrounds specific virtues and affects through which women built new practices and networks of Muslim piety. These pious practices subvert American feminist conceptions of autonomy and freedom, revealing a much wider set of religious desires and motivations. In this chapter, I build on Mahmood's theoretical attention to affect in order to trace the wide intellectual and religious terrain of Jameelah's gendered politics.

As a case study, however, Jameelah's writings on gender reveal a distinct thread of revivalism that quite directly challenged Western liberalism in general and feminism in particular. Jameelah contested foundational liberal ideals such as freedom, individualism, and choice as false. To do so, Jameelah relied on an American middlebrow framework—periodicals such as *Reader's Digest*, her personal observations of Pakistani society, and feminist critiques of American culture—to generate shame. That is, instead of excavating Islamic theology or spiritual practice, Jameelah mobilized shame as a potent anti-modern affect in two main directions. One, she argued that Muslims ought to feel shame for these collective shortcomings to implement essential Islamic obligations around gender and sexuality; she also invoked shame to demarcate the moral boundary between "Islam" and the "West." Two, Jameelah evoked shame to accentuate what she saw as the emasculating effects of ongoing Western cultural dominance.[3] In contrast to theories of affect that presume that communities need to expel shame, Jameelah demanded that her readers first experience and dwell in it.[4] For Jameelah, shame was productive, and she sought to intentionally cultivate it.

We cannot understand the religious work of shame, which Jameelah coded as feminine, without considering its opposing affect—pride—which she framed as masculine. By invoking models of masculinity that could free female bodies from sticky shame, Jameelah further reinforced the boundaries around Islam and gender.[5] To that end, she wrote extensively about male exemplars, both past and present. In opposition to women, who symbolized the shame of colonial subjugation, exemplary men embodied the intellectual, military, and religious capacity that was necessary to revive Islam. The shame that Muslim women brought to the umma could only be restored through the valiant actions of great male revivers. In this way, male revivers embodied "normative Muslimness."[6]

What ties Jameelah's affective vision to other revivalist efforts, then, is a much broader affective economy centered on the restoration of Muslim pride.[7] As we have seen, while Jameelah regularly invoked universalist rhetoric, she believed that "true" Muslims constituted a small slice of the global Muslim community. As such, the task of revival necessitated sweeping collective shame, but the task of restoring pride rested with a much smaller group of vanguard revivalists.

After analyzing Jameelah's use of the shame-pride progression, I consider the ways that Muslim women in Pakistan in the 1960s and 1970s—including Jameelah herself—subverted the gendered norms and practices that she sought to uphold. While Jameelah sought to restrict women's mobility, the Jamaat-i-Islami sought women's participation in Muslim revivalist spaces outside the home. Additionally, women were already active in intellectual debates, political action, and educational initiatives in the decades prior to Jameelah's arrival in Pakistan, a fact that she barely acknowledged in her near-total elision of actual women and female authors from her writings. As a result, Jameelah's lack of attention to women's contributions to the very causes she believed in considerably limited her appeal beyond Jamaat-i-Islami networks. Jameelah saw these subversions (with the exception of her own) as reasons to feel badly about the state of modern Islam. And yet, women's direct involvement in the revivalist movement was necessary to achieve the global solidarity that she sought to enact.

The Failures of the Nation-State

When Jameelah arrived in Pakistan in 1962, the government was in the process of revising its family law code. While she generally supported the implementation of Muslim criminal, commercial, and family law in Pakistan, she was skeptical that state institutions could serve as instruments for achieving a just Muslim society. So, once she was settled and ready to more fully embark on her writing career, she seized on the opportunity to generate collective shame by highlighting the inability of governments to protect Islamic laws: "It is a matter of shame and regret that the family laws are being mutilated in Muslim countries so that the Holy Prophet, His Companions, and our greatest divines, who nearly all married more than one wife, would be considered as 'criminals' under contemporary legislation!"[8] The goal of Jameelah's arguments was not to realize specific legal reforms, but rather to generate negative collective emotions around them to galvanize Muslim solidarity. While this passage was prompted by specific political debates in Pakistan, Jameelah saw the country's legal reforms as a source of collective shame for all Muslims. These legal debates signaled that Muslims had acquiesced to the "exaggerated individualism" on which the critique of polygamy was made. They chose to reject the collective benefits of polygamy—namely, the universal obligation to enact God's laws and to provide the protection of the family to all Muslim women. (In other words, polygyny offered protection to the women who would otherwise have been forced to remain single.) According to Jameelah, not one modern Muslim society had properly maintained Islamic prescriptions around family through the law. The entire umma was thus subject to the collective shame of failing to restore fundamental religious laws and practices.

Jameelah's focus on polygamy reflects the durability of the "status of women" discourse, which became prominent among colonial administrators in South Asia as well as a key feature of religious and nationalist opposition to colonial rule. Later, women and gender figured prominently in discussions about the role of religion in public life. Postcolonial Muslim thinkers also debated over the presence of women in public space and the regulation of their bodies within those spaces, including educational institutions and the workplace. For example, Egyptian thinkers of the 1970s and 1980s, from seemingly opposite poles of the ideological spectrum—Islamic reformers and socialist feminists—concurred that modernity had degraded women by forcing them to display their bodies publicly.[9] Not surprisingly, the various proposed solutions to this "problem" diverged sharply. Was women's dignity best restored through the renewal of Islam in politics? Or would the embrace of socialist ideals promise better outcomes? Participants in these debates shared the assumption that the declining position of women indexed the dire state of modern society generally—perpetuating key assumptions within the colonial paradigms that had portrayed women as the benchmark of "civilization." Such discourses simultaneously decried the objectification of women and utilized them as symbols of progress and liberation.

In Pakistan, where Jameelah explicated most of the ideas discussed here, women and girls were highly visible objects in nation-building projects and in the construction of a religious and national identity.[10] Jameelah entered a local political context (whose particulars she only marginally grasped) in which the "status" of women and girls was being used to advance a range of social aims. In the 1950s and 1960s the Pakistani government adopted a modernization program to attract business, tourists, investment, and partnership with British and American allies. Representations of women in Pakistani media, advertising, and government reports set up a binary between the modern woman, who was the desired subject for a modern Pakistan—and the secluded woman, or the "failed subject." And yet, women and girls who were seen as "too" modern, especially if they appeared "hyper-sexualized," were also failed subjects—because they disrupted the ideal role of a wife and mother who reproduces national subjects. According to this mindset, the fate of the nation rested on the fate of its women.

Sara Ahmed's analysis of shame in the context of Australia illustrates the unifying political aims that Jameelah sought to accomplish through cultivating collective emotion. According to Ahmed, the idea that a collective entity feels shame is linked to the perception that its members are unable to "live up to" its shared values: "By witnessing what is shameful about the past, the nation can 'live up to' the ideals that secure its identity or being in the present. In other words, our shame means that we mean well and can work to reproduce the nation as an ideal. . . . The national ideal is shaped by taking some bodies as its form and not others. The pride of some subjects is in a way tautological: they feel pride at approximating an ideal that has already taken their shape."[11] Ahmed explains that white Australians experience shame when they perceive that they have failed to live up to the multicultural ideal by inflicting harms on Indigenous and non-white people through colonialism. Given this, we might expect that such collective feelings of shame would lead to a reckoning over Australian national identity and perhaps an expansion of the national project to include Indigenous peoples. But the inverse is true; no reckoning and no expansion of the nation takes place. Only a more limited group feels collective shame because they are the ones who ultimately inhabit the ideal that has been compromised. In this way, the expression of national shame is really a conservative project that restores white Australians' feeling of pride in their nation and the centrality of their place within that nation. White Australians' shame in failing to uphold national values reaffirms their attachment to the nation yet does not dislodge their status as the ideal national subjects.

Similarly, Jameelah viewed collective shame as a productive register through which to restore pride and dignity in the umma. However, she believed that the nation-state, at least in any of its current manifestations, could not be the instrument for restoring Muslim pride. In surveying the state of Muslim gender practices in the 1960s, Jameelah saw only the failure to uphold the gender norms of the original community of Muslims during the life of the Prophet Muhammad. In some nation-states, such as Tunisia, polygamy had been outlawed altogether. In other places, such as Egypt and Pakistan, the practice was allowed but only under certain conditions. She viewed any restrictions on the practice as an affront to the Muslim family itself. The failure to live up to what Jameelah considered to be original Muslim gender practices was the source of the umma's shame. Restoring dignity through revival was the only way to avert the ongoing corrosive effects of the nation-state's regulation of Islamic law. But instead of seeking to reform the state, Jameelah focused her energy on the family as the institution through which to foster pride in the umma.

The Failures of Modernism

As we have seen, very few Muslims lived up to Jameelah's ideals. The incapacity to feel shame was one indicator that a Muslim had abandoned Islam. She singled out unnamed "modernists" who were particularly unlikely to feel shame around the erosion of traditional gender roles in Muslim communities because they had already succumbed to "mental slavery" and capitulated to Western cultural dominance.[12] Modernists had become pawns of imperialism by embracing "perverted cultural values" that led to the mixing of proper gender roles. Jameelah argued that for modernists, "a woman is entitled to honour and respect to the extent to which she succeeds in performing the functions of a man while at the same time exhibiting her maximum beauty and charm to the public."[13] Jameelah thus used shame to draw stark lines between those Muslims who were committed to living out the ideals of the Prophet Muhammad and those who had abandoned the original teachings of Islam. While claiming to speak on behalf of all Muslims, Jameelah's affectsphere hinged on such exclusions.

Jameelah identified several key figures that she labeled as "modernist" and, as such, beyond the pale—ranging from the Indian scholar and Muslim reformer Sayyid Ahmed Khan (d. 1898) to the Turkish nationalist and sociologist Ziya Gokalp (d. 1924) to the Indian diplomat and Islamic legal thinker Asaf Fyzee (d. 1981).[14] She was particularly incensed by the work of Ghulam Ahmad Parvez (d. 1985), who had served as an official in the Pakistani government and wrote a four-volume commentary of the Qur'an, *Ma'arif al-Qur'an*, published in Urdu in the 1940s; as well as *Islam: A Challenge to Religion*, published in English in 1968. Jameelah was unflinching in her appraisal that "nowhere has the Qur'an suffered a more mutilated and distorted interpretation than by the pen of Parvez."[15] She took issue with Parvez's distinction "between *Mudhab* [*madhab*] which he translates as 'religion,' and *din* or the faith of Islam."[16] Jameelah was even more outraged by what she saw as his complete omission of hadith—sayings and deeds of the Prophet Muhammad—from his articulation of "permanent divine values" such as tolerance and justice.[17] She asked rhetorically, "If the sources of the Tradition are so defective . . . how can such an emasculated faith provide the human race with a sound code of life? Who would be prepared to struggle and make sacrifices for such watered-down modernism?"[18] Modernists feminized Islam, stripping it of its civilizational strength through "radical amputation" of what was at its heart a strong, implicitly masculine tradition.

In contrast to feminine "modernists," she coded as masculine those Muslims who upheld "traditional" gender norms and supported laws for enforcing them—and thus contributed to rebuilding the past. Such "real" Muslims worked for glory of the umma and sought to reverse the decline of Islam under colonialism and modernization. Jameelah argued that, since the late nineteenth century, the vanguard of the Islamic Revival had been engaged in an existential battle for the survival of their religion. Quite often, their battle was against fellow Muslims such as thinkers like Qasim Amin (d. 1908), the prominent Egyptian scholar and nationalist figure who sought to eliminate practices such as seclusion and veiling because he believed those practices had no place in a modern society.[19] Amin's arguments about the need to end seclusion were also predicated on a shame/pride progression in which Islam itself should not be blamed for the degraded status of women. Amin argued that Islam had emancipated women by ending female infanticide and establishing their property rights long before any European nation conferred similar rights. "Despotic" governments, not Islam, were to blame for the position that twentieth-century Muslim women found themselves in, lagging as they did behind European women in terms of political rights, education, and economic well-being. The exercise of raw political power had led men to "despise" women. It was the conduct of despots that warranted shame for excluding women from educational and other public institutions and demanding that wives serve their husbands as head of the household. The only way to restore the Egyptian nation—and by extension, the umma as a whole—was to return women to the original, vaulted status they enjoyed in the time of the Prophet Muhammad.

Although Jameelah was staunchly opposed to modernism, her arguments and affective framework echoed key assumptions of modernist thought. First, she concurred with the general contours of Amin's declension narrative and the need to restore Islam in the wake of decline. In addition, she similarly understood the "status of women" as a key metric through which to measure collective strength and unity.[20] She also placed enormous affective weight on the role of the nuclear family as the building block of a robust society. In this way, Jameelah tapped into powerful affective attachments around female bodies and the family that resonated across multiple ideological projects.

Ultimately, Jameelah's universalism was predicated on divisions within the umma that she wished to uplift, not gloss or repair. Only certain Muslims—those who shared Jameelah's complementarian view of gender roles and the necessity of religious strictures to maintain them—could make this revivalist mission a reality. The affect of shame did not merely help to instantiate the Islam/West binary; generating shame also positioned a limited group of Muslims as the true inheritors of the legacy of the Prophet Muhammad. Other Muslims, most notably modernists, posed an existential threat to the survival of Islam. While the language of the umma at first glance seems to be an inclusive, universal category, invoking shame created and solidified boundaries within the umma. Jameelah used the anti-modern affect to recognize those Muslims who were committed to the revivalist project and who inhabited a special role in maintaining, preserving, and ultimately reestablishing the glory of Islam.

Domestic Space and Religious Renewal

For Jameelah, women occupied an ambivalent position as idealized yet subordinate members of the global Muslim community. She sought to define and uplift complementary gendered roles, which she believed was the basis for preserving a Muslim way of life: "While men are the actors on the stage of history, the function of the women is to be their helpers, concealed from public gaze from behind the scenes—a less exciting and more humble role perhaps, but no less essential for the preservation of our way of life."[21] In making this case, Jameelah contributed to an emerging set of revivalist publications in the 1960s and 1970s that emphasized domestic space as an essential site for reinvigorating Islam. Female authors were instrumental in articulating the Islamic vocabulary around the primacy of the home and women's contributions within it. For Jameelah, the Muslim mother must ensure the stability of the family, unified in their obedience and devotion to God, and the home as a place where the "instructions" contained in the Qur'an and Hadith would be "practically *implemented* in their everyday lives."[22] Within the space of the home, Jameelah cast the mother's role as reproductive in two primary ways: birthing children and ensuring the transmission of Islamic norms and practices among those children. Women were thus tasked with ensuring the continuity of religious practice. The domestic space functioned as a primary political arena for the preservation of tradition. It was the best place to ensure compliance with Islamic regulations and prohibitions and, in the process, ensure the distinctiveness and superiority of "Muslim civilization."[23]

The problem, Jameelah believed, was that women had become disconnected from their most fundamental roles as caregivers. Late capitalism eroded women's capacity to perform their primary responsibilities. Even worse, some women now pursued different aspirations. In a fiery pamphlet published in 1978, Jameelah proclaimed that Western business investment in Pakistan portended an all-out "cultural invasion":

> It is not exaggeration to assert that *Western big business is their chief medium of cultural invasion*. . . . Foreign-dominated business and industry insist that women leave the home and compete with men for jobs in offices and factories; thus our women are transformed from chaste wives, mothers, sisters, and daughters into ticket collectors on buses and trains, bank-clerks, telephone-operators, sales-ladies, air-hostesses . . . and consequently *Purdah*, the home and the family are destroyed with illicit sex and children mature into vicious "teddies" and juvenile delinquents.[24]

In Jameelah's account, some Muslim women had been lured into the trap of earning money and seeking professional advancement. In the process, such women not only abandoned their "natural" functions, but they also diminished the potential for men to fulfill theirs by competing for the same jobs. Thus, women entering the workforce disrupted the complementary vision for gender roles—that she believed were foundational to Islam—and created new resentments between men and women.

According to Jameelah, the expansion of the female workforce was the result of "foreign" interests, and governments like Pakistan's that had been swayed by such interests and preyed upon unsuspecting, highly impressionable Muslim women. Not only did such jobs take women out of their rightful place in the home, but even worse, they also encouraged women to abandon Islamic norms around sexuality. According to Jameelah, who cited no evidence, anecdotal or otherwise, women who worked in paying jobs were more likely to abandon their "chaste" natures and engage in illicit sex. In turn, such immoral practices further undermined the integrity of the nuclear family and the purity of the home. As a result, such women became accomplices to the "enemies" of Islam, or the "imperialists" who "are trying to degrade us morally and spiritually and enfeeble us in body and mind."[25] Whatever economic conditions led women to seek employment outside the home, Jameelah argued that such realities must be subordinated to what she saw as immutable ethical obligation to prioritize the labor of women within the home.

Drawing on Mawdudi's notion of the term, Jameelah was primarily concerned with outlining the requirements of purdah, the practice of maintaining gender separation among men and women who were not close family members and restricting female presence in public space. Jameelah took purdah to mean that women should spend most of their time in their homes in order to avoid unwanted male attention, preserve their sexual virtue, and ensure they had properly fulfilled their caregiving and domestic tasks.[26] When they did leave the home, women needed to dress modestly to avoid attracting unwanted male attention and to prevent untoward interactions between the genders. Jameelah largely adhered to Mawdudi's approach to the practice of purdah but sought to intensify the collective emotions around the concept. Many back covers of her books emphasize that her "hatred" of materialism led to her "strict" observance of purdah.[27] While Jameelah exhorted her readers that modest dress was a strict obligation, she cast that requirement within a broader set of rules around separating men and women and maintaining the purity of the home as a bulwark against encroaching materialism and secularism.

Jameelah's intense focus on the female body also resonated with that of other women revivalists who were articulating their own polemics against the new visibility of Muslim women in public space.[28] These female authors largely did not recognize or refer to one another. Yet in their respective revivalist networks, they helped to generate a cohesive affective terrain of the revival, amplifying the emotional stakes around the female body and the home. For example, in Egypt the author and preacher Ni'ma Sadiq, a contemporary of Jameelah, began publishing books, essays, pamphlets, and sermons that were translated into multiple languages and achieved a transnational reach. Sadiq saw the female body in a similar way to Jameelah, as a "a site of the sacred unseen, challenging the value of the exposed body, displayed like a commodity in the marketplace."[29] Such a critique found traction across revivalist organizations, functioning as a key framework through which to understand the erosion of Islamic values and practices. At the same time, Jameelah's conceptual landscape was quite distinct from Sadiq's, who was much more interested in sharing insights from exegetical traditions and exploring the sensory dimensions of female piety.

Jameelah's critique of materialism as the primary conduit for disrupting the divinely sanctioned gender order reflected the more direct influence of Iranian American scholar Seyyed Hossein Nasr (b. 1933). Jameelah's reliance on Nasr demonstrates that she came to her views on gendered roles and responsibilities through a varied set of influences. A key figure in perennialist philosophy, Nasr developed an Islamic metaphysical approach that drew heavily on Traditionalism and its critiques of modernity.[30] What drew Jameelah to Nasr's thought was not his perennialism; it was his affectsphere. Nasr's views on gender, as articulated in his 1966 *Ideals and Realities of Islam*, took center stage in Jameelah's work. She marshaled key features of his arguments: the patriarchal family was the "natural" building block of any functioning society; modernity had oppressed women by destabilizing the financial protections afforded to them in traditional societies; and complementary gender roles ensured security and tranquility between men and women.[31] The dire condition of modernity—encapsulated for Jameelah by the erosion of the fundamental hierarchies of social arrangements between genders—represented a profound rupture of what Traditionalists imagined as a "sacred order" upon which civilization rested.[32] Due to the erosion of religious ideals and practices in modernity, many women suffered from alarming "anxiety" and other mental illnesses that Jameelah believed were a hallmark of the modern world. Most importantly, many women experienced spiritual disillusionment and alienation from Islam.[33]

Popular Culture and the Corruption of the Home

Increase in female employment was not the only threat to the reproductive functions of women and the sanctity of feminized domestic space. Working for wage labor also exposed women to media and art that Jameelah deemed threatening forms of "dirt." To use Mary Douglas's classic formulation, Jameelah called pop culture "dirty" to signal to her readers that any consumption of pop culture was "out of place" in an authentic religious community. While her readers might have thought taking in a film was an acceptable pastime, Jameelah wanted to underscore that such activities threatened the foundation of a Muslim way of life.[34] Practices that she identified as "dirty" were cause for collective shame. Nowhere was this association between dirt and shame more apparent for Jameelah than in the realm of pop culture: film, television, music, and magazines. As she frequently emphasized, these media served only to wantonly display the female body and to objectify women. She declared that "no poison was more deadly for Islamic moral values than the cinema" and called for a ban on foreign movies to stem the tide of illicit sex and immoral relations between sexes that she saw as directly caused by this form of entertainment.[35]

It was not just that Jameelah considered pop culture to be un-Islamic; it was also that music and movies confounded the firm boundaries that Jameelah imagined between Islam and the West. She lamented that Muslims *liked* American movies and those desires created a robust demand for American and European films in Pakistan. In this way, Jameelah ascribed enormous power to pop culture, arguing that the ubiquity of rock and roll and romantic movies threatened an Islamic way of life. Music and movies were more than mere entertainment; they were "vulgar" and "dirty" forms that threatened to destroy the "whole moral and social framework" of Muslim societies.[36]

By calling out pop culture as a perilous social domain, Jameelah amplified an emerging Islamic politics around "fun." While Jameelah was drawn to Arab culture as a young girl through the music of Umm Kulthum, she took an increasingly hardline stance against forms of enjoyment that did not align with her narrow conceptions of Islamic normativity. Asef Bayat traces this phenomenon across Saudi Arabia, Egypt, and Afghanistan in the late twentieth century, arguing that this diffuse opposition represents an effort to curtail a "happy culture of Islam."[37] In this vein, Jameelah attacked pop culture to argue that Western imperialism was alive and well in the cultural domain and that even a nation that staked its identity on Islam, such as Pakistan, could not hold back its tides. Only a rigid set of constraints—a long list of what *not* to do—could resist the destructive force of "Western culture." Jameelah's anti-fun stance thus depended on a significant dose of fear to invoke collective shame. The proliferation of objects and spaces that brought diversions into modern Muslim life, from movie theaters to radios to makeup, made the task of rooting out fun a particularly daunting yet necessary one. What differentiates these modern critiques of fun from earlier examples was both the central place they assumed in Islamist politics and their potency in generating collective movements.[38] Jameelah's panic over the destructive capacity of entertainment suggested the need for increased surveillance of Muslims who participated in these forms of entertainment, whether as producers or as consumers. Her critiques represent her recognition of the affective potency of the politics of fun as a key site for cultivating the negative feelings that distinguished "us" from "them."

It was up to mothers to mount the moral defense to the threat posed by pop culture; shame was a primary tool in their arsenal: "Under no circumstances should she permit "pop" music to be heard in the house because this is the worst possible moral influence on the children. If ever children start singing these vulgar songs that they have heard and learned from their neighbors' radios and television sets, she [the mother] should hush them and tell them how ashamed they should feel to be heard singing such dirt!"[39] Her denigration of pop music was not just about it being inappropriate and immoral from an Islamic point of view. Jameelah constantly reminded her readers that Islam simply had no space for frivolity. Exposure to Western culture eroded the capacity of Muslim families to focus on their children's moral development. There was no time for such entertainment if families were properly focused on children's religious education. In cultivating shame around watching television or listening to the radio, mothers were also engaged in the crucial political aim of retaining the correct boundaries around Islam.

Despite Jameelah's declarations that such prescriptions represent unchanging tradition, the notion that women's (unpaid) domestic and caregiving labor is a metric of civilizational progress represents a thoroughly modern construction of the family. Women were simultaneously held responsible for enabling Western norms to take hold and held the key to fortifying the home against their influence. Here, Jameelah advocated for the role of shaming in the domestic space as both a tool to compel children to conform and a key practice for the rearing of devout Muslim children.

This polemic reinforced the idea that women functioned as the measure of a society's worth. Muslim women continued to have the capacity to feel shame as well as to deploy it within their domain of the home when they redoubled their adherence to Islamic beliefs and practices. Due to the incursions of Western influence, which Jameelah observed in the availability of American films and music in Pakistan, Muslim women were subject to the same kinds of temptations as European and American women. Yet Muslim women possessed the capacity to resist by being chaste, modest, and pure. Unlike women who had abandoned their faith, Muslim women who had prioritized religion over all other forms of identity acted out of obligation. As a result, they were more likely to assume their proper place within the home and focus on the primary task of reproducing Islamic norms and practices through their children.

However, according to Jameelah, Muslim women did not feel enough shame. Nowhere was this more apparent than in her description of the state of Pakistani households. Like many American and European observers, Jameelah railed against what she saw as the lack of hygiene and cleanliness in the homes that she frequented: "Most Pakistani homes, even those of middle-class people, are dingy and dirty. Too many Pakistani women I know have the dirty habit of continuously littering the floors of their homes, particularly the courtyards and kitchens, with garbage and rubbish. They would rather live in filth than clean it up themselves. Islamic education should teach girls cleanliness and orderliness. Women should not feel ashamed to clean and sweep the house themselves. They should not depend on servants to do it for them."[40] For Jameelah, a wife who ensured a clean home fulfilled her religious and moral aspirations.

While Jameelah proclaimed herself to be an ardent anti-imperialist, she frequently deployed colonial and class-based logics to critique Muslim women in Pakistan. The cleanliness of Pakistani homes indexed the degree to which commitment to Islam could be measured, rather than representing an accurate description of the state of homes that Jameelah frequented (or possibly did not frequent). Thus, the dirtier the household, the more its inhabitants had fallen away from Islam. As a result, Islamic educational initiatives had to redress this lapse in women's attention to the cleanliness of their homes. The emphasis on hygiene as an Islamic practice has its roots in colonial-era ideologies that cast the lack of cleanliness as both a moral and public health crisis. British colonial officers and educators imposed Victorian ideals of health on local communities by framing hygiene as an Islamic virtue. Gregory Starrett argues that such efforts recast the meaning of ritual practices such as ablutions (*wudu'*) in order to "put Islam to work."[41] These measures instrumentalized religious practices toward new political and social ends that served colonial powers.

To this colonial construct, Jameelah added the American Cold War image of an ideal, white, middle-class housewife and mapped it on to the Pakistani women that she observed. Ideally, a woman should complete all household tasks herself. She should not avail herself of paid labor. From this perspective, the ideal Muslim wife and mother was self-reliant and hardworking, fulfilled by her proper role as caregiver and homemaker in the nuclear family. This vision of femininity and domesticity resonated with the suburban norms of Jameelah's childhood.[42] Her use of the term "middle-class" signaled an aspirational gendered ideal, one embedded in racial and class structures that upheld a largely unattainable familial model as universal. Within this model, male breadwinners performed wage labor to provide for their dependent wives and children, and the labor of women was unpaid, outside of market forces. Rather than being compensated through currency, domestic labor in the US involved affective exchange of comfort, security, and affirmation.[43] While Jameelah railed against American materialism, she invoked the term "middle-class" to suggest that the fulfillment of Islamic norms around cleanliness and self-reliance (as she understood them) was more attainable by Muslims who had accrued the requisite socioeconomic status. Women from wealthier households were not exempt from household labor; they should sweep the floors themselves.

By invoking Cold War gender ideology and imposing it as an Islamic norm, Jameelah perpetuated the same kind of cultural imperialism that she claimed to detest. Her understanding of household labor and the ideal Muslim wife further aligned with Cold War justifications for fostering economic and social progress through development projects in societies that were deemed "beneficiaries." While Jameelah conveyed her disdain for "cultural imperialism" in Pakistan and elsewhere, her assessment of domestic spaces as "dirty" employed the same logic that Western observers used to offer moral critiques of the problems plaguing developing societies. Jameelah offered up a different solution through her revivalist vision of Islam, but the diagnosis tracked along prevailing US and European discourses that promoted cleanliness and hygiene for intertwined projects of public health and civilizational progress.

Most importantly, Jameelah's connection between shame, women, and domestic space demonstrates how she used affect to bridge the many cultural differences among her varied audiences. The shame that Jameelah invoked was not anchored in the genealogy of Islamic notions of shame. Instead, she constructed a transnational ideal that she hoped would be legible for Muslims living in a wide variety of cultural contexts. Castigating Muslim women for failing to adhere to Islamic standards of cleanliness underscored their simultaneous status as the paragons of Islamic civilization. When a Muslim mother and wife did not adhere to such standards, she then contributed to the shame of the entire umma. Precisely because women were the guardians of this boundary between Islam and the West, and between committed and non-committed Muslims, their actions necessitated intense scrutiny and correction. The attachments that Jameelah sought to build to the umma and the revivalist project therefore revolved around a "durable" colonial logic in which the measure of a society depended on the rendering of women as potent signs of decline and degradation.[44]

Restoring Pride Through Masculine Revival

Jameelah interchangeably used two terms—"revival" and "renewal"—that she considered essential for redressing the shameful decline of Islamic civilization. If the decline of Islam was collectively felt as shame through what she deemed as feminine/female spaces, then robust revival, and its associated affect of pride, was a decidedly masculine project. Jameelah invoked two distinct meanings of revivalism in her writing. The first meaning reflected an Islamic genealogy. The second encompassed American revivalist traditions.

In the first sense, Jameelah applied the term *mujaddid* to describe revivers such as Mawdudi and other revivalist figures that I discuss below. The term is widely attributed to a hadith that promises the rise of a pious figure who brings renewal to the faith by eliminating practices seen as innovations and, in the process, restores Islam to the original example set by the Prophet Muhammad. Following this usage, Jameelah understood revival to be cyclical, happening at regular intervals due to the heroic actions of prominent men. Although their backgrounds and actions differed, every renewer sought to correct and strengthen adherence to Islamic ritual practice and cultivate stronger attachments to the umma. The task of revival was necessary because the Muslim community regularly endured periods of degeneration that required correction. Jameelah was able to invoke the term's elastic qualities to encompass aspirational notions of renewal that she believed had the potential to engender robust pride in the umma.

In the mid-twentieth century, "revival" also took on particular political connotations that Jameelah's framework reflects. For thinkers such as Qutb and Mawdudi, the restoration of the original glory of the umma required the total reform of society according to Islamic principles. As we have seen, modernity represented an all-out catastrophe for Jameelah because it destroyed the religious foundations of a just society. Only the restoration of the practices and values of the Prophet Muhammad and his closest companions could make humanity whole again.

Jameelah's concept of revival had two distinctive elements. The first was that revival should have no fixed geographic center. All Muslims needed revival; this was one universal. Materialism everywhere threatened a Muslim way of life. While Jameelah invoked examples from Africa to Europe to the Middle East to make her case that revival was necessary, she never engaged in a sustained analysis of a particular national or cultural context. Rather, she moved between and among multiple settings to establish the necessity of mobilizing behind a global revival. She sought to first generate shame, and then pivoted toward male exemplary revivalists to inspire collective pride.

From this perspective, revivalism had the potential to overcome sectarian divisions. Jameelah was outright dismissive of the relevance of sectarian divisions, for example, between Sunni and Shia communities in Pakistan. She was also not particularly engaged in contemporary debates about Sufism and its status in modern Muslim communities, a debate that was particularly religiously and politically potent in the South Asian context.[45] For her, such divisions should never stand in the way of Muslim unity, and she was curiously indifferent to (or possibly ignorant of) their implications, either historically or in the contemporary period.

For Jameelah, revivalism had a broader connotation, that of "awakening." This valence was more appealing in diasporic Muslim contexts in Europe and North America. Starting in the late 1960s, on the back of each of her pamphlets Jameelah exhorted her audience to "awake" to the dangers posed by their internal and external enemies, which was the first step toward uniting behind a common Muslim identity and restoring the "path to the Quran and Sunnah." Revival began with a political and moral awakening, a state that each individual Muslim needed to inhabit before pride could be restored. While she berated fellows Muslims constantly for failing to comply with their religious obligations, her praise for revivalists—the great men of the past and the present—provided a counternarrative of Muslims who did the right thing when their societies faced existential threats from anti-Islamic elements, whether from within or without. Her biographies of great Muslim men provided the model for other male Muslims, who could then contribute to the cycle of renewal that Muslims before them had undertaken in service of the umma.

In the mid-1970s, Jameelah began to chronicle the lives of renewers, who she referred to as "great men." She wrote several books about historical and contemporary exemplars whom she believed embodied the characteristics of the ideal Muslim man. She wrote short biographies of the leader of the Sokoto jihad in

West Africa, Usman dan Fodio (d. 1817); the Turkish religious figure and political dissident Said Nursi (d. 1960); the founder of the Muslim Brotherhood, Hassan al-Banna (d. 1949); and her mentor, Mawdudi. Of these, Dan Fodio is the only mujaddid who lived before the twentieth century, but his example was especially important for Jameelah because of the political and eschatological implications of his life. Taken together, this list of luminaries underscores the lack of ideological uniformity at the heart of Jameelah's project and instead reinforces the affective dimensions of her revivalism. Despite the different life trajectories that each of these men followed, Jameelah identified four common threads that make for a great man and a true mujaddid: education, rejection of materialism, physical strength, and opposition to the status quo. I next analyze each in turn.

The first thread is education: in the Qur'an, Sunna, the Islamic sciences such as law, and the Arabic language—through a multiplicity of paths—as well as education in a broader set of knowledge, including science and philosophy (including European and American philosophy). In her biographies, Jameelah foregrounded learning as a key attribute possessed by every renewer. However, as this list of renewers suggests, learning could be acquired through any number of paths that need not be traditional modes of Islamic learning. While Usman dan Fodio was trained by traditional Muslim authorities, Hassan al-Banna received his "pure Islamic education" solely at home through his father. Rather than focusing on a common pedagogical foundation for renewal and received certifications in Islamic sciences such as *fiqh* (Islamic law and ethics), Jameelah was much more focused on the result—mastery of the Qur'an and Sunnah, knowledge of Islamic law, and a commitment to bringing Islamic education to others. Her embrace of multiple pedagogical methods and institutions reflects the fragmentation and diversification of Muslim learning in the twentieth century. And of course, this model fits Jameelah herself, who was largely self-taught.

The second criterion was a mujaddid's rejection of materialism in his everyday life, satisfying only basic needs in terms of dress, food, and housing. She portrayed Dan Fodio, Nursi, al-Banna, and Mawdudi as living simple lives free from the attachment to wealth and this-worldly desires. In describing Nursi, she proclaimed, "He led a very simple, honest, and self-restrained life. . . . He refrained from taking food when he was doubtful about it and satisfied himself by eating vegetables and even grass. It was customary to give a part of his food to the ants."[46] This rejection of materialism came out of the mujaddid's commitment to Islam as a way of life that governed all his political and religious activities.

Third, a mujaddid embodied physical strength that only men possessed; this could include athletic prowess, ability to withstand torture and imprisonment—even willingness to make the ultimate sacrifice through martyrdom. About Hassan al-Banna's capacity to travel and preach late into the night, Jameelah wrote: "Shaikh Hassan al-Banna was magnificently equipped for his task. He was not only endowed with a razor-sharp intelligence but an exceptionally strong body as well. Despite his short stature, he was the epitome of virile manhood. Throughout his life, he was blessed with exuberant, radiant health, his energy and capacity for endurance inexhaustible. . . . Illiterate laborers and learned shaykhs [scholars] alike flocked to him, irresistibly drawn by his powerful oratory and magnetic personality."[47] Al-Banna's physical and intellectual capacities went hand in hand, enabling him to mobilize all sectors of Egyptian society, from scholars to peasants. Only charismatic, masculine power was up to the task of confronting the evils of colonialism and materialism, and overcoming the shame that saturated feminine, domestic space. To return to Ahmed's theory of the shame-pride relationship, the male revivalist figure functioned as the "assumed form" of an idealized umma—the strong, robust, and united version of a global community.

The final characteristic of a mujaddid was his willingness to fervently oppose the political and religious status quo—through spoken, written, and even violent resistance. Jameelah praised each of her exemplary Muslim men for their oratorial skills. She celebrated Said Nursi's ability to explain deeper meanings of the

Qur'an and to show the "beauty of the verses, laying special stress on their spiritual, physical, and mental significance in reference to the present life and life Hereafter."[48] She was keen to emphasize Mawdudi's ability to reach large audiences with the beauty of his prose and his capacity for distilling profound religious truth into a universal message. Jameelah also extolled him for uniting scholars and leaders from across South Asia behind efforts to restore Islam in public life, such as the 1951 Karachi conference that brought together representatives from the Deobandi, Barelvi, and Shia communities to set down Islamic principles for a constitutional government.[49] This capacity to unify Muslims stemmed from a renewer's educational prowess, but it was also linked to his embodied presence and charisma that inspired others to engage in renewal in their everyday lives. In the midst of a shameful present, a mujaddid articulated a compelling vision for a proud future.[50] In fact, Jameelah's imagined shame-to-pride progression depended on this vanguard of exceptional men. Yet, as I explore in the next section, during the height of Jameelah's popularity as an author, women were already playing increasingly public roles spreading the revival. These subversions created new tensions that demonstrate the limits of her vision.

Subverting the Shame-Pride Progression

The affective economy of shame and pride, as articulated by Jameelah, rested on multiple overlapping binaries: male/female, shame/pride, private/public, and so on. Women belonged in domestic space, while men occupied the public domain of politics, commerce, and religious institutions. For Jameelah, the only way to progress from the collective shame of decline wrought by colonialism was to reinvest in these binaries. Female bodies were marked with collective shame; male exemplary figures could restore the pride that contemporary Muslims had lost. Strongly echoed by Jameelah, Jamaat-i-Islami writings from this period presented the entry of women into public life in South Asia and other Muslim societies as a departure from Islamic tradition and a Western import. Jameelah took up this strain while also making feminism the enemy of the revivalist cause: a new imperialist, materialist threat that needed to be stamped out before it took further hold on Muslims. She identified only a limited set of contributions that women could make to the revivalist project beyond their domestic and childrearing responsibilities.

Despite Jameelah's insistence that revivalist communities relegate women to domestic space on account of unchanging Islamic norms, the reality on the ground was far more complicated. In practice, the Jamaat-i-Islami actively recruited female members to assist with educational efforts. Mawdudi and other male leaders saw women as integral to reinvigorating and spreading their message. As Irfan Ahmad has argued, Mawdudi's views on women were "Janus-faced."[51] On the one hand, Mawdudi argued that women had no place in the public sphere; their presence portended total civilizational collapse. On the other, the Jamaat-i-Islami became the first Muslim organization in India to recruit female members, who served as active participants even if they could not hold leadership roles during its early years of operation.

Mawdudi adopted this strategy because female members were seen as key players in the project of recruiting others, especially their families, to the organization's cause. Female members were instructed to challenge their male family members on questions of doctrine, ritual practice, and ideology if they did not agree with the Jamaat-i-Islami's approach. This directive sat in tension with Mawdudi's insistence on male dominance over women. Religious practice and doctrine stood out as a domain in which women could exert moral authority within their domestic space. In this circumscribed way, the organization's interests took precedence over concerns about women overstepping the boundaries of their divinely sanctioned gender roles within the family and asserting themselves over fathers, brothers, and husbands on questions related to religious observance. That precedence also unintentionally created an opening for future Jamaat-i-Islami cadres and members to challenge Mawdudi on the question of female leadership starting in the 1970s, paving the way for female Jamaat-i-Islami members to assume more public roles, such as holding political office, which Mawdudi considered improper.

Jameelah's own role within the movement also had unintended consequences. As an American woman who had made an indisputably difficult choice not just to become a Muslim but also to leave behind a life of comfort, Jameelah served as a model within the organization. She also became one of Mawdudi's "most influential disciples," helping to disseminate his call for revival to new audiences, including to other women.[52] At the same time, her own relationship to domestic labor starkly contrasted the prescriptions that she made for other women. Jameelah's most prolific period came during her childbearing years, suggesting that she had quite a bit of help caring for her five children. Moreover, her husband supported her endeavors by publishing her books under a Jamaat-i-Islami imprint. Her unique position within Mawdudi's household and within the organization meant that she did not perform the same kind of household labor that was expected of other women in Lahore. Jameelah—largely disconnected from the material circumstances of her audiences—retained the pretense of ideological purity even as her own story was rich with nuances and contradictions that ruptured the wall between "Islam" and the "West" that she constantly tried to reinforce.

At the same time, Jameelah's status as a public intellectual, one who defied her birth family to become Muslim, served as inspiration for women in the Jamaat-i-Islami to assume greater leadership roles in the organization's branches throughout South Asia. Given that Jamaat-i-Islami presses translated her work into Urdu, she was able to spread her influence to other women affiliated with the organization while rarely leaving her house. Amina Jamal argues that Jameelah earned the admiration of female Jamaat-i-Islami members for being a key "translator" of Mawdudi's ideas to broader audiences around the world. She also stood out on account of having joined the organization as a convert—unlike the majority of women connected to the organization through their families. Jameelah's familial relationships were neither the primary cause for her affiliation with the organization nor her status within it. Her choice inspired other women to similarly choose to be part of the cause.

Indeed, Jameelah's intellectual prowess and capacity to become a public scholar were facilitated by the broader participation and leadership of Muslim women—especially educated, elite women—in the public sphere through political organizations, development work, educational institutions, and the like. Elora Shehabuddin has documented the extent of elite Muslim Pakistani women's participation in twentieth-century transnational networks—which connected them with activists and leaders throughout South and Southeast Asia, as well as the United States and Europe. These networks took on issues such as women's rights, reproductive health, poverty, and education from a variety of ideological perspectives. Through travel supported by organizations such as the Ford Foundation and government entities like the State Department, different Pakistani and American women's groups exchanged proposals about everything from women's health to economic development to political engagement.[53] Contrary to Jameelah's portrayal of these transnational actors as having capitulated to Western imperialism, South Asian Muslim female intellectuals, authors, and leaders did not adopt American culture wholesale. Rather, they critiqued the elements they found problematic, such as the decline of extended family structures among Americans, and embraced those aspects they found beneficial for their communities and resonant with their conceptions of justice.

Global Cold War politics also amplified the "status of women" discourse beyond the specific category of the "Muslim woman." The transnational discourse around women's rights during the 1960s and 1970s largely did not treat Muslim women as distinct from other communities in the Global South or "Third World" that needed economic, educational, and political development. Muslim women themselves often worked in this space in South Asia, for example, arguing for the need for better working conditions, improving the infrastructure of rural communities, and expanding educational access. They established relationships and partnerships with various Western and Soviet NGOs, as well as aid organizations working toward improving the material conditions of women. For Jameelah, however, such development projects smacked of neocolonialism because they did not always invoke religious identities or texts. Moreover, in her critique of women who participated in these transnational projects, Jameelah dismissed other forms of identity and community that were salient to South Asian Muslim women, including nation, ethnicity, and class. Instead, she worked very hard to foreground the category of "Muslim woman" as a distinct group who had suffered the most under the weight of colonialism *and* could only be redeemed through Muslim renewal.

Even as Jameelah took other Muslims to task for drawing on European and American culture, she was herself embedded in feminist thought and its transnational networks. These ongoing connections explain why Shehabuddin includes Jameelah in her account of transnational feminism—even though Jameelah was an ardent anti-feminist whom South Asian Muslim feminists saw as an opponent. Shehabuddin notes that, though Jameelah was no longer in the United States when Betty Friedan's *The Feminine Mystique* was published in 1962, "she would have embraced emerging feminist critiques of the beauty industry and beauty contests."[54]

In fact, Jameelah drew inspiration from the same feminist bestseller that Friedan had—Simone de Beauvoir's *The Second Sex*. In her 1970 book *Western Civilization Condemned to Itself*, Jameelah used a lengthy passage from de Beauvoir to argue that the West had subjugated and oppressed women and that a radical, structural change was needed. She also employed critiques fashionable within American and European feminist circles, especially those with a Marxist and existentialist bent, because they tied female oppression to capitalism and had similarly catastrophic undertones. For Jameelah, such critiques were the most powerful because they exposed the rot from within, and this was the basis for her appeal as an insider critic. The fact that Jameelah believed feminists such as de Beauvoir were destroying modern civilization did not stop her from quoting de Beauvoir directly and extensively to diagnose the ills of the "West." Jameelah was keen to use European and American thinkers' insider critiques of their birth countries as evidence of the West's degradation.

Jameelah thus pulled on multiple affective threads to show her readers that the tentacles of Western feminism had infiltrated Muslim communities. Relaying major social developments in her adopted home and the country of her birth, she reported to her readers that feminists continued to make significant legal and political gains. In the United States, new laws barred workplace discrimination against women and pregnant workers; divorce was more easily attained; *Roe v. Wade* (1973) instituted a federal right to abortion; and laws such as Title IX (1972) facilitated the entry of women en masse to higher education and into the workforce. In Pakistan, feminists were also making inroads through civil society organizations focused on education, professional advancement, and economic opportunities. In 1975, Pakistan signed on to the Mexico Declaration at the conclusion of the International Women's Year conference in Mexico City.

The rising social power of feminists in the US and in South Asia confirmed for Jameelah that materialism continued to run roughshod over pious Muslims. In her 1976 pamphlet *Islam and the Muslim Woman Today* Jameelah anticipated, and sought to amplify, her audience's discomfort with women's entry into higher education and the workforce. She presented aspirations of gender equality and female advancement as "cheap slogans" that obscure "a malignant conspiracy to destroy the home and family and eventually wreck our entire society."[55] Jameelah also gave her readers a target for that anxiety—Pakistani feminists. She took aim at the All-Pakistan Women's Association (APWA), which was the most prominent women's rights organization of the 1970s in Pakistan and which operated within the umma space that Jameelah and the

Jamaat-i-Islami were determined to occupy. Starting in 1952, the APWA hosted a series of international conferences to identify challenges and goals shared by Muslim women around the world. Singling out Mrs. Satnam Mahmud, a prominent speaker at the meeting, Jameelah reported that Mahmud "frankly admitted that though Western women are blessed with material plenty and complete social freedom and equality, they are not necessarily happy. If peace of mind is the aim, then the path of so-called emancipation may not be the answer."[56] Jameelah, very much following Mawdudi, argued that this unhappiness stemmed from feminist social reforms, which had created a situation in which, "modern women must bear the *double burden* of professional employment, being a wife to her husband, and keeping a spotless house single-handed! Is this justice?"[57] The clear Marxist undertones here, focused on the commodification and objectification of women, demonstrate the convergence of feminist and revivalist rhetoric, marshaled to very different ends.

For Jameelah, no critique was more emotionally compelling than one that came from inside the house. Deploying her trademark approach, Jameelah used middlebrow sources to clue her audience into the calamitous effects of loosening social restrictions around sexuality. She provided a lengthy quotation from "Our Anything Goes Society—Where Is It Going?" by the American journalist Max Lerner, printed in *Reader's Digest* in April 1968, nearly ten years prior. Invoking the outrage and indignation that Jameelah very much shared, Lerner lamented the decline of institutions—family, religious community, and government—that could control sexuality. Inverting the modernization theories that she so despised, Jameelah instead offered a narrative of inevitable Muslim collapse should they mistake the promise of women's liberation for something other than what it was—a sign of social collapse. In contrast to other female revivalists who excavated Islamic virtues and cultivated affects toward an alternative spiritual politics, Jameelah kept the object of her critique very close at hand, along with the shame that this closeness elicited.

Conclusion

For Jameelah, Muslims had to *feel* the collective weight of modernity's destruction if they were to rebuild their unity and recover the lost glory of the Muslim past. As a result, the umma's collective recognition of its failure, experienced as shame, became the first step for religious revival. Existential threats warranted repeated warnings about their dangers, and those dangers were most visible in domestic spaces. For Jameelah, addressing these existential threats meant cultivating an affectsphere—a constellation of negative collective emotions—that served as the prerequisite for political action.[58]

Castigating Pakistani feminists on affective grounds, Jameelah allowed that many modern people, including the enemies of Islam, end up feeling quite negatively. However, she differentiated between those bad feelings that were the inevitable pathologies of modern life on the one hand, versus bad collective feelings that came out of right moral and political principles, on the other: "Almost anyone living in the giant urban centers subconsciously feels an intuitive emptiness in his days," she opined, "which no amount of material goods and the frantic chase after 'happiness' or enjoyment of sensual pleasures can satisfy."[59] From this perspective, happiness was an immoral pursuit, thus effectively erasing joyous affects from her vision of Islam. Materialist ideologies such as nationalism, socialism, and feminism could never deliver on the promise of happiness because they were antithetical to the transcendental aspirations of the umma. Only the vanguard, as represented by the masculine revivalists dedicated to the cause of religion, could first direct other Muslims toward shame in their present condition, in their torpor and feeble-mindedness, and then lead the umma toward the restoration of pride.

By engaging and appropriating feminist critiques, Jameelah sought to render feminism—a diffuse, internally diverse movement—into a singular affective flashpoint in the broader struggle to combat modernity's evils. Inversion functioned as the primary tool in Jameelah's kit, as she cast women's empowerment as their enslavement and the entry of women into public spaces as the demise of civilization. She thus inculcated anxiety and fear about initiatives that claimed to provide advancement for Muslim women, many of which were advanced by Muslim women themselves. Jameelah called on her fellow Muslims to hear those terms such as "liberation" and "progress" as meaning their opposite: degradation and shame.

The next chapter traces how Jameelah's anti-modern affects were taken up and reworked in American Muslim communities. In doing so, I show that while gender and sexuality remain key nodes of global revivalism, other prominent thinkers began to offer a much more optimistic orientation toward American culture that hewed more closely to the lived experiences of Muslim families.

6

Crisis Narratives and Prescriptive Literature in American Islam

JAMEELAH'S LIFELONG engagement with American ideas also made her work increasingly relevant to Muslims back in the US. As we have seen, her proximity to American culture was a core reason why she had become a prominent revivalist Muslim intellectual in the first place. She excelled at "talking back" to American politics as the foil against which she built her vision for global Muslim solidarity. To her readers in South Asia, in other words, she functioned as an inside reporter of an America in precipitous moral decline. But to her American Muslim readers, her writings functioned more as a guide for how recent immigrants should engage American culture firsthand.

As a result, Jameelah's work had an enduring legacy in the birth country that she had so vociferously rejected. In this chapter, I trace her impact on American Islam through prescriptive literature—which she published mainly in articles and short books—on women, gender, and the family from the late 1960s to the early 1970s. Less than a decade after she left the US, Jameelah's writing began to recirculate in revivalist-oriented Muslim American communities, and she became particularly influential within the Muslim Students Association (MSA). By the time her work was exported back to the US, Jameelah's revivalist project—and the affective politics around which it was built—landed in a significantly transformed American religious context. Following the 1965 Immigration and Nationality Act, the influx of Muslim immigrants from South Asia and Arab countries had challenged proponents of religious diversity to expand beyond their "tri-faith" model.[1] Jameelah's insider knowledge of American culture, combined with her potent affectsphere, appealed to new Muslim immigrants and helped them navigate their position as religious and racial minorities while maintaining connections to the umma.[2]

Tracing the circulation and impact of Jameelah's vision reveals that American Muslim thinkers were far more engaged in the emergent culture wars around gender and sexuality than we have previously acknowledged. I argue that Jameelah's affectsphere shared key features with evangelical Christian and conservative Catholic thinkers who constructed a crisis narrative around the erosion of "traditional" family values, the rise of feminism, and the expansion of reproductive rights.[3] As a female intellectual calling for the exclusion of women from public space, Jameelah used her platform in the same way as did other religious conservatives who wanted to curtail sexual experimentation, limit women's economic power, and restrict access to abortion.

At the same time, Jameelah's brand of revivalism coalesced with American Muslims' understanding of themselves as a "counterpublic" that was rooted in the affective framing of the US as, paradoxically, an "object of disdain and desire."[4] In this way, she provided a framework through which Muslims could challenge American exceptionalism. In the second half of the chapter, I explore how Jameelah's affectsphere and her middlebrow approach dovetailed with the emotional framing of other popular prescriptive texts. The MSA distributed a wide variety of such literature, primarily centered on family life and devotional practice. These short pamphlets and paperbacks became a popular format because they could be cheaply produced and easily distributed. Even without large budgets, these distribution networks connected geographically disparate Muslim communities with one another. This prescriptive literature sought to guide recently arrived students and young professionals on topics such as living authentically and how to educate non-Muslims about Islam.

These short books and pamphlets notably deployed Jameelah's trademark negative emotions around gender and sexuality. To illustrate the ways that her writing resonated with and amplified the crisis narratives articulated by other prominent US Muslim authors, I put Jameelah's work in conversation with three well-known prescriptive texts published in 1971–1972: the MSA's *Parents' Manual: A Guide for Muslim Parents Living in North America*, Muhammad Abdul Rauf's *Marriage in Islam*, and Jamal Badawi's *The Status of Women in Islam*.[5] Using a middlebrow voice that combined Islamic texts, academic literature, and personal observations, these pamphlets and manuals roused strong emotions over the threats posed by changing gender norms. In stark contrast to Jameelah's writings, however, all of these texts portrayed the United States as a place where Muslims could potentially thrive.

This chapter thus demonstrates a shifting affectsphere in American Muslim revivalism, away from the catastrophic rendering of modernity and toward a more hopeful register. In fact, we now know what Jameelah thought was impossible—Muslim flourishing in America—was actually becoming a reality for many of her cosmopolitan, college-educated, middle-class readers. Vigilance against the excesses of American gender norms and sexualities thus remained an important feature of prescriptive literature, even as Jameelah's structural critiques of materialism gradually became less prevalent.

Jameelah and US Muslim Revivalist Networks

Despite all her disavowals of Western culture and influence, Jameelah's position as an American with insider access to her home society's pathologies made her a compelling figure in the country of her birth. One important group was the Muslim Students Association (MSA), which reprinted many of Jameelah's articles in the 1960s and 1970s in its magazine *Al-Ittihad* (Unity). The MSA's publishing apparatus thus introduced Jameelah's ideas to a new set of revivalist-minded readers. The organization's revivalist activities centered on *daʿwa* or "calling" others to Islam. Adopting an activist ethos, the MSA pursued daʿwa by seeking to educate other Muslims about Islamic ritual practice and religious values, as well as creating more accurate perceptions of Islam among non-Muslim Americans. In its founding period in the late 1960s and early '70s, the MSA was part of a diffuse network of transnational revivalist communities. The MSA saw itself as leading a vigorous renewal of Islam and articulated ambitious aspirations for a united global Muslim community. Founded in 1963 at the University of Illinois Urbana-Champaign by students hailing primarily from Arab and South Asian countries, the MSA mostly drew adult graduate students from a range of national backgrounds into its orbit.

Several trends in postwar higher education facilitated greater entry of Muslim students to American universities. The GI Bill accelerated the demand for university education, and new and growing universities met that demand by appealing to broader constituencies in terms of race, class, and gender. Meanwhile, the 1965 Hart-Celler Act lifted longstanding quotas and ushered in thousands of immigrants from Asia and the Middle East, many of them professionals recruited to take white-collar jobs and to meet the burgeoning demand for scientific and technical training in their countries of origin and in the United States. The national organization, led by a board, was responsible for coordinating chapter activities around common goals; raising funds; publishing and distributing books, journals, and other print materials; and planning national conferences and retreats.

A significant portion of MSA programming centered on nuclear-family activities involving wives and children, such as educational programs, social events, and summer camps. The newly created H1-B and student visas, through which many Muslims immigrated and then often stayed in the United States, made it possible for entire families to come together. As a result, the MSA saw itself as serving a far wider community than just students enrolled in university courses. College campuses had ample facilities for hosting events, financial resources to support various kinds of student initiatives, many campus religious groups committed to missionary and devotional activities, and a base of operations to generate enthusiasm for the revivalist cause.

Publishing was a key dimension of the MSA's efforts to achieve its goals of unifying and reinvigorating the global Muslim community. The organization established its own distribution networks that sold Islamic books, pamphlets, and correspondence courses to promote ritual practice. In addition to publishing works by MSA members, the organization reprinted excerpts by prominent Muslim intellectuals who were also part of Jameelah's orbit, such as Mawdudi and Qutb. The periodicals and magazines of this early period had a revivalist bent, but they also represented the idiosyncratic interests of early MSA board members who wanted to promote their particular causes. In this way, rather than presenting a unified ideological program, MSA publications offered a forum through which its members sought to enact an activist, grassroots vision of Islam. MSA publications also emphasized academic expertise, including the writings of scholars who incorporated economics, sociology, and history into their interpretations of Islam. As we have seen, Jameelah exemplified this kind of religious authority, having constructed her vision out of a wide range of academic and middlebrow sources.

Jameelah was one of the few female writers to appear in *Al-Ittihad*, and she was the most frequently published. The female-authored articles focused on gender and family issues because these domains were seen as essential for maintaining an Islamic way of life in a cultural climate that, on the one hand, was perceived as hostile to revivalism and, on the other, presented a vital venue for renewing and restoring Islamic practice. Most of the other female authors were members of the MSA Women's Committee, which was formed in 1965, and coordinated da'wa initiatives for women and children through the national MSA. Articles and other publications authored by women tended to be focused on domestic and everyday issues, such as childrearing, cooking, and fulfilling ritual and other obligations (for instance, wearing modest dress). Jameelah stood out because she directly addressed contemporary American politics in her work. Many more pieces in *Al-Ittihad* concerned international politics, especially events surrounding state suppression of Islam around the world; the periodical mostly did *not* engage key domestic events during the tumultuous 1960s, such as the Vietnam War or the civil rights movement. Jameelah's detailed discussions of American feminist initiatives represented a significant exception.

As a convert, Jameelah was useful to the MSA in another way. The MSA embraced converts out of the same revivalist principle that we saw among the Jamaat-i-Islami: the necessity of intentionally and deliberately *choosing* Islam. The pivotal role of universities as conduits for future converts to learn about Islam also encouraged this trend. Converts like Jameelah were seen as particularly helpful to the work of daʿwa because they demonstrated the appeal of Islam as a faith that was freely and intentionally chosen.

Notably, *Al-Ittihad* did not telegraph Jameelah's identity as a convert. Unlike her other publications, which as we have seen, always included a short biography and conversion narrative, the MSA did not provide any of her biographical details. Jameelah's work appeared alongside reprints of writings by Mawdudi and Qutb, who needed no introduction. In this way, her authority as an author was taken for granted without explanation. At the same time, it is possible that some MSA members, particularly those who did not have links to the Jamaat-i-Islami, may not have known who Jameelah was. The omission of her biography may have been in service of a different revivalist strategy—to deemphasize individual authorship in order to present Islam as a universal set of principles and practices.

Jameelah and the American Culture Wars

One important thread that Jameelah contributed to MSA literature was her overt anti-feminism. In 1973, *Al-Ittihad* reprinted an excerpt of Jameelah's *Criterion* article "The Feminist Movement

Versus the Muslim Woman." In this piece, Jameelah expressed horror at the rise of "radical feminism," which she presented as calling for the abolition of marriage, "unqualified equality for men and women," and unrestricted access to contraception and abortion. She traced the history of feminism through a decidedly white and middle-class trajectory: through the nineteenth-century women's suffrage movement, John F. Kennedy's Commission on the Status of Women, and finally the 1960s reinvigoration of feminism on college campuses.[6] The thrust of this narrative emphasized feminism as solely a Western product that had been imposed on Muslims in the form of cultural imperialism. The possibility of a feminist trajectory in South Asia or elsewhere, or as embodied by women of color in the United States, was absent from this article. As the previous chapter explored, Jameelah was keenly aware of feminist thinkers and movements in Pakistan. In this case, she argued that the rising tide of feminism should strike fear into the heart of every Muslim, especially those living in the US, where feminism and its related ills, such as homosexuality, had moved to the center of public life.

By naming feminism as an enemy within American culture, Jameelah's writing demonstrates how affective politics works: attaching certain emotions to objects so as to facilitate their circulation and repetition. When Jameelah wanted to instill a sense of crisis in her audiences, she linked feminism to various kinds of "dangerous" sexualities. "The Feminism Movement Versus the Muslim Woman" brought together Jameelah's characteristic affective matrix of disgust, outrage, and shame—all aimed at amplifying her audience's negative emotions. Feminism, she maintained, was an "unnatural, artificial, and abnormal product of contemporary social disintegration, which in turn is the result of all transcendental, absolute moral and spiritual values." She added that "the disintegration of the home and the family, the loss of the authoritarian role of the father, and sexual promiscuity, have been directly responsible for the decline and fall of every nation in which these evils became prevalent."[7] As we saw in the previous chapter, the stakes were existential because feminism's influence and visibility meant that secularism and materialism were winning the battle over religion.

With prose animated by American Cold War anxieties about enemy infiltrators, Jameelah linked feminism to communism in order to make the case that it was bent on destroying both capitalism and Islam. In "Islam and the 'Emancipation' of the Muslim Woman," Jameelah argued that *The Communist Manifesto* had paved the way for modern feminism because it "insisted that women must be 'liberated' from domestic servitude and achieve full economic independence."[8] She decried the many other "communist" policies that she cast as feminist goals, namely, "contraceptives, sterilization, and abortion to prevent unwanted pregnancies" as well as "state-controlled nurseries and public boarding schools assuming the responsibility for the rearing of children. . . . This is in essence what the modern concept of 'women's rights' amounts to."[9]

This passage brought 1970s American policy debates to the fore of MSA publications. She was unflinching in her appraisal: these proposals and views were "evil" because they opened too many possibilities for women to choose a path other than the one set by God—fulfilling their role as caregivers for their husband and children. The specter of state-run daycares loomed particularly large in Jameelah's work because she believed that they relieved mothers of the moral responsibility to raise their children. Jameelah saw entrusting that religious responsibility to the state as deeply flawed and morally bankrupt, whether in the US or in Pakistan. She blasted "radical feminists" for promoting alternative family arrangements such as communes and for proposals "where the welfare and rearing of the children would be a public responsibility. They are demanding that child-care centres are made available to parents on a 24-hour basis provided to the public as free on demand just as parks, libraries, and recreation facilities are taken for granted in most American communities."[10] These were, in fact, proposals made by organizations such as the National Organization for Women (NOW). In the 1970s, several efforts were underway for the federal government to fund universal childcare for American children. Feminist organizers led a variety of grassroots initiatives around funding and supporting childcare initiatives at the federal and state levels. As legal historian Deborah Dinner argues, Congress's passage of the 1971 Comprehensive Child Development Act (CCDA) represented the success of feminist organizing at all levels of politics and across economic and racial lines. While this legislation proposed federal support to address the changing socioeconomic realities of American families—specifically the prevalence of women in the workforce and their contributions to the American economy—its opponents cast the measure as a radical feminist proposal. The New Right's opposition to the legislation hinged on the association of universal childcare with what it saw as "radical elements," such as communism and feminism, and then helped to justify Nixon's veto of the legislation in 1971.

Jameelah also took on a core principle of second-wave feminism: choice. Drawing on Traditionalist inversions, she was unequivocal: choice was no liberation; it was the path toward continued Muslim political and religious weakness in relation to the West, sure to be followed quickly by total social destruction. She warned her audience that what feminists were really proposing by focusing on choice was the destruction of the nuclear family; complete women's bodily autonomy and freedom, including the right to contraception and abortion; the option to pursue any professional career; the ability to take an active role in sex and to engage in sexual activity with both men and women; and an end to sex segregation in schools and sports.

Jameelah allowed that Muslims had not yet embraced such policies, but she warned that more relaxed social norms placed them on a perilous path toward destruction.[11] Gayle Rubin calls this logic the "fallacy of misplaced scale," in which "small differences in value or behaviour are experienced as cosmic threats."[12] To Jameelah's audiences who might be tempted to allow their daughters to attend a school dance or wear a skirt above the knee, she warned that this was the first step down the road to premarital sex or, worse, lesbianism. The inability of Muslim communities to regulate female sexuality through modest dress was one such example of everyday practices that Jameelah framed in existential terms.

At the same time as she spoke to her fellow Muslims, Jameelah generated a bundle of negative feelings that flowed directly into a specific kind of 1970s American anti-feminism. Jameelah's version of this grand narrative was that "the student of anthropology and history can be certain of the abnormality of the Feminist movement because all human cultures that we know of throughout prehistoric and historic times make a clear-cut distinction between 'masculinity' and 'femininity' and pattern the social roles of men and women accordingly." Feminism was not a unique danger to Islam; it was a unique danger to *any* healthy society, which required the nuclear family with the heterosexual, companionate couple to serve as its center.[13] As such, this struggle wasn't specifically a Muslim one, it was about humanity. Within this narrative, Muslims, possessing the distinctive, superior religious framework, had a special responsibility to salvage what was left of civilization. While Jameelah had always been critical of what she saw as excessively loose sexual mores in American society, with the growth and success of feminism she had the added ammunition, shared among feminists' critics across religious lines, that those fears had been realized.

Jameelah never acknowledged her affinity with other American religious conservatives, yet her approach mirrored that of other thinkers who argued that feminism posed an existential threat.[14] Evangelical Christian and Catholic thinkers of the 1960s and 1970s decried the "acids" of modernity that were eating away at Christian morality, which was the cornerstone of a functional American society: "Society can be good or depraved, civilized or uncivilized. It either possesses order or chaos depending on the degree to which male and female sex roles are accepted or rejected."[15] At the center of these emerging culture wars was an affective matrix that hinged on amplified negative emotions aimed at unifying disparate audiences and groups behind feeling bad about the decline of American culture, which in turn fostered the desire to return to a white, Christian America.

This politics of fear united multiple communities across ideological lines, from Catholics and evangelicals to supply-side economists and neoconservatives. Historian Marie Griffith emphasizes the affective tissue that brought these disparate groups together:

> For those who worked to sustain the old sexual order and resisted models for sexual relationships and behavior outside traditional marriage, a driving force has been fear. That is, fear of certain kinds of changes has aroused passionate defiance, motivated acts of resistance, and galvanized political support for the anti-change side . . . a widespread and easily stoked fear that America is a once great nation now pitched into grave decline, largely because of the evil activities (very often, evil *sexual* activities) of some of its citizens. So women, nonwhites, and homosexuals and other "non normative" sexual actors (the transgendered, the fluid, the flagrant) have repeatedly represented something like the enemy within, shredding the sacred fabric binding together a God-blessed nation.[16]

Indeed, Jameelah marshaled this same affective economy linking nonnormative sexualities to evil and the disintegration of society. In this way, her emphasis on "traditional" gender arrangements stemmed not only from her engagement with Islamic thinkers and movements, but also from an American affective politics in which the existential stakes were highest when gender and sexuality were on the table.

Like other female conservative thinkers, Jameelah saw her public work as necessary for ensuring the primacy of women in the home. Phyllis Schlafly and other prominent women of the New Right used their public position as highly educated intellectuals and activists to promote "traditional family values" and to argue that women's interests and aspirations were best protected and fulfilled when they focused on domestic and caregiving responsibilities.[17] Similarly, as we have seen, Jameelah far preferred her typewriter to domestic labor. I have been unable to locate any evidence that Jameelah read Schlafly directly, though it would not surprise me if she did, or at least followed her trajectory. The two women embraced a remarkably similar affective and rhetorical strategy around communism, feminism, and childcare. Jameelah was certainly current on American debates in the early 1970s about women's liberation, family, reproduction, and women's labor. Thus, it is not surprising that we find echoes of Schlafly's affect of fear in Jameelah's rhetoric.

Such resonances are important because they point to a deeper US Muslim engagement in the culture wars than has previously been understood. Focusing on affect enables us to trace unlikely religious and political convergences around a shared sense of anxiety over the consequences of modernity. When Jameelah's reprinted article "Islam and the Muslim Woman Today" appeared in the pages of *Al-Ittihad*, it was read by students and their families in light of an American religious politics over gender, one that placed sexuality, the female body, and the nuclear family at the center of a new "culture war" that Americans were waging over the future of the country. Maintaining the purity of the female body was essential for preserving society itself. Jameelah's article appeared in the pages of *Al-Ittihad* in 1973, the same year that the Supreme Court's *Roe v. Wade* decision marked a turning point in American politics—in which anti-feminist forces argued that the state waged an anti-Christian agenda that threatened to plunge US society into the depths of moral depravity.

The same politics of fear around the existential stakes of preserving gender and sexuality along "traditional" lines emerges in response to an increasingly visible feminist movement. To borrow again from Sara Ahmed's language, in the 1970s anxiety affixed itself to female and queer bodies, objects that were especially "sticky," in response to structural legal and political changes that had opened up new political rights for women and minorities. Conservative Christian figures such as Jerry Falwell cast feminists as the enemy of the family, pointing to feminist critiques of inequality and sexism as the reason for the decline of the American family. Jameelah's anti-feminism had a similar bent. While she prided herself on reading and commenting on works of sociology and economics, the causal factors she focused on regarding the decline of America were nearly all cultural rather than economic.

We might be tempted, then, to say that Jameelah was a kind of Phyllis Schlafly or Anita Bryant; however, there was a stark divide between Jameelah's end goal and that of these Christian thinkers. Whereas Schlafly and others used American institutions, laws, and policies in their efforts to restore Christian supremacy, it was inconceivable to Jameelah that Muslims could benefit from, much less pull the levers of, American state power. This divergence stems from the conservative anti-colonialism that undergirded Jameelah's religious imagination, namely her outright rejection of American nationalism as that handmaiden to colonialism. Due to her unflinching castigation of American neo-imperialism, she never engaged with legal or governmental institutions or electoral politics as the Christian Right did during this period.

As such, Jameelah's affective matrix aimed at reinvigorating Islamic practice and Muslim identity through strategies that she believed could not and should not be subsumed within national politics. Her call was aimed at mobilizing Muslims to shore up their families' defenses around their most important principles and practices, with gender and sexuality norms being among those most in need of protection. What was paramount was the unity of Muslims—not of Americans or Pakistanis or Palestinians. The most aspirational dimensions of her religious imagination encapsulated the entire umma, which she maintained should not be limited by the narrowness of national politics.

An Optimistic Opening Through Relationship Building

Jameelah's work found an audience with recently arrived immigrants seeking to carve out a Muslim "way of life" as religious and ethnic minorities. Her new readers were pursuing the same sort of life that in the late 1950s that Jameelah had deemed impossible for herself, and for any devout Muslim. In the 1970s, MSA publications expressed a mix of enthusiastic optimism and serious trepidation over the challenges of being Muslim in America.

One such publication was the MSA's 1972 *Parents' Manual: A Guide for Muslim Parents Living in North America,* which painted a dire picture of American gender and sexual mores, especially the "vulgar, foul, and incorrect attitudes so common among young people today." Using language that mirrored Jameelah's, the manual called out contemporary sartorial practices that "Muslims can only consider grossly insulting and regard as the degradation of the woman into a sex object."[18] Like Jameelah, the manual's authors attributed these evils to the excesses of materialism, which they saw as ushering in social disintegration, injustice, and sexual decadence.

The *Parents' Manual* likewise extolled a vision of Islam as fundamentally distinct from Western culture, declaring that "the Islamic attitude toward relations between the sexes, modesty, propriety, and dress—and thereby toward family life and the life of the entire society—is directed toward a completely different goal."[19] This goal was serving God, a task that could be accomplished by upholding "Islamic attitudes" through pious Muslim practice. The manual shared Jameelah's emphasis on the nuclear family as the basis for a strong religious community. This orientation was particularly compelling to a revivalist-oriented community for whom the possibility of transforming state structures or institutions was out of reach or undesirable. This goal, which was promoted by some revivalists in their home countries, was obviously impossible to imagine in the United States.

At the same time, the *Parents' Manual* deviated from Jameelah's vision in an important way, by portraying the US as a flawed but promising site for reform and renewal of Islam. Its opening lines affirmed this ambitious outlook: "As pioneer Muslim parents in the Western hemisphere, we will demonstrate to ourselves and to our children that Islam is as practicable and as valuable today as it has been and will always be until the end of the world. To the waiting eyes of the world we will show both that it can be done and that *it is being done,* insha'Allah (God-willing), with great success."[20] By invoking the language of "pioneer," the *Parents' Manual* called up the founding myths of the US as a place where religious aspirations could be achieved and serve as a model for others to emulate.

While Jameelah insisted on the inability of other religious communities to find common ground with non-Muslims, other MSA authors were far more open to the possibility of connection and relationality to other pious Americans with whom they identified a common commitment to family life. The *Parents' Manual* argued that Muslims had partners in their quest to undermine materialism by centering religion in all aspects of daily life. Devout, "strongly religious circles" represented potential kindred spirits in navigating the moral hazards of the Cold War as shared partners against the collective dangers that their families faced. The manual's authors found within other religious communities the ideals that they wanted to implement and grow in the American context.

The MSA Women's Committee publications made much use of this relational opening, seeking to establish relationships and friendships with other Americans who shared their religious framework—one that was much more flexible and accommodating of American culture than Jameelah's unflinching opposition. These multiple visions, which existed uneasily alongside one another in the pages of the MSA publications in the 1970s, were all threaded together with an aspirational vision, a religious path that could withstand the negative sides of materialism, that root cause that threatened to destroy an Islamic way of life. They also speak to the ambivalent place of American Muslims in US public life: as one among many groups of newly arrived immigrants, as ethnic and racial minorities, and as a religious community with strong emotional attachments to a transnational community.

As we have seen, the nation-state was never Jameelah's principal focus; she concentrated on protecting the nuclear family from the perils of popular culture and the materialism it represented. The irony here is plain: for all of Jameelah's disavowal of the "West," her thoroughgoing Americanness enabled her to tap into the family as a major flashpoint of American religious politics in the US, which then made her a compelling observer for other Muslim Americans. At the same time, while other American Muslims took up her critique of American culture, they embraced a very different approach to ameliorating the excesses of materialism, one that emphasized relationship-building over oppositional affects.

Durable Negative Emotions

This emphasis on the nuclear family is reflected in another important prescriptive text from this period: Muhammad Abdul Rauf's 1971 *Marriage in Islam*. The short book was marketed as a comprehensive, practical manual for Muslim marriage in the US.[21] Published when Abdul Rauf was serving as the imam for the Islamic Center in Washington, DC, the manual positions marriage as a key institution through which US Muslims could successfully and confidently live out their obligations to one another and to God. Given that the Islamic Center was one of the largest US Muslim congregations at the time, and located near the center of American state power, Abdul Rauf was one of the most prominent US Muslims of this period. Born in Egypt in 1917, Abdul Rauf trained at Al-Azhar before beginning his career in Malaysia, where he was sent to found Muslim College. He taught in Malaysia through the 1950s before immigrating to the United States, where he became the director of the Islamic Foundation in New York City in 1963.[22]

Abdul Rauf was a frequent officiant of Muslim marriages. By his count, he had conducted over five hundred weddings. He thus offered his readers not only his expertise in Islamic texts, but also his on-the-ground knowledge of marriage in the US. Several photos from these weddings were printed in his manual. These photos portray happy couples who are embarking on a new life together. Many of the couples are from different ethnic backgrounds; including Muslim men who are marrying Christian women. Abdul Rauf provided guidance for bridging cultural differences around dowries, wedding ceremonies, and familial relationships. Similar to Jameelah, Abdul Rauf saw marriage as rooted in complementarian notions of rights and responsibilities within the home. He argued that complementarianism stemmed from inherent, biological differences between men and women, which he understood to be articulated in both Islamic texts and in science. Similarly, he presented patriarchal family structures as both religiously sanctioned and proven by academic arguments to serve as the foundation for a functioning, stable society.

In addition to its offering as a guide for a happy marriage, Abdul Rauf's manual also starkly rendered the stakes about *why* its readers needed to double down on companionate marriage. In making this case, Abdul Rauf employed an affectsphere that echoed Jameelah's bundling of negative affects:

> I am extremely perturbed by the shameless open demonstrations by homosexuals and by the audacity of some corruptive writers who stand to defend this "gay liberation" movement, seeking to argue that homosexuality is not unnatural, not immoral, and not a sickness. . . . It is unnatural not only because it is unproductive but also because it is perverse. . . . The inherently indisputable evil and filth of homosexuality for its own sake make it comparable to such disputable institutions as polygamy, which is digestible in some cultures and indigestible in others.[23]

Abdul Rauf's analysis invoked the same tropes, including the use of "evil" and "filth," to separate out authorized practices from un-Islamic ones. Like Jameelah, he was particularly troubled by public displays of queer sexualities because he saw them as destabilizing otherwise functioning heterosexual relationships—which had already been weakened by the rise of materialism.

Although he held out the possibility of cultural relativism with respect to sexuality, Abdule Rauf's argument inverted the colonialist charges against Muslims as violating moral law through the practice of polygyny, and instead upheld homosexuality as evidence of Western immorality and the perversion of "natural" sexuality. If Americans charged that polygamy was uniquely patriarchal and backward to women, Abdul Rauf countered that the practice—documented in various forms as practiced by different cultures—was far superior to "homosexuality for its own sake," which was, as quoted above, "unnatural, not only because it is unproductive but also because it is perverse."[24]

For Abdul Rauf, abortion further raised the specter of catastrophe. Abortion access portended grave threats to marriage by providing "adulterers and fornicators [with] an easy solution to their illegitimate pregnancies and an encouragement to their immoral pursuits."[25] The manual was published in the wake of the expansion of abortion access and just prior to the 1973 *Roe v. Wade* decision. Abdul Rauf briefly acknowledged that some Muslim texts seem to allow for the termination of pregnancy up to the fourth month of pregnancy. For example, he mentioned the prophetic tradition that "*ruh*, or the spirit of life" is breathed into the fetus at 120 days. But Abdul Rauf did not believe that this and other traditions permitted modern abortion procedures, noting that other scholars thought that abortion constituted the taking of a human life. He did make exceptions for when the life of the mother was "really threatened" and in the case of rape.[26]

Notably, Abdul Rauf did not dwell on the specifics of these theological and legal arguments, which for him were incidental to the affective urgency of this extended critique: "Thousands of babies are daily murdered unduly; morality is continuously and openly butchered unashamedly; and big money is greedily grabbed undeservedly. And yet the conscience of the world is unperturbed! May God preserve us, Muslims, from this contagious and inhuman genocide!"[27] Abdul Rauf's argument hinged on a critique of materialism as triumphing over religious imperatives and norms, a move that should now be familiar as Jameelah's calling card. By invoking the greed of corporations and doctors, whom Abdul Rauf imagined benefiting from reproductive care, he invoked a familiar affective framework rooted in fear over the existential survival of religion posed by the powerful forces of capitalism.

This framing mirrored that of evangelical and Catholic activists and intellectuals who opposed legal abortion in the 1970s. Abdul Rauf invoked two primary tropes of pro-life activism from this period: the threat of contagion and portraying abortion as genocide. The framework of contagion hinges on what Kristen Luker calls the "tip of the iceberg" model for understanding opposition to legal abortion as deeply invested in a broader politics of motherhood.[28] During this period, pro-life activists also began to invoke the Holocaust to paint a dystopian, catastrophic vision for America if abortion were to be legalized. Anti-abortion organizations increasingly labeled their opponents as "Nazis" and argued that the only way to prevent a fascist future was to organize strong collective resistance.

Both abortion and homosexuality were objects of disgust around which attachments could be forged. Abdul Rauf and Jameelah both understood "the power of an object of disgust closely held."[29] For Abdul Rauf, homosexuality and abortion represented two interrelated threats to the institution of marriage: they were simultaneously signs of a decaying society and its cause. They signaled the disintegration of proper sexuality, gender roles, and the nuclear family, all of which portended the internal collapse of modern society. Abdul Rauf's writings on abortion reveal that some key American Muslim leaders were rather attuned to American culture wars around gender, which were refracted through the politics of recognition around immigration and religious minorities. Prescriptive literature was part of the broader effort by Muslim American immigrants to determine, according to Grewal, "how (and how not) to become American, albeit with a wistful nostalgia for their homelands."[30] Family life was seen as a primary way to maintain connections to immigrant homelands. The phrase "wistful nostalgia" points to one affective thrust of these texts, which were centered on which practices should be upheld as normative and authoritative to preserve Muslim unity. But family and gender simultaneously functioned as key affective sites for Muslims to navigate American political debates and to negotiate their recognition in relation to them.

Indeed, most Muslim American thinkers rejected Jameelah's complete disavowal of the "West," seeking instead to become part of the American social fabric—benefiting from its economic promises and political protections while retaining an aspirational attachment to a global Muslim community.[31] What is more, figures like Abdul Rauf were far more optimistic about the prospects for Muslim engagement with American society. As we have seen, his efforts to promote interreligious dialogue within Muslim communities drew Jameelah's ire in the wake of the Six-Day War. Moreover, Abdul Rauf saw few impediments to the formation of strong Muslim families who prospered economically. At the end of the twentieth century, this hopeful orientation began to displace the anti-modern affects that Jameelah had sought to instill.

The Status of Women and the Logics of Religious Outsiderhood

This section turns to a short, influential book, *The Status of Women in Islam*, by Jamal Badawi, to further explore this affective shift in American Muslim prescriptive literature. Badawi spent his early life in Cairo, where as a child he had been fascinated by an array of Islamic texts—including hadith and biographies of the Prophet Muhammad (*sira*). It was also there that he developed an admiration for the daʿwa initiatives of the Muslim Brotherhood, especially the organization's capacity to reach a wide swath of Egyptians through multiple kinds of programs and initiatives, such as publishing, youth camps, and preaching. As an adult in the early 1960s, enduring President Gamel abd-al Nasr's suppression of religious and political opposition, Badawi and his wife left Egypt to pursue graduate study at Indiana University Bloomington. There he became a leading figure in the fledgling national MSA, and later in the 1982 founding of the Islamic Society of North America

(ISNA), as well as in Canadian Muslim organizations. Badawi was part of a generation of US Muslim leaders whose religious authority was derived from a combination of both Islamic learning and professional achievements.

In 1971, Badawi published an article, "The Status of Women in Islam" in *Al-Ittihad*, followed by an extended pamphlet version in 1972, which was also published through the MSA. A popular text, it was reprinted and reissued through the 1980s.[32] Twenty-eight pages in length, the short book's objective was to provide a "fair evaluation of what Islam contributed (or failed to contribute) toward the restoration of women's dignity and rights."[33] For Badawi, an "objective" treatment was necessary because Muslim women had been portrayed inaccurately in Western media. In turn, this biased representation distorted non-Muslims' perceptions of their American Muslim neighbors and coworkers.[34] The text thus functioned to instruct Muslims on their own tradition, but also to provided arguments to challenge anti-Muslim views in the US.

Badawi's approach echoed that of Jameelah in several ways. First, the two authors presented "Islam" as a comprehensive, total system that was distinct and monolithic in contentious relation to the "West." Two, Badawi and Jameelah argued that a woman's spiritual and emotional fulfillment came through her caregiving responsibilities, particularly for her children. Like Jameelah, Badawi argued that "with regard to the woman's right to seek employment, it should be stated first that Islam regards her role in society as a mother and a wife as the most sacred and essential one. Neither maids nor babysitters can possibly take the mother's place as the educator of upright, complex-free, and carefully reared children."[35] Third, Badawi believed that it was desirable to restrict women's leadership in certain public roles, citing the now-controversial hadith that reported that, on hearing that a woman had been appointed as queen of Persia, the Prophet Muhammad had said, "A people will not prosper if they let a woman be their leader."[36] To this scriptural justification, he added the view that women's psychological and physiological changes during menstruation would affect their decision-making capacities in emergency situations that "require a maximum of rationality and a minimum of emotionality—a requirement which does not coincide with the instinctive nature of women."[37] Adopting a middlebrow approach similar to Jameelah's, Badawi engaged a variety of sources, from the Qur'an and the Bible to *Encyclopaedia Britannica* to quotes from thinkers such as John Stuart Mill—to argue that this constellation of views was rooted in religious texts, science, and common sense.

Badawi's use of the term "status" reveals that his more measured approach is also shot through with the same anxieties around gender that animated Jameelah's revivalism. Status is a deeply affective category because it entails comparison across social groups. First, the status of women in Islam discourse reflects a colonial logic in which the status of women marks Islam as superior or inferior in relation to the "West." Women, sexuality, and gender were central to the civilizing mission of colonialism—to which, as has been extensively documented elsewhere, Muslim scholars and writers produced an avalanche of counterresponses. Indeed, the studies of the "status of women in Islam" are too vast to fully engage here. But I do want to underscore that the "status of women" necessarily implies a comparison between Islam and the West as monolithic entities. Contrary to colonial critiques of Muslims' "backward" gender practices, MSA pamphlets and articles extolled the much higher "status" of Muslim women—because they were able to devote themselves to the tasks that most suited their natural, innate qualities and were afforded rights such as inheriting property long before European women were granted those same economic privileges.

Countering this colonial logic carried particular affective resonance for Muslims living in Europe and North America. Educating non-Muslims about Islam was a centerpiece of daʿwa among revivalist communities during the Cold War, and this dimension of the project had major implications for the affective dimensions of revivalist texts.[38] By seeking to depict a "true" or "complete" Islam, MSA publications sought Islam as a religion that could be recognizable to other Americans.[39] As the authors of these prescriptive texts rightly noted, American audiences tended to have negative associations when it came to Muslim women. In other words, these texts extolled the beneficial aspects of Muslim family life in order to create positive associations between Islam and gender for both Muslim and non-Muslim audiences.

Second, the status of women took center stage in other struggles between "civilizations," namely between Soviet-style socialism and American democratic capitalism. The glossy advertisements in magazines of the 1960s promised American families not just the ease and efficiency brought about by modern amenities and appliances, but also American superiority over communism. Domestic life promised emotional security for men seeking a refuge from new bureaucratic demands, and emotional reward and fulfillment for women performing caregiving labor within their homes. In this way, the "status" of women was a common thread among multiple "systems"—whether political or religious—that were viewed as locked in existential battles for survival, a zero-sum game in which there could be only one victor. Amid these Cold War struggles between superpowers, MSA publications, like other revivalist organizations, proposed a "third way" in the form of Islam. Within this system's logic, whether the Islam/West binary or the struggle between global superpowers locked in a cold war, domestic space served as a key site through which the aspirations of a unified umma could become fulfilled.

Finally, "status" talk reflected the racial, classed, and gendered politics of the US. As such, status is constructed in that ambivalent space between self-perception and the structural categories that shape the political and economic possibilities for communities and individuals. "Status" is distinct from socioeconomic class in that it is not wholly determined by income, educational level, or profession, though all these markers help to determine a person's status in conjunction with race, gender, ablebodiedness, and the like.[40] Experiencing anxiety and fear over losing one's status shapes American politics in profound ways. A person who perceives a loss of status need not have experienced, say, the loss of a job. Rather, one's sense of status depends on how individuals and communities *feel* about their position in society. Moreover, American communities have strong feelings of attachment to certain status categories; belonging to the "middle class," for example, is much more about affective, aspirational attachment to a shared identity than about an actual income level or tax bracket.

Such attachments drive powerful political movements. In the 1970s, the perceived loss of status among white American Protestants galvanized the affective politics of gender and sexuality. For example, Phyllis Schlafly's STOP ERA movement succeeded, in part, on the fear that its proponent cultivated that women would lose their status as protected, vulnerable members of society once sex-based differences were no longer in place in institutions such as the miliary or in spaces like bathrooms. Fears over status helped to mobilize disparate groups who were interested in protecting women's status—from segregationists alarmed by the civil rights gains of the 1960s, to major labor unions worried about losing employment protections, to feminists in fear of the unraveling of hard-fought gains.

For US Muslims in the 1970s, the "status of women" discourse marked their ambivalence toward the contemporary politics in which they were embedded: the long reach of colonialism, the politics of postcolonial states, and the Cold War dynamics of 1970s America. In the 1970s, prescriptive literature was fraught with anxieties about whether it was possible to retain transnational aspirations for the Muslim umma in the American context. From this position, it was unnecessary for Badawi to drum up intense emotions over the challenges that his readers faced. Invoking the "status of women" tapped into a deep well of converging anxieties about the integrity of Islam and its future in the modern world.

In this way, revivalist-oriented American Muslims constituted a counterpublic that was united not just by ideology or negotiations over tradition but also by their affective orientation to modernity. The anxious politics surrounding gender and sexuality were shared across geographic boundaries, traversing distinct legal systems and political institutions. Where was the Muslim family strong? Where were women being honored and treated as they should? Where were Muslim norms being upheld? The answer was, "Nowhere."

At the same time, Badawi's prescriptions for American Muslims elevated a more optimistic set of collective emotions. He left considerably more room than Jameelah did for the entry of women into public life. It was permissible, even advantageous, he argued, for women to seek employment "where there is a necessity for it, especially in positions which fit her nature and in which society needs her most . . . nursing, teaching (especially for children), and medicine . . . moreover there is no restriction on benefiting from women's exceptional talent in any field."[41] He saw women's education as socially beneficial for Muslims and women's presence in education and medical institutions as a social good. Moreover, in a recent interview Badawi claimed he never wanted to upbraid other Muslims or impose a set of narrow ritual prescriptions.[42] As should be clear by now, there were no minor infractions in Jameelah's eyes—and she took no hesitation in condemning Muslims for all their failings.

Whereas Jameelah largely seemed to foreclose the possibility of living a pious Muslim life in the "West," Badawi saw a genuine opportunity for Muslims to thrive under American capitalism and the protections afforded by religious freedom, and even serve as model revivalists for other Muslims.[43] By cultivating a particular vision of the nuclear family, centered on companionate marriage as the bulwark against social collapse, thinkers such as Badawi mainstreamed Islam by making it more legible within American politics.

Conclusion

Attending to the affective economy of revivalism thus allows us to discern the emotional connective tissue that brings together seemingly disparate, discordant political and religious actors.[44] While Jameelah did not have any direct connection to anti-feminist

Christians in the 1960s and 1970s, her work, and that of some Muslim American authors, nevertheless contributed to the negative affectsphere that came to typify the culture wars of the 1980s and 1990s. In the decades after the circulation of Jameelah's work, urgent affective rhetoric was no longer required to galvanize these strong emotions around gender and family. That affective groundwork, and its catastrophizing of religious survival, had already been laid.

One recent example illustrates this complex affective terrain of religious outsiderhood. On May 23, 2023, a group of nearly a hundred primarily US-based Muslim leaders, intellectuals, academics, scholars, and shaykhs signed an online statement titled "Navigating Differences: Clarifying Sexual and Gender Ethics in Islam."[45] The statement was presented as a "collective, non-partisan articulation of Islam's position on sexual and gender ethics."[46] It was released following several high-profile controversies surrounding public school curricula that included LGBTQ stories. Social debates concerning gender identity also ramped up with the passage of many state bills restricting trans health care, especially for minors, as well as protracted public debates about the rights of parents and the authority of doctors. It was in this social context that the statement sought to articulate a clear, concise Islamic position on sex, arguing that these social developments subvert "the agency of Muslim parents to teach their children their religiously grounded sexual ethics, violate their constitutional right to freely practice their religion, and contribute to an atmosphere of intolerance toward faith communities."[47] The logic of religious diversity hinges on a simultaneous position of national belonging and marginality.

Similar to the earlier prescriptive texts that we have examined in this chapter, the statement attempted to delineate a universal Islamic position. At first glance, its rhetoric sounded fairly measured. The "non-partisan" approach sought to underscore that its authors were not moved by emotional attachments or political affiliation. While acknowledging the diversity of Islamic legal discourse, the statement invoked what it describes as the authoritative position of the Qur'an, namely that "God explicitly condemns sexual relations with the same sex (see, e.g., Quran, *al-Nisā'*: 16, *al-A'rāf*: 80–83, and *al-Naml*: 55–58)." By emphasizing the divine origin of this position, the statement thus drew hardened boundaries around what is authentically Muslim—and what is not.

The "Navigating Differences" statement therefore underscore how religious thinkers and scholars are constantly *feeling* their way through shifting political contexts. These legal and scriptural arguments implicitly marshaled the deeply affective crisis narrative around gender that Jameelah and other authors had pioneered more than fifty years ago. Even when couched in neutral and objective language, legal arguments about gender and sexuality always have an affective thrust. While these shifting political allegiances appear confusing at first glance, excavating the affective economies at play demonstrates the durable legacy of thinkers like Jameelah, who raised the catastrophic stakes around gender and sexuality in the decades prior—and did so in ways that resonated across religious boundaries. As a result, it is no longer necessary to invoke or amplify those stakes as forcefully or as explicitly as Jameelah did in order to rouse strong collective emotions about gender and the survival of "traditional" religious values. Such negative affects are always close to the surface, ready to be activated when the next crisis emerges.

Conclusion

GENDER AND THE AFFECTIVE ECONOMIES OF RELIGION

MARYAM JAMEELAH recognized that religious revivals are generated by collective emotions. Her intellectual project was thus animated by the effort to make her readers *feel something*. By analyzing the role of affect in the global Islamic Revival, I have offered a case study in how transnational religious movements bridge cultural boundaries by creating a "felt sense of us."[1] Jameelah envisioned a global Muslim community that was bound together by its shared understanding of modernity as a hostile place where materialism was the root cause of all evils—the destruction of the family, colonial oppression, nationalism, racism, and above all, the decline of religion. Within Jameelah's framework, Islam was the only way to protect civilization from moral collapse.

This case study has also demonstrated that being part of a religious community does not always feel good. For Jameelah, committed Muslims needed to feel badly about the world around them. She constantly castigated readers for their enjoyment of modern amenities. Her work foreclosed affects such as joy, tenderness, and humor. Any community that was optimistic about the future portended by late capitalism, she believed, had abandoned religion altogether.

When I first encountered Jameelah's writings, they made me feel not just pessimistic, but also a bit defensive. I felt like

Jameelah was writing *to me* specifically, as an American, scholar, woman, mother, and feminist. Her writing struck a discordant yet familiar chord for me across these social roles. I imagine that many readers of this book may have experienced a similar feeling, finding aspects of Jameelah's thought compelling, even prescient, while also recoiling from many of her positions. In particular, I would wager that some may relate to the grief and anguish that Jameelah expressed about a world that is falling apart. Some fifty years later, many of us feel like we are struggling against prevailing political headwinds, impending social collapse, rising authoritarianism, armed conflicts, and insurmountable environmental calamities.

Jameelah's corpus surfaces these emotions because she effectively tapped into the affects of catastrophe. Her ability to rouse collective feelings across disparate cultures testifies to the imaginative depth of her work. Jameelah had an aspirational, expansive vision for religious revival across all Muslim societies. She connected her readers to distant peoples and places, and she wanted them to think, feel, and act on behalf of their fellow Muslims, whether in Pakistan or Palestine or Paris.

At the same time, I have tried to uplift the unresolved tension between the expansiveness of Jameelah's religious imagination and the narrowness of her affective range. Even as I have highlighted the broad affective appeal of her critiques of modernity, I want to underscore that Jameelah's vision was also deeply exclusionary. For Jameelah, being a good Muslim required you to feel bad about modernity. The select few, or the vanguard of revival, constituted a community bound not just by a set of ideological commitments but also by a bundle of negative emotions—anxiety, disgust, shame—out of which Jameelah imagined the umma could rise as an alternative to liberal democratic capitalism, communism, and pan-Arab nationalism. As we have seen, this negative affectsphere helped to forge her relationship to Mawdudi and bolstered her appeal among revivalists in Pakistan and beyond.

For Jameelah, the most obvious place to bear witness to the catastrophe of modernity was the female body, and the family was the only site through which true Islam could be restored and revived. Her use of affect illuminates the paths through which gender, the family, and female sexuality became integral to Muslim politics in the twentieth century. Alongside other revivalists, she fashioned the nuclear family into the linchpin of religion itself. The transmission of correct Islamic practices thus required that women stay in their rightful social roles. Rather than cultivating feminine virtues or spirituality, Jameelah constructed women's bodies as "sticky" objects for generating collective emotion. These negative affects made women into yardsticks for measuring modernity's ill effects.

Unlike many of the Islamists from whom she drew inspiration, Jameelah's focus, and indeed the affective heart of her work, was the family, not the state. Because she saw the nation-state as an inherently anti-religious institution, she was largely uninterested in questions of sovereignty, legal reforms, or policy debates. Instead, Jameelah singled out popular culture as a particularly egregious site for promoting immoral gender relations and sexual promiscuity. Her entire political project called upon women to double down on caregiving and domestic responsibilities to protect their families from cultural imperialism. Just as American popular culture had gone global in the twentieth century, Jameelah believed that its excesses merited an urgent transnational Muslim response.

As her work was reprinted and recirculated back in the US, Jameelah brought these emergent culture wars into American Muslim politics. Her deeply gendered politics spoke to her lifelong affinity with other American religious conservative thinkers. Like evangelical and Catholic anti-feminists, she elevated the nuclear family as the institution that would safeguard morality and contain modernity's extremes. Jameelah's assumption that societies shared a universal affective register around sexuality and family reflected, in fact, America's gendered hierarchies.

Jameelah's affectsphere of Palestine might also prompt us to explore key questions about the politics of grief. In the aftermath of the horrific attacks perpetuated by Hamas on October 7, 2023, and as the devastating Israeli war on Gaza that has resulted in unfathomable suffering, I found myself returning often to Jameelah's drawings of Ahmad Khalil, as well as her renderings of Israeli soldiers as Holocaust survivors. Her artwork depicts a direct connection between the near annihilation of the Jewish people in the 1940s and the existential threat facing Palestinians in the 1960s. Such depictions *destabilize* the hardened boundaries that Jameelah constructed through her writing. They reveal, in fact, an emotional reservoir that exceeded the grief and outrage that she always demanded of her readers. The fact that Jameelah continued to produce drawings and paintings from her novel until very late in her life suggests that she, too, found spiritual meaning in the suffering of all peoples. As far as I can tell, most of her audiences never saw these drawings; they appear instead to have been intended only as private acts of mourning—a mourning for modernity that transcended the actions of any one community or government.

Through *Ahmad Khalil*, Jameelah plumbed the appalling consequences of displacement and death: physical, material, psychological, spiritual. When I first read the novel, in 2016, I thought it seemed overwrought. The sheer number of calamities that Ahmad Khalil and his family endured seemed completely implausible. Today, I experience the novel quite differently. The endless bombings, starvation, exile, injury, illness, and mass death experienced by Palestinian families are even worse than the imagined fate of Ahmad Khalil's family. Jameelah's novel is a contribution to a sustained outpouring of Muslim grief over the wanton killing of Palestinian men, women, and children—and the global community's paralysis and complicity.

Jameelah's affectsphere around Palestine thus invites us to reflect on the collective emotions that continue to structure our own world: Which lives are mourned? Which deaths move us to political action? What does it mean to grieve on behalf of others? Which collective emotions are effective in building solidarity? Ahmad Khalil could never adequately grieve the destruction of his village, the trauma of the Nakba, and the death of his family.[2] Like many of us, Jameelah had very little agency over the actions of leaders who waged wars in the name of her birth country and her religion(s). What she could do was devote her creative energies to mourning the catastrophic effects of modernity on behalf of the Palestinian families that she imagined and loved.

As her writings on Palestine evince, one of the more unexpected elements of Jameelah's career was that American culture and Judaism continued to shape her life long after she converted to Islam and left the United States. Indeed, her corpus reveals unexplored convergences of postwar American Judaism, Islamic revivalism, and transnational feminism. Years after she left the US and formally eschewed ties to her Jewish childhood, Jameelah continued to see the world largely through the national and religious cultures that she had left behind. Her ongoing connections to American culture, refracted through her Jewish background, were also a large part of what made her so appealing to other Muslims. Emphasizing her insider status as an American Jewish woman amplified the significance of her choice to become Muslim. Her *choice* served as inspiration, even for those born into Islam, to more deliberately embrace religious activism. Religious conversion never entails a complete break with the past.

Other aspects of Jameelah's biography further underscore the variety of religious, academic, and political networks that shaped her as a Muslim intellectual. Her childhood was defined by the rising affluence of America's Jewish communities and the growing diversity of its suburbs. New York City provided the ideal intellectual launching point for Jameelah's later foray into the literary world, and a variety of religious communities that were quite different from the Jewish milieu in which she was raised. The city's many universities and the New York Public Library, in particular, afforded her expansive access to Muslim thinkers and texts, providing her with a potent set of tools. With this matériel, Jameelah channeled her personal disaffection into an overarching narrative of moral decline.

Jameelah's conversion also illustrates the importance of interpersonal relationships, and the affective ties that structure them, in forging religious and political movements.[3] Her rise to intellectual prominence came through an unlikely set of relationships with key Muslim figures of the twentieth century—Shaykh Daoud Faisal and Mother Khadija in New York, and Abul A'la Mawdudi in Pakistan. Her unlikely relationship with Mawdudi, in particular, underscores the contingent social connections that often undergird global solidarity movements. Moreover, Mawdudi's and Jameelah's unexpected mutual recognition was more than just an ideological alignment. Instead, their life-changing relationship was forged through the expression of shared anxieties about modernity's dire consequences.

Focusing on the trajectory of a single religious actor thus enables us to tease out the multiple threads that shape our contemporary religious lives. Stories such as Jameelah's defy easy characterization as either Jewish or Muslim. As such, they complicate our understanding of the boundaries around these two traditions. Jameelah's story, like that of many converts, points to the instability of religious identities, even among those thinkers who are most intent on drawing sharp borders around them. As we have seen, Jameelah's boundary crossing and maintenance amplified, rather than detracted, from her affective appeal as a global Muslim intellectual. Even though Jameelah insisted on rigid boundaries, the way she moved between Islam and Judaism captures the generative possibilities of engaging across lines of difference. At times, Jameelah leaned on the multiplicity of her religious perspectives, while in others, she tried to render her rejection of Judaism absolute. She came to Islam out of a profound aversion to colonialism and yet romanticized Arab lands and peoples as authentic sites and timeless characters.[4]

While Jameelah's rise to prominence was remarkable, her story also demonstrates the precarious position that female intellectuals often occupy. She had no female role models to follow. Her path was bound to be unconventional. As a perpetual convert,

Jameelah's position in the revivalist movement was inextricably bound to the American context. Never quite belonging to a particular place, her authority as a Muslim woman was predicated on traversing cultural and political boundaries that she both solidified and subverted.

For a person so preoccupied with enforcing rigid norms, one of the central ironies of Jameelah's story was her own propensity to break the rules. She refused the easy materialism of suburban life, rejected the norms of an assimilated Jewish home, and challenged the neo-colonial logic of middlebrow intellectuals who saw the US as the pinnacle of civilization. Jameelah's penchant for refusing conformity and critiquing her own communities made her a perennial outsider. As a prolific writer who was utterly devoted to her career, she actually did not uphold the gender norms and practices that she demanded her readers enact.

Maryam Jameelah died in Lahore in 2012. As I reflect on her wider legacy, I want to conclude by dwelling on Jameelah's complicated relationship to feminism. As this book has explored, Jameelah saw revivalism as the antidote to materialism, and she saw feminism as one of the worst manifestations of the erosion of religion and the family. As these categories illustrate, while Jameelah loathed the women's liberation movement, she intimately understood the feminist project. So why would I, a feminist scholar, find her so interesting and compelling? Because: studying anti-feminist thinkers, I argue, is actually essential for understanding the impact and influence of feminism on religious communities. Furthermore, as Jameelah's life so vividly illustrates, the political and religious terrain across which gender is defined and contested is far more expansive than it is typically understood to be. Jameelah's trajectory is part of a much larger trend. Like her, many American female intellectuals who make women's liberation the target of their ire often embody feminist ideals in their own careers.

While feminists served as her foil, Jameelah's writing was simultaneously infused with feminist affects that resonated with her identity as a convert. One way of understanding feminist affect is the impulse to "see the world *as if* for the first time" and "to notice that which is there, is made, has arrived, or is extraordinary." This "surprise of wonder," Sara Ahmed astutely notes, "is crucial to how [feminism] moves bodies."[5] Jameelah's books exude a convert's wonder at discovering a new cultural and religious world—that of Islam, that of a non-Western society—and she fell in love with a vision of creating that better world for women. Through religious revival, she wanted her readers to discover, intellectually and affectively, why modernity was so broken and to feel anger at ways that injustice persisted. She also wanted to renew her readers' awe at the beauty and perfection of Islam.

Taken together, Jameelah's work remains a biting yet insightful critique of modern capitalism: its wars and genocides; its commodification of *everything*; its environmental destruction; and above all, its embrace of materialism over religious meaning. The singular focal point of Jameelah's critique, and the unrelenting commitment with which she pursued that critique, should not distract us from the bricolage of experiences, sources, relationships, and texts through which she crafted her call for Islamic revival. When we ignore anti-feminists and their publics, we risk losing sight of one of the most significant features of the modern world: gender, women, and the family often form the central node through which transnational religious identity is forged. So often religious thinkers like Jameelah present a clarity of purpose and a purity of vision. As scholars, our job is to uncover the messy underside of the modern religious imagination.

NOTES

Introduction

1. Amina Jamal, *Jamaat-e-Islami Women in Pakistan: Vanguard of a New Modernity?* (Syracuse University Press, 2013).

2. Nathan Glazer, *American Judaism* (University of Chicago Press, 1957).

3. Maryam Jameelah, *Islam and Modernism*, 4th ed. (Muhammad Yusuf Khan, 1977), vi–xiii.

4. Rachel Gordan, "The Sin of American Jewish Exceptionalism," *AJS Review*, 2021, 1–20; David Sorkin, *Jewish Emancipation: A History Across Five Centuries* (Princeton University Press, 2019).

5. Lila Corwin Berman, "American Jews and the Ambivalence of Middle-Classness," *American Jewish History* 93, no. 4 (2007): 409–34.

6. Eric L. Goldstein, *The Price of Whiteness: Jews, Race, and American Identity* (Princeton University Press, 2006).

7. Maryam Jameelah, *Islamic Culture in Theory and Practice*, 2nd ed. (New Crescent Publishing Company, 2006), 14.

8. Samuli Schielke, *Egypt in the Future Tense: Hope, Frustration, and Ambivalence Before and After 2011* (Indiana University Press, 2015), 70–75.

9. Zaid Adhami, *Dilemmas of Authenticity: Inside the Muslim Crisis of Faith* (University of North Carolina Press, 2025), 71–75.

10. Benjamin E. Zeller, "American Postwar 'Big Religion': Reconceptualizing Twentieth-Century American Religion Using Big Science as a Model," *Church History* 80, no. 2 (2011): 321–51.

11. Zeller, "American Postwar 'Big Religion,'" 330–32; Jonathan Sarna, *American Judaism* (Yale University Press, 2004), 274–82.

12. Kevin Schultz, *Tri-Faith America: How Catholics and Jews Held Postwar America to Its Protestant Promise* (Oxford University Press, 2011).

13. Schultz, *Tri-Faith America*, 7.

14. Aaron Rock-Singer, "The Salafi Mystique: The Rise of Gender Segregation in 1970s Egypt," *Islamic Law and Society* 23, no. 3 (2016): 279–305; Saba Mahmood, *Politics of Piety: The Islamic Revival and the Feminist Subject* (Princeton University Press,

2011); Charles Hirschkind, *The Ethical Soundscape: Cassette Sermons and Islamic Counterpublics* (Columbia University Press, 2006); Ellen McLarney, *Soft Force: Women in Egypt's Islamic Awakening* (Princeton University Press, 2015).

15. Muhammad Qasim Zaman, *The Ulama in Contemporary Islam: Custodians of Change* (Princeton University Press, 2002).

16. Dale F. Eickelman and James P. Piscatori, *Muslim Politics* (Princeton University Press, 2004); Gregory Starrett, *Putting Islam to Work: Education, Politics, and Religious Transformation in Egypt* (University of California Press, 1998); Jeanette S. Jouili, *Pious Practice and Secular Constraints: Women in the Islamic Revival in Europe* (Stanford University Press, 2015).

17. Deborah Baker, *The Convert: A Tale of Exile and Extremism* (Graywolf Press, 2012), 17.

18. Humaira Iqtidar, "Conservative Anti-Colonialism: Maududi, Marx and Social Equality," *Journal of the Royal Asiatic Society*, series 3, vol. 32, no. 2 (2022): 297–98.

19. Jameelah, *Islamic Culture in Theory and Practice*, back cover.

20. Mark Sedgwick, *Against the Modern World: Traditionalism and the Secret History of the Twentieth Century* (Oxford University Press, 2004), 25; Mark Sedgwick, *Traditionalism: The Radical Project of Restoring Sacred Order* (Oxford University Press, 2023), 102–4.

21. Sedgwick, *Traditionalism*, 103.

22. Maryam Jameelah, *Westernization Versus Muslims* (Muhammad Yusuf Khan, 1978), 63.

23. Sara Ahmed, *The Cultural Politics of Emotion*, 2nd ed. (Routledge, 2014); Donovan O. Schaefer, *The Evolution of Affect Theory: The Humanities, the Sciences, and the Study of Power* (Cambridge University Press, 2019).

24. Kambiz GhaneaBassiri, *A History of Islam in America: From the New World to the New World Order* (Cambridge University Press, 2010), 252.

25. Omid Safi, ed., *Progressive Muslims: On Justice, Gender, and Pluralism* (Oneworld, 2003).

26. Sara Ahmed, "Affective Economies," *Social Text* 79, no. 22.2 (2004): 117–39.

27. Ahmed, "Affective Economies," 118.

28. Donovan O. Schaefer, *Religious Affects: Animality, Evolution, and Power* (Duke University Press, 2015), 75.

29. Shenila Khoja-Moolji, *Sovereign Attachments: Masculinity, Muslimness, and Affective Politics in Pakistan* (University of California Press, 2021), 5.

30. Khoja-Moolji, *Sovereign Attachments*, 15.

31. Schaefer, *Religious Affects*, 67.

32. Cemil Aydin, *The Idea of the Muslim World: A Global Intellectual History* (Harvard University Press, 2017).

33. Darryl Li, *The Universal Enemy: Jihad, Empire, and the Challenge of Solidarity* (Stanford University Press, 2020), 14.

34. Li, *The Universal Enemy*, 14.

35. Schaefer, *Religious Affects*, 124–25; Lauren Berlant, *Cruel Optimism* (Duke University Press, 2011).

36. Sianne Ngai, *Ugly Feelings* (Harvard University Press, 2005).

37. Jameelah, *Islamic Culture in Theory and Practice*, 6.

38. Ahmed, *The Cultural Politics of Emotion*, 50.

39. R. Marie Griffith, *Moral Combat: How Sex Divided American Christians and Fractured American Politics* (Basic Books, 2017); Andrew Hartman, *A War for the Soul of America: A History of the Culture Wars*, 2nd ed. (University of Chicago Press, 2019); Elaine Tyler May, *Homeward Bound: American Families in the Cold War Era* (Basic Books, 2008).

40. Roxanne Euben, *Enemy in the Mirror: Islamic Fundamentalism and the Limits of Modern Rationalism* (Princeton University Press, 1999), 51.

41. Rebecca Solnit, *Men Explain Things to Me* (Haymarket Books, 2014).

42. Junaid Rana, *Terrifying Muslims: Race and Labor in the South Asian Diaspora* (Duke University Press, 2011).

43. Julia Stephens, *Governing Islam: Law, Empire, and Secularism in South Asia* (Cambridge University Press, 2018), 17.

44. Evelyn Alsultany, "Evoking Sympathy for the Muslim Woman After 9/11," in *Evoking Sympathy for the Muslim Woman After 9/11*, ed. Michael W. Suleiman, Suad Joseph, and Louise Cainkar (Syracuse University Press, 2021), 373.

45. Marcia Hermansen, "Roads to Mecca: Conversion Narratives of European and Euro-American Muslims," *Muslim World* 89, no. 1 (1999): 56–89.

46. John L. Esposito and John Voll, *Makers of Contemporary Islam* (Oxford University Press, 2001).

47. Abraham Rubin, "Muslim Identity on the Suburban Frontier: The American-Jewish Context of Maryam Jameelah's Conversion to Islam," *Journal of Jewish Identities* 12, no. 2 (2012): 125–48.

48. Sarah Imhoff, *The Lives of Jessie Sampter: Queer, Disabled, Zionist* (Duke University Press, 2022), 3.

49. Imhoff, *The Lives of Jessie Sampter*. The biographies of Sampter and Jameelah also overlap in fascinating ways, as they were both American women authors from German-Jewish backgrounds from the New York City area. Both women participated in the Ethical Culture movement and developed an enduring fascination with Palestine.

50. Lois Banner, "Biography as History," *American Historical Review* 114, no. 3 (2009): 582.

51. Marc David Baer, *German, Jew, Muslim, Gay: The Life and Times of Hugo Marcus* (Columbia University Press, 2020), 11–12.

52. Rubin, "Muslim Identity on the Suburban Frontier," 129.

53. Baker, *The Convert*, 207.

54. Rubin, "Muslim Identity on the Suburban Frontier," 129. Rubin argues that Baker's focus on the letters' fraudulence misses the fact that they nonetheless provide

a valuable window into how Jameelah portrayed her conversion as "an autobiographical solution to problems stemming from her American-Jewish background."

55. Rubin, "Muslim Identity on the Suburban Frontier," 128.

56. *Correspondence Between Abi-i-A'la al-Maudoodi and Maryam Jameelah* (Abul-Qasim Publishing, 1992).

Chapter 1. A Jewish Youth Adrift in Suburban America

1. Rachel Kranson, *Ambivalent Embrace: Jewish Upward Mobility in Postwar America* (University of North Carolina Press, 2017), 3.

2. Berman, "American Jews and the Ambivalence of Middle-Classness," 411.

3. Rubin, "Muslim Identity on the Suburban Frontier," 142. Rubin argues with regard to Jameelah's Jewish roots, "Ironically, the manner in which Jameelah disaffiliates from American Judaism and asserts her Islamic identity reveals her at her most Jewish."

4. Judith Goldstein, *Inventing Great Neck: Jewish Identity and the American Dream* (Rutgers University Press, 2006); Riv-Ellen Prell, "Triumph, Accommodation, and Resistance," in *The Columbia History of Jews and Judaism in America*, ed. Marc Lee Raphael (Columbia University Press, 2008); Matthew Lassiter, *The Silent Majority: Suburban Politics in the Sunbelt South* (Princeton University Press, 2006); Kenneth T. Jackson, *Crabgrass Frontier: The Suburbanization of the United States* (Oxford University Press, 1985); Lisa McGirr, *Suburban Warriors: The Origins of the New American Right* (Princeton University Press, 2001); Adam Rome, *The Bulldozer in the Countryside* (Princeton University Press, 2001).

5. Maryam Jameelah, *Islam Versus the West* (Abul-Qasim Publishing, 1994), 1.

6. Rachel Deblinger, *Saving Our Survivors: How American Jews Learned About the Holocaust* (Indiana University Press, 2025).

7. Hasia R. Diner, *We Remember with Reverence and Love: American Jews and the Myth of Silence After the Holocaust, 1945–1962* (New York University Press, 2009), 2; Deborah E. Lipstadt, *Holocaust: An American Understanding* (Rutgers University Press, 2016). Diner and Lipstadt challenge what they see as a consensus among historians that the Holocaust was absent from American Jewish life in the postwar period. Jameelah's autobiographical writings confirm not just the visibility of the Holocaust but also profound emotional grappling with the catastrophic event especially among coming-of-age Jews during this period.

8. Schultz, *Tri-Faith America*, 99–117.

9. Elizabeth Kolbert, "If You're Thinking of Living in Larchmont," *New York Times*, February 24, 1985.

10. Zeller, "American Postwar 'Big Religion,'" 336–40.

11. Kranson, *Ambivalent Embrace*, 49–50.

12. Sarna, *American Judaism*, 277–82.

13. Glazer, *American Judaism*, 106–26.

14. Jameelah, *Islam Versus the West*, 2.

15. Maryam Jameelah, *Islam Versus Ahl al-Kitab* (Muhammad Yusuf Khan, 1968), xxvii.

16. Valerie Hoffman-Ladd, "Polemics on the Modesty and Segregation of Women in Contemporary Egypt," *International Journal of Middle East Studies* 19, no. 1 (1987): 33; Asef Bayat, "Islamism and the Politics of Fun," *Public Culture* 19, no. 3 (2007): 433–59.

17. Will Herberg, *Protestant-Catholic-Jew: An Essay in Religious Sociology* (University of Chicago Press, 1955).

18. Herberg, *Protestant-Catholic-Jew*, 54.

19. Maryam Jameelah, *Why I Embraced Islam* (Muḥammad Yusuf Khan, 1975), 4.

20. Berman, "American Jews and the Ambivalence of Middle-Classness," 411.

21. Berman, "American Jews and the Ambivalence of Middle-Classness," 428.

22. Kranson, *Ambivalent Embrace*, 18.

23. Maryam Jameelah, *Islamic Culture in Theory and Practice*, 2nd ed. (New Crescent Publishing Company, 2006), 3–4.

24. John D. Carlson and Jonathan H. Ebel, "John Brown, Jeremiah, and Jihad: Reflections on Religion, Violence, and America," in *From Jeremiad to Jihad: Religion, Violence, and America*, ed. John D. Carlson and Jonathan H. Ebel (University of California Press, 2012), 10.

25. For example, Jameelah's critique here echoes that of Abraham Joshua Heschel, who argued in the 1950s that American Jews were losing touch with the transcendental dimensions of religious life as they moved in more symbolic and humanistic directions. See Edward K. Kaplan, *Spiritual Radical: Abraham Joshua Heschel in America, 1940–1972* (Yale University Press, 2007), 164.

26. Rubin, "Muslim Identity on the Suburban Frontier," 135.

27. Rachel Gordan, "The 1940s as the Decade of the Anti-Antisemitism Novel," *Religion and American Culture: A Journal of Interpretation* 31, no. 1 (2021): 33–81.

28. Jameelah, *Islamic Culture in Theory and Practice*, 3–5.

29. Kranson, *Ambivalent Embrace*, 97–113; Berman, "American Jews and the Ambivalence of Middle-Classness," 430; Riv-Ellen Prell, *Fighting to Become Americans: Jews, Gender, and the Anxiety of Assimilation* (Beacon Press, 1999).

30. Correspondence between Maryam Jameelah and Abul A'la Mawdudi, box 1, folder 5, Maryam Jameelah Papers, Manuscripts, Archives, and Rare Books Division, New York Public Library.

31. May, *Homeward Bound*, 162–82.

32. Jameelah, *Islam and Modernism*, ix.

33. Jameelah, *Islam and Modernism*, ix.

34. Robert S. Ellwood, *The Fifties Spiritual Marketplace: American Religion in a Decade of Conflict* (Rutgers University Press, 1997).

35. Jameelah, *Islam and Modernism*, ix.

36. Rubin, "Muslim Identity on the Suburban Frontier," 133.

37. Emily Sigalow, *American JewBu: Jews, Buddhists, and Religious Change* (Princeton University Press, 2019).

38. Umar F. Abd-Allah, *A Muslim in Victorian America: The Life of Alexander Russell Webb* (Oxford University Press, 2006); Justine Howe, *Suburban Islam* (Oxford University Press, 2018).

39. Lynn Davidman, *Tradition in a Rootless World: Women Turn to Orthodox Judaism* (University of California Press, 1991). Lynn Davidman makes a similar point about late twentieth-century women who embrace Orthodox Judaism. The women in her study gradually moved toward ritual observance over a several month period.

40. Lincoln Mullen, *The Chance of Salvation: A History of Conversion in America* (Harvard University Press, 2017).

41. Hermansen, "Roads to Mecca," 80.

42. Historians of psychiatry continue to debate why conditions such as "hysteria" and "schizophrenia" were more commonly diagnosed among particular groups in the twentieth century. One theory is that women who flouted social conventions were more likely to be diagnosed due to their refusal to conform to social norms. Another theory is that social conditions amplified emotional distress in women and thus resulted in increased mental illness rates. These explanations, among others, are possible in Jameelah's case. Either way, it is impossible to determine the causal relationship between her lack of conformity to social norms, the causes of her illnesses, her experiences of illness, and the symptoms that led to her diagnosis as schizophrenic. For an example of this debate, see Jonathan Metzl, *The Protest Psychosis: How Schizophrenia Became a Black Disease* (New York: Beacon Press, 2009); Tanya Luhrmann, review of *The Protest Psychosis: How Schizophrenia Became a Black Disease*, *American Journal of Psychiatry* 167, no. 4 (April 2010): 479–80.

43. Judith Weisenfeld, *Black Religion in the Madhouse: Race and Psychiatry in Slavery's Wake* (New York University Press, 2025), 17; Jonathan Sadowsky, *Imperial Bedlam: Institutions of Madness in Colonial Southwest Nigeria* (University of California Press, 1999), 5.

44. Baker, *The Convert*, 209.

45. Janis H. Jenkins, *Extraordinary Conditions: Culture and Experience in Mental Illness* (University of California Press, 2015).

46. Jameelah, *Islam Versus the West*, 5.

47. Richard Noll, *American Madness: The Rise and Fall of Dementia Praecox* (Harvard University Press, 2011), 235–39.

48. Noll, *American Madness*.

49. Lauren Hirshbein, *American Melancholy: Constructions of Depression in the Twentieth Century* (Rutgers University Press, 2009); Joel Braslow, *Mental Ills and Bodily Cures: Psychiatric Treatment in the First Half of the Twentieth Century* (University of California Press, 1997).

50. Metzl, *The Protest Psychosis*, 94, 37.

51. Hirshbein, *American Melancholy*, 94–96.

52. Metzl, *The Protest Psychosis*, 37.

53. Metzl, *The Protest Psychosis*, 101, 165. Notably, she does not report that her conversion to Islam raised fears about potential violent propensities, as did conversions to Islam by Black leaders such as Malcolm X. Similar to other white women who received a diagnosis of schizophrenia, Jameelah was released to her family's care, presumably because she was not perceived as a threat to herself or others.

54. Jameelah, *Islam Versus the West*, 5.

55. Marmaduke Pickthall, *The Meaning of the Glorious Koran: An Explanatory Translation* (Alfred A. Knopf, 1930).

56. Jameelah, *Islamic Culture in Theory and Practice*, 14.

57. Imhoff, *The Lives of Jessie Sampter*, 20.

58. Hermansen, "Roads to Mecca," 78.

59. Emily Mace, "Feminist Forerunners and a Usable Past: A Historiography of Elizabeth Cady Stanton's *The Woman's Bible*," *Journal of Feminist Studies of Religion* 25, no. 2 (2009): 5–23.

Chapter 2. Discovering Islam in New York City

1. Zareena Grewal, *Islam Is a Foreign Country: American Muslims and the Global Crisis of Authority* (New York University Press, 2014), 82.

2. Donovan O. Schaefer, *Wild Experiment: Feeling Science and Secularism After Darwin* (Duke University Press, 2022), 5.

3. Patrick Bowen, *A History of Conversion to Islam in the United States: White American Muslims Before 1975* (Brill, 2015), 240–41.

4. Bowen, *A History of Conversion*, 239.

5. The number of Jewish converts to Islam during this period is difficult to quantify, and Bowen, who has done the most extensive research on this area, does not provide an actual figure. Jameelah mentions another female Jewish convert, though not by name.

6. GhaneaBassiri, *A History of Islam in America*, 151.

7. Correspondence between Maryam Jameelah and Abul A'la Mawdudi, Maryam Jameelah Papers.

8. Correspondence between Maryam Jameelah and Abul A'la Mawdudi, Maryam Jameelah Papers.

9. Marc Ferris, "To 'Achieve the Pleasure of Allah': Immigrant Muslims in New York City, 1893–1991," in *Muslim Communities in North America*, ed. Jane I. Smith and Yvonne Hazbeck Haddad (State University of New York Press, 1994), 209–30.

10. GhaneaBassiri, *A History of Islam in America*, 155–264.

11. Correspondence between Maryam Jameelah and Abul A'la Mawdudi, Maryam Jameelah Papers.

12. Patrick Bowen, "The Search for 'Islam': African-American Islamic Groups in NYC, 1904–1954," *Muslim World* 102, no. 2 (2012): 264–83.

13. Patrick Bowen, "Satti Majid: A Sudanese Founder of American Islam," *Journal of Africana Religions* 1, no. 2 (2013): 202.

14. Judith Weisenfeld, *New World A-Coming: Black Religion and Racial Identity During the Great Migration* (New York University Press, 2017), 18; Bowen, "The Search for 'Islam,'" 267–68.

15. Rasul Miller, "Black Muslim Cosmopolitanism: The Global Character of New York City's Black Muslim Movements, 1929–1990" (PhD diss., University of Pennsylvania, 2019).

16. Weisenfeld, *New World A-Coming*, 5.

17. GhaneaBassiri, *A History of Islam in America*, 251–54. Members of the Islamic Mission were also inspired by Mawdudi to form their own distinct groups. For example, in 1968 a group of Islamic Mission congregants who thought that Shaykh Daoud was too focused on gaining acceptance in the American mainstream split off to form a new organization called Dar ul-Islam. The organization was deeply influenced by Mawdudi and argued that Islam should take a much more prominent role in daily life. It also saw Islam as a potent framework to challenge structural racism and the legacies of imperialism.

18. Rasul Miller, "Black Muslim Racial Reimagining: Traditions of Racial and Religious Self-Making Among Black Sunni Muslims in the US," *Journal of Africana Religions* 12, no. 2 (2024): 223–51.

19. Miller, "Black Muslim Racial Reimagining," 240.

20. Jameelah, *Islam and Modernism*, 45.

21. Amy Aisen Kallander, *Tunisia's Modern Woman: Nation-Building and State Feminism in the Global 1960s* (Cambridge University Press, 2021), 157–96.

22. Maryam Jameelah, *Islam and Western Society* (Adam Publishers and Distributors, 2010), 82.

23. Edward Curtis IV, *Muslims of the Heartland: How Syrian Immigrants Made a Home in the American Midwest* (New York University Press, 2022); Sarah Gualtieri, *Between Arab and White: Race and Ethnicity in the Early American Syrian Diaspora* (University of California Press, 2009).

24. Khaled A. Beydoun and Erika K. Wilson, "Reverse Passing," *UCLA Law Review* 282 (2017): 291.

25. There is a robust literature on Jewish practices of "passing" that demonstrates the complex and shifting relationship of race, ethnicity, and religion within Jewish communities in different social contexts. Susan A. Glenn, "'Funny, You Don't Look Jewish': Visual Stereotypes and the Making of Modern Jewish Identity," in *Boundaries of Jewish Identity*, ed. Susan A. Glenn and Naomi B. Sokoloff (University of Washington Press, 2010); Judith Ruderman, *Passing Fancies in Jewish American Literature and Culture* (Indiana University Press, 2019).

26. Rubin, "Muslim Identity on the Suburban Frontier," 127.

27. Sylvia Chan-Malik, *Being Muslim: A Cultural History of Color in American Islam* (New York University Press, 2018), 10, 15–16.

28. Chan-Malik, *Being Muslim*, 15. Sara Ahmed also engages the concept of "againstness," theorizing anger as the key expression that "energizes" feminist opposition to racism and sexism. See Ahmed, *The Cultural Politics of Emotion*, 174–75.

29. Chan-Malik, *Being Muslim*, 12.

30. Ula Yvett Taylor, *The Promise of Patriarchy: Women and the Nation of Islam* (University of North Carolina Press, 2017); Chan-Malik, *Being Muslim*, 24.

31. Chan-Malik, *Being Muslim*, 77.

32. Taylor, *Promise of Patriarchy*; Edward Curtis IV, *Black Muslim Religion in the Nation of Islam, 1960–1975* (University of North Carolina Press, 2006).

33. Sherman A. Jackson, *Islam and the Blackamerican: Looking Toward the Third Resurrection* (Oxford University Press, 2005).

34. Taylor, *Promise of Patriarchy*, 104–24.

35. Jameelah, *Islam and Western Society*, 29–30.

36. Grewal, *Islam Is a Foreign Country*, 111–13.

37. Grewal, *Islam Is a Foreign Country*, 221.

38. Grewal, *Islam Is a Foreign Country*, 221.

39. Sarah Imhoff, "The Creation Story, or How We Learned to Stop Worrying and Love Schempp," *Journal of the American Academy of Religion* 84, no. 2 (2016): 474.

40. Abraham Katsch, *Judaism in Islam* (New York University Press, 1954).

41. Jameelah, *Islam and Modernism*, x.

42. Schaefer, *Wild Experiment*, 8.

43. Kranson, *Ambivalent Embrace*, 35.

44. Jameelah, *Islam Versus the West*, 4.

45. Lila Corwin Berman, *Speaking of Jews: Rabbis, Intellectuals, and the Creation of a Public Identity* (University of California Press, 2009), 10.

46. Jameelah, *Islam and Modernism*, 105–6.

47. Jameelah, *Islam and Modernism*, 121.

48. Correspondence between Maryam Jameelah and Abul A'la Mawdudi, Maryam Jameelah Papers. I was unable to acquire additional biographical information about Mr. Parr.

49. Hermansen, "Roads to Mecca," 69.

50. Jameelah, *Why I Embraced Islam*, 4.

51. Hermansen, "Roads to Mecca," 61.

52. Correspondence between Maryam Jameelah and Abul A'la Mawdudi, Maryam Jameelah Papers.

53. Baer, *German, Jew, Muslim, Gay*, 4–5.

54. Sigalow, *American JewBu*.

55. Matthew Hedstrom, *Rise of Liberal Religion: Book Culture and American Spirituality in the Twentieth Century* (Oxford University Press, 2011). Hedstrom has

documented the robust middlebrow reading culture that was created by liberal Protestants starting in the 1920s and was widely embraced across middle-class publics by the 1950s.

56. Rachel Gordan, *Postwar Stories: How Books Made Judaism American* (Oxford University Press, 2024); Gordan, "The Sin of American Jewish Exceptionalism," 6–7.

57. Joanne P. Sharp, *Condensing the Cold War: Reader's Digest and American Identity* (University of Minnesota Press, 2000); Joanne Meyerowitz, "Beyond the Feminine Mystique: A Reassessment of Postwar Mass Culture, 1946–1958," *Journal of American History* 79, no. 4 (1993): 1455–82.

58. Sharp, *Condensing the Cold War*, xii; Christina Klein, *Cold War Orientalism: Asia in the Middlebrow Imagination, 1945–1961* (University of California Press, 2003), 61–99.

59. Brannon Ingram, *Revival from Below: The Deoband Movement and Global Islam* (University of California Press, 2018), 7–9.

60. Ingram, *Revival from Below*, 7–9.

61. Maryam Jameelah, "A Critique of Islam in Modern History," *Muslim Digest* 10, no. 8 (1960): 187.

62. McLarney, *Soft Force*, 10–12.

63. McLarney, *Soft Force*, 5.

64. Michael Warner, *Publics and Counterpublics* (Zone Books, 2002), 76. Warner argues that a social form constituted through voluntary forms of attention "requires our constant imagining."

65. Grewal, *Islam Is a Foreign Country*, 83.

66. Imhoff, *The Lives of Jessie Sampter*, 57–60.

Chapter 3. Generating a Shared Emotional Vocabulary Around Modernity

1. Correspondence between Maryam Jameelah and Abul A'la Mawdudi, Maryam Jameelah Papers.

2. Irfan Ahmad, *Islam as Critique* (University of North Carolina Press, 2017).

3. Baker, *The Convert*, 42.

4. Iqtidar, "Conservative Anti-Colonialism."

5. Iqtidar, "Conservative Anti-Colonialism," 297.

6. Muhammad Qasim Zaman, *Islam in Pakistan: A History* (Princeton University Press, 2018), 141–52.

7. Zaman, *Islam in Pakistan*, 136.

8. Zaman, *Islam in Pakistan*, 162.

9. Maryam Jameelah, *Western Civilization Condemned by Itself: A Comprehensive Study of Moral Retrogression and Its Consequences* (Muhammad Yusuf Khan & Sons, 1979), x.

10. Baker, *The Convert*, 43.

11. Jan-Peter Hartung, *A System of Life: Mawdudi and the Ideologisation of Islam* (Oxford University Press, 2014).

12. Ahmad, *Islam as Critique*, 100.

13. Correspondence between Maryam Jameelah and Abul A'la Mawdudi, Maryam Jameelah Papers.

14. Correspondence between Maryam Jameelah and Abul A'la Mawdudi, Maryam Jameelah Papers.

15. Correspondence between Maryam Jameelah and Abul A'la Mawdudi, Maryam Jameelah Papers.

16. Imhoff, *The Lives of Jessie Sampter*, 6.

17. Correspondence between Maryam Jameelah and Abul A'la Mawdudi, Maryam Jameelah Papers.

18. Correspondence between Maryam Jameelah and Abul A'la Mawdudi, Maryam Jameelah Papers. Emphasis added.

19. Kallander, *Tunisia's Modern Woman*, 163–64. Betty Luther Hillman, *Dressing for the Culture Wars: Style and the Politics of Self-Presentation in the 1960s and 1970s* (University of Nebraska Press, 2015).

20. Kate Manne, *Down Girl: The Logic of Misogyny* (Oxford University Press, 2018), 20.

21. Correspondence between Maryam Jameelah and Abul A'la Mawdudi, Maryam Jameelah Papers.

22. May, *Homeward Bound*; Griffith, *Moral Combat*; Janet R. Jakobsen, *The Sex Obsession: Perversity and Possibility in American Politics* (New York University Press, 2020).

23. Euben, *Enemy in the Mirror*, 123–52.

24. Khoja-Moolji, *Sovereign Attachments*, 18.

25. Correspondence between Maryam Jameelah and Abul A'la Mawdudi, Maryam Jameelah Papers.

26. Schaefer, *Religious Affects*, 123.

27. Ingram, *Revival from Below*, 148.

28. Schaefer, *Religious Affects*, 126.

29. Correspondence between Maryam Jameelah and Abul A'la Mawdudi, Maryam Jameelah Papers.

30. Correspondence between Maryam Jameelah and Abul A'la Mawdudi, Maryam Jameelah Papers.

31. Correspondence between Maryam Jameelah and Abul A'la Mawdudi, Maryam Jameelah Papers.

32. Amanullah De Sondy, *The Crisis of Islamic Masculinities* (Bloomsbury Academic, 2014), 38.

33. J. Barton Scott and Brannon Ingram, "What Is a Public? Notes from South Asia," *Journal of South Asian Studies* 38, no. 3 (2015): 357–70.

34. Jameelah, *Westernization Versus Muslims*, ix.

35. Schneur Zalman Newfield, *Degrees of Separation: Identity Formation While Leaving Orthodox Judaism* (Temple University Press, 2020).

36. Maryam Jameelah, *Shehu Uthman Dan Fodio: A Great Mujaddid of West Africa* (Muhammad Yusuf Khan, 1978), 4.

37. Baker, *The Convert*, 209–12.

Chapter 4. The Affectsphere of Suffering

1. Maryam Jameelah, *Ahmad Khalil: The Biography of a Palestinian Arab Refugee* (Muhammad Yusuf Khan, 1968), v.

2. Derek J. Penslar, *Zionism: An Emotional State* (Rutgers University Press, 2023), 150; Amy Kaplan, *Our American Israel: The Story of an Entangled Alliance* (Harvard University Press, 2018), 59.

3. Maryam Jameelah Papers, series 2, box 4, Manuscripts and Archives Division, The New York Public Library.

4. Jonathan Marc Gribetz, *Defining Neighbors: Religion, Race, and the Early Zionist-Arab Encounter* (Princeton University Press, 2014), 6. Gribetz demonstrates that late nineteenth-century Jews and Arabs more commonly invoked religious and racial categories as they encountered one another in Palestine, rather than nationalism. He shows how relying on religious narratives and concepts did not necessarily lead to conflict; instead, such frameworks sometimes created the potential for mutual recognition. By the time Jameelah invoked primordial religious narratives, however, such possibilities had largely been foreclosed.

5. Schaefer, *Religious Affects*, 124; Berlant, *Cruel Optimism*.

6. Jameelah, *Islam Versus Ahl al-Kitab*, 320.

7. Jameelah refers to the conflict as the "Six-Day War." The conflict is also referred to as the June War. The mass displacement of Palestinians in 1967 is also referred to as the *Naksa*, or setback.

8. Penslar, *Zionism*; Mark Raider, *The Emergence of American Zionism* (New York University Press, 1998).

9. Imhoff, *The Lives of Jessie Sampter*, 15.

10. Penslar, *Zionism*, 1. Penslar conceives of Zionism as both a movement and an ideology rooted in the conviction that "Jews constitute a nation that has a right and need to pursue collective self-determination within historic Palestine."

11. Geoffrey Levin, *Our Palestine Question: Israel and American Jewish Dissent, 1948–1978* (Yale University Press, 2023), 6. Levin uses the terms "anti-Zionist" and "non Zionist" to refer to American Jewish voices who advocated for Palestinian rights.

12. Edward Said, "Zionism from the Standpoint of Its Victims," *Social Text* 1 (winter 1979): 7–58; Rashid Khalidi, *The Hundred Years' War on Palestine: A History of Settler Colonialism and Resistance, 1917–2017* (Picador, 2020); Rashid Khalidi,

Palestinian Identity: The Construction of Modern National Identity (Columbia University Press, 1997).

13. David Nirenberg, *Anti-Judaism: The Western Tradition* (W. W. Norton, 2013).

14. Gordan, "The 1940s as the Decade of the Anti-Antisemitism Novel," 10–11.

15. Gordan, *Postwar Stories*, 3–4; Jonathan Sarna, "Antisemitism in America, 1654–2020," in *Cambridge Companion to Antisemitism*, ed. Steven Katz (Cambridge University Press, 2022); Leonard Dinnerstein, *Anti-Semitism in America* (Oxford University Press, 1994).

16. Suha Taji-Farouki, "Thinking on the Jews," in *Islamic Thought in the Twentieth Century*, ed. Suha Taji-Farouki and Basheer N. Nafi (I. B. Tauris, 2004), 328.

17. Taji-Farouki, "Thinking on the Jews," 328.

18. Jameelah, *Ahmad Khalil*, 58–59.

19. Jameelah, *Ahmad Khalil*, 33–34.

20. Alex Winder, "Nakba Diaries: Unsettling the Scale and Temporality of Historical Writing," *AlMuntaqa* 2, no. 2 (2019): 24–39. Winder emphasizes the central role of the affect, especially grief, in firsthand accounts of the Nakba.

21. Jameelah, *Ahmad Khalil*, v.

22. Typescript of *Ahmad Khalil*, 1961, Mss Col 1545, series 2, box 3, folder 3, Maryam Jameelah Papers, Manuscripts and Archives Division, The New York Public Library.

23. Roxane Euben and Muhmmad Qasim Zaman, eds., *Princeton Readings in Islamist Thought: Texts and Contexts from al-Banna to Bin Laden* (Princeton University Press, 2009), 107–11.

24. Typescript of *Ahmad Khalil*, 1979, Mss Col 1545, series 2, box 3, folder 1, Maryam Jameelah Papers, Manuscripts and Archives Division, The New York Public Library.

25. Typescript of *Ahmad Khalil*, 1991, Mss Col 1545, series 2, box 3, folder 2, Maryam Jameelah Papers, Manuscripts and Archives Division, The New York Public Library.

26. Ted Swedenburg, "The Palestinian Peasant as National Signifier," *Anthropological Quarterly* 63, no. 1 (1990): 18–30.

27. "A Note on these Illustrations," 1988, Ms Coll 1545, series 2, box 4, Maryam Jameelah Papers, Manuscripts and Archives Division, The New York Public Library. In this same note, Jameelah cited another source for these childhood drawings: The leftist artist Käthe Kollwitz's drawings and etchings of workers and displaced persons in post–World War I Germany. Kollwitz's etchings often depicted mothers who had lost children to the ravages of war, whether in combat or as civilians. Reflecting on this inspiration thirty years later, Jameelah stated that she similarly wanted to grapple with the destructive effects of war, especially the emotional toll of loss on the human body.

28. Per-Olow Anderson, *They Are Human Too: A Photographic Essay on the Palestinian Arab Refugees* (Henry Regnery Company, 1957), 10.

29. Catherine A. Lutz and Jane L. Collins, *Reading National Geographic* (University of Chicago Press, 1993), 7.

30. Jameelah, *Ahmad Khalil*, vi.

31. M. M. Silver, *Our Exodus: Leon Uris and the Americanization of Israel's Founding Story* (Wayne State University Press, 2010), 2.

32. Kaplan, *Our American Israel*, 59–60.

33. Silver, *Our Exodus*, 3–4.

34. Jameelah, *Ahmad Khalil*, vii.

35. Kaplan, *Our American Israel*, 65; Melani McAlister, *Epic Encounters: Culture, Media, and U.S. Interests in the Middle East Since 1945*, Updated edition, with a Post-9/11 chapter (University of California Press, 2005), 44–46.

36. Rubin, "Muslim Identity on the Suburban Frontier," 137.

37. Rubin, "Muslim Identity on the Suburban Frontier," 138.

38. Hugh Wilford, "American Friends of the Middle East: The CIA, US Citizens, and the Secret Battle for American Public Opinion in the Arab-Israeli Conflict, 1947–1967," *Journal of American Studies* 51, no. 1 (2015): 102.

39. Wilford, "American Friends of the Middle East," 115.

40. Jameelah, *Ahmad Khalil*, 31.

41. Jameelah, *Ahmad Khalil*, vii–ix.

42. Khalidi, *Palestinian Identity*, 191.

43. Khalidi, *Palestinian Identity*, 195.

44. Jameelah, *Islam Versus Ahl al-Kitab*, 119.

45. Sara Hirschhorn, *City on a Hilltop: American Jews and the Israel Settler Movement* (Harvard University Press, 2017), 32. Hirschhorn argues that American Jews before the 1967 war were largely "bystanders" to the events that first created the State of Israel. Even in the postwar period, few organizations and religious leaders were active in or openly intervened in Israeli politics.

46. Nouri Gana, *Melancholy Acts: Defeat and Cultural Critique in the Arab World* (Fordham University Press, 2023).

47. Jameelah, *Islam Versus Ahl al-Kitab*, 4.

48. Taji-Farouki, "Thinking on the Jews," 319.

49. Yvonne Haddad, "Islamists and the 'Problem of Israel': The 1967 Awakening," *Middle East Journal* 46, no. 2 (1992): 271.

50. Taji-Farouki, "Thinking on the Jews," 323, 338.

51. Jameelah, *Islam Versus Ahl al-Kitab*, 4–5.

52. Jameelah, *Islam Versus Ahl al-Kitab*, 12.

53. Taji-Farouki, "Thinking on the Jews," 328.

54. Jameelah, *Islam Versus Ahl al-Kitab*, 10–11.

55. Gudrun Kramer, "Anti-Semitism in the Muslim World: A Critical Review," *Die Welt Des Islams* 46 (2006): 257; Norman A. Stillman, "Antisemitism in the Arab and

Islamic World Prior to 1948," in *Antisemitism: A History*, ed. Albert S. Lindemann, and Richard S. Levy (Oxford University Press, 2010), 218–19; Derek J. Penslar, "Antisemitism and Anti-Zionism: A Historical Approach," in *Contemporary Antisemitism: Canada and the World*, ed. Derek J. Penslar, Michael R. Marrus, and Janice Gross Stein (University of Toronto Press, 2005); Taji-Farouki, "Thinking on the Jews."

56. Taji-Farouki, "Thinking on the Jews," 336.

57. Jameelah, *Islam Versus Ahl al-Kitab*, 10.

58. Abdul Majid, "The Zionist Conspiracy," *Pakistan Times*, June 29, 1967.

59. Jameelah, *Islam Versus Ahl al-Kitab*, 59.

60. Jameelah, *Islam Versus Ahl al-Kitab*, 133–34. In order to "liberate Palestine," Jameelah argued that, first, Arab countries had to reconcile their differences; second, that the "Muslim World" needed to extract itself from economic dependence on America and Russia; and third, that Muslims needed to break the economic links between Israel, Europe, and America—such as via an "intensive propaganda campaign" to "drive a wedge in between Jewry and Christendom" with a program of sanctions, boycotts, and nationalization of industries such as oil.

61. Jameelah, *Islam Versus Ahl al-Kitab*, 134–35, 312.

62. Qutb saw jihad unfolding in stages, with the community first coming together around the "commitment" to jihad, then emigrating away from the corrupting society, then waging the military and political battles necessary to bring about an Islamic state.

63. Taji-Farouki, "Thinking on the Jews," 336. Jameelah does not quote from Qutb's writings that specifically focus on Jews, but her works echo his framework.

64. Since 9/11, scholars have returned extensively to many of these debates, including distinctions between offensive and defensive jihad, as well as the multivalent meanings of jihad as armed fighting and spiritual struggle. For example, see Asma Asfaruddin, *Striving in the Path of God: Jihad and Martyrdom in Islamic Thought* (Oxford University Press, 2013); and David Cook, *Understanding Jihad* (University of California Press, 2005).

65. Roxane Euben, "Killing (for) Politics: Jihad, Martyrdom, and Political Action," *Political Theory* 30, no. 1 (2002): 22.

66. For example, Jameelah noted that the Qur'an contained complex portrayals of Jews, noting that "not all of them were guilty." Jameelah regularly invoked these exceptions alongside statements that suggested that Jews had been working against Muslims in all times and all places. Jameelah, *Islam Versus Ahl al-Kitab*, 136.

67. Schaefer, *Religious Affects*, 146.

68. Mark Dollinger, *Black Power, Jewish Politics: Reinventing the Alliance in the 1960s* (Brandeis University Press, 2018).

69. Shaul Magid, *Meir Kahane: The Public Life and Political Thought of an American Jewish Radical* (Princeton University Press, 2021), 5–10.

Chapter 5. Leveraging Shame to Build Global Muslim Solidarity

1. Portions of this chapter were previously published in Justine Howe, "Maryam Jameelah and the Affective Economy of Islamic Revival," *International Journal of Religion* 33, no. 2 (2022): 49–61.

2. McLarney, *Soft Force*, 5.

3. Gana, *Melancholy Acts*, 4.

4. Schaefer, *The Evolution of Affect Theory*.

5. De Sondy, *The Crisis of Islamic Masculinities*, 45–50.

6. Khoja-Moolji, *Sovereign Attachments*, 16–18.

7. Schaefer, *The Evolution of Affect Theory*, 61.

8. Maryam Jameelah, *Islam and the Muslim Woman Today* (Muhammad Yusuf Khan, 1976), 7.

9. Hoffman-Ladd, "Polemics on the Modesty and Segregation of Women in Contemporary Egypt," 25.

10. Shenila Khoja-Moolji, *Forging the Ideal Educated Girl: The Production of Desirable Subjects in Muslim South Asia* (University of California Press, 2018), 6.

11. Ahmed, *The Cultural Politics of Emotion*, 109.

12. Jameelah, *Islam and the Muslim Woman Today*, 6.

13. Jameelah, *Islam and the Muslim Woman Today*, 9.

14. Jameelah, *Islam and Modernism*, xv–xvi.

15. Jameelah, *Islam and Modernism*, 99.

16. Jameelah, *Islam and Modernism*, 98.

17. Jameelah, *Islam and Modernism*, 101–3.

18. Jameelah, *Islam and Modernism*, 102.

19. Leila Ahmed, *Women and Gender in Islam: Historical Roots of a Contemporary Debate* (Yale University Press, 1993), 144–68.

20. Beth Baron, *The Women's Awakening in Egypt: Culture, Society, and the Press* (Yale University Press, 1994).

21. Jameelah, *Islam and the Muslim Woman Today*, 9.

22. Jameelah, *Islam and the Muslim Woman Today*, 11.

23. Marion Holmes Katz, *Wives and Work: Islamic Law and Ethics Before Modernity* (Columbia University Press, 2022), 3–5; Kecia Ali, *Marriage and Slavery in Early Islam* (Harvard University Press, 2010). It is important to point out that Islamic studies scholars disagree about the extent to which, and on what terms, Muslim wives were and are expected to complete household work as part of their marital obligations. Marion Katz observes that in fact the prevailing consensus among scholars of Islamic law was that premodern Muslim marriage contracts did *not* require women to perform domestic labor. As Katz points out, Islamic conceptions of household labor reflect broader ethical assumptions that wives performing household labor is a social good.

24. Jameelah, *Westernization Versus Muslims*, 11–12.

25. Jameelah, *Westernization Versus Muslims*, 12.

26. Jameelah, *Islam and the Muslim Woman Today*, 21.

27. Maryam Jameelah, *The Resurgence of Islam and Our Liberation from the Colonial Yoke* (Muhammad Yusuf Khan, 1980), back cover.

28. Fedwi Malti-Douglas, *Medicines of the Soul: Female Bodies and Sacred Geographies in Transnational Islam* (University of California Press, 2001).

29. Hoffman-Ladd, "Polemics on the Modesty and Segregation of Women in Contemporary Egypt," 29–31; McLarney, *Soft Force*, 103–42.

30. Sedgwick, *Against the Modern World*, 154–55.

31. Jameelah, *Islam and Western Society*, 153–55; Sayyid Hossein Nasr, *The Encounter of Man and Nature* (George Allen & Unwin Ltd., 1968).

32. Sedgwick, *Traditionalism*, 4.

33. Jameelah, *Islam and the Muslim Woman Today*, 44–47; Seyyed Hossein Nasr, *Ideals and Realities of Islam*, 4th ed. (George Allen & Unwin Ltd., 2000), 105–8.

34. Mary Douglas, *Purity and Danger* (Routledge, 2002).

35. Jameelah, *Islamic Culture in Theory and Practice*, 21.

36. Jameelah, *Islam and the Muslim Woman Today*, 31.

37. Bayat, "Islamism and the Politics of Fun," 435.

38. Bayat, "Islamism and the Politics of Fun," 445.

39. Jameelah, *Islam and the Muslim Woman Today*, 14.

40. Jameelah, *Islam and the Muslim Woman Today*, 14.

41. Starrett, *Putting Islam to Work*.

42. Carolyn Herbst Lewis, *Prescription for Heterosexuality: Sexual Citizenship in the Cold War Era* (University of North Carolina Press, 2010).

43. Katz, *Wives and Work*, 7–8.

44. Ann Laura Stoler, *Duress: Imperial Durabilities in Our Times* (Duke University Press, 2016), 5–9.

45. Ingram, *Revival from Below*; SherAli Tareen, *Defending Muhammad in Modernity* (University of Notre Dame Press, 2020). The vibrant intellectual, religious, and political debates described in these books are entirely absent from Jameelah's writing.

46. Maryam Jameelah, *A Great Islamic Movement in Turkey: Badee-u-Zaman Said Nursi* (Muhammad Yusuf Khan, 1976), 6.

47. Maryam Jameelah, *Shaikh Hassan al Banna & Al Ikwan Al Muslimun* (Muhammad Yusuf Khan, 1976), 8.

48. Jameelah, *A Great Islamic Movement in Turkey*, 11.

49. Maryam Jameelah, *Who Is Maudoodi* (Muhammad Yusuf Khan, 1973), 10.

50. Hartung, *A System of Life*, 166.

51. Ahmad, *Islam as Critique*, 100–109.

52. Seyyid Vali Reza Nasr, *Mawdudi and the Making of Islamic Revivalism* (Oxford University Press, 1996), 52; Jamal, *Jamaat-e-Islami Women in Pakistan.*

53. Elora Shehabuddin, *Sisters in the Mirror: A History of Muslim Women and the Global Politics of Feminism* (University of California Press, 2021), 168–206.

54. Shehabuddin, *Sisters in the Mirror*, 231.

55. Jameelah, *Islam and the Muslim Woman Today*, 30–31.

56. Jameelah, *Islam and the Muslim Woman Today*, 30.

57. Jameelah, *Islam and the Muslim Woman Today*, 29.

58. Schaefer, *The Evolution of Affect Theory*, 57.

59. Jameelah, *Westernization Versus Muslims*, 61.

Chapter 6. Crisis Narratives and Prescriptive Literature in American Islam

1. R. Stephen Warner and Judith G. Wittner, eds., *Gatherings in Diaspora: Religious Communities and the New Immigration* (Temple University Press, 1998); Carolyn Chen, "The Religious Varieties of Ethnic Presence: A Comparison Between a Taiwanese Immigrant Buddhist Temple and an Evangelical Christian Church," *Sociology of Religion* 63, no. 2 (summer 2002): 215–38.

2. Portions of this chapter were first published in Justine Howe, "Daʿwa in the Neighborhood: Female-Authored Muslim Students Association Publications, 1963–1980," *Religion and American Culture: A Journal of Interpretation* 29, no. 3 (2020): 291–325.

3. Hartman, *A War for the Soul of America*, 135–40.

4. Grewal, *Islam Is a Foreign Country*, 83.

5. Adhami, *Dilemmas of Authenticity*, 5–6; Grewal, *Islam Is a Foreign Country*, 36–39. These ethnographies attest to the ongoing resonance of crisis narratives among American Muslims into the twenty-first century.

6. Maryam Jameelah, "The Feminist Movement Versus the Muslim Woman," *Al-Ittihad*, fall 1973, 14–15. This article was later reprinted in *Islam and the Muslim Woman Today* (1976).

7. Jameelah, "The Feminist Movement Versus the Muslim Woman," 15.

8. Jameelah, *Islam and the Muslim Woman Today*, 26.

9. Jameelah, *Islam and the Muslim Woman Today*, 27.

10. Jameelah, *Islam and the Muslim Woman Today*, 36–37.

11. Jameelah, *Islam and the Muslim Woman Today*, 35.

12. Gayle S. Rubin, "Thinking Sex: Notes for a Radical Theory of the Politics of Sexuality," in *Culture, Society, and Sexuality: A Reader*, ed. Richard Parker and Peter Aggleton (University College London Press, 1999), 151.

13. Hartman, *A War for the Soul of America*, 135.

14. Hartman, *A War for the Soul of America*, 140.

15. Hartman, *A War for the Soul of America*, 135.

16. Griffith, *Moral Combat*, ix.

17. Emily Suzanne Johnson, *This Is Our Message: Women's Leadership in the New Christian Right* (Oxford University Press, 2019).

18. Muslim Students' Association Women's Committee, *Parents' Manual: A Guide for Muslim Parents Living in North America* (Crescent Publications, 1972), 75.

19. Muslim Students' Association Women's Committee, *Parents' Manual*, 76.

20. Muslim Students' Association Women's Committee, *Parents' Manual*, 1.

21. Abdul-Rauf, *Marriage in Islam*, 11–12.

22. Muhammad Abdul-Rauf, *From the Nile to the Potomac: Autobiography of an Azharite American* (Universiti Sains Islam Malaysia, 2012).

23. Abdul-Rauf, *Marriage in Islam*, 71–72.

24. Abdul-Rauf, *Marriage in Islam*, 71.

25. Abdul-Rauf, *Marriage in Islam*, 70.

26. Abdul-Rauf, *Marriage in Islam*, 70.

27. Abdul-Rauf, *Marriage in Islam*, 70.

28. Kristin Luker, *Abortion and the Politics of Motherhood* (University of California Press, 1985).

29. Jennifer L. Holland, *Tiny You: A Western History of the Anti-Abortion Movement* (University of California Press, 2020), 15.

30. Grewal, *Islam Is a Foreign Country*, 137.

31. Grewal, *Islam Is a Foreign Country*, 140.

32. Jamal Badawi, "The Status of Women in Islam," *Al-Ittihad* 8, no. 2 (1971).

33. Jamal Badawi, *The Status of Women in Islam* (Muslim Students Association of the United States and Canada, 1972), 5–6.

34. Badawi, *The Status of Women in Islam*, 5.

35. Badawi, *The Status of Women in Islam*, 22.

36. Fatima Mernissi, *The Forgotten Queens of Islam* (University of Minnesota Press, 1997). This hadith has been interpretated in a variety of ways. Some interpreters and scholars think it applies to all women and all kinds of political leadership; others that it applies only to the position of the caliphate; and still others that it is fabricated, having been transmitted by only a single Companion of the Prophet rather than having a strong *isnad*, or chain of transmission.

37. Badawi, *The Status of Women in Islam*, 25.

38. Grewal, *Islam Is a Foreign Country*.

39. GhaneaBassiri, *A History of Islam in America*, 267.

40. Tressie McMillan Cottom, *Thick: And Other Essays* (The New Press, 2019).

41. Badawi, *The Status of Women in Islam*, 22.

42. "Interview with Dr. Jamal Badawi: A Pioneer of Islam in America," YouTube, October 15, 2021, https://www.youtube.com/watch?v=RyJ4rrFV2yg. For an analysis

of Qadhi's impact on contemporary American Islam, see Grewal, *Islam Is a Foreign Country*, 305–10.

43. Grewal, *Islam Is a Foreign Country*, 153.

44. Ahmed, *The Cultural Politics of Emotion*, 180.

45. "Navigating Differences: Clarifying Sexual and Gender Ethics in Islam," *Navigating Differences*, accessed November 18, 2025, https://navigatingdifferences.com/clarifying-sexual-and-gender-ethics-in-islam/. Most signatories were from the United States; however, several Canadian religious figures signed on as well. For further analysis of the statement, see Kecia Ali, *The Woman Question in Islamic Studies* (Princeton University Press, 2024).

46. "Navigating Differences."

47. "Navigating Differences."

Conclusion: Gender and the Affective Economies of Religion

1. Schaefer, *Religious Affects*.

2. Abdaljawad Omar, "Can the Palestinian Mourn?," *Rusted Radishes: Beirut Literary and Art Journal*, November 27, 2023, https://rustedradishes.com/can-the-palestinian-mourn/; Reem Kassis, "The Cruel Calculus of Palestinian Grief," *Atlantic*, October 11, 2025, https://www.theatlantic.com/family/2025/10/palestinian-grief-grandmother-death/684521/.

3. Rachel B. Gross and Sarah Imhoff, "Friends Are the Cream of Life: Mary Antin and Jesse Sampter's Religious Creativity," *Religion and American Culture: A Journal of Interpretation* 33, no. 3 (2025): 354–84; Constance Furey, "Body, Society, and Subjectivity in Religious Studies," *Journal of the American Academy of Religion* 80, no. 1 (2012): 7–33.

4. Baer, *German, Jew, Muslim, Gay*, 11.

5. Ahmed, *The Cultural Politics of Emotion*, 180.

REFERENCES

Abd-Allah, Umar F. *A Muslim in Victorian America: The Life of Alexander Russell Webb*. Oxford University Press, 2006.

Abdul-Rauf, Muhammad. *From the Nile to the Potomac: Autobiography of an Azharite American*. Universiti Sains Islam Malaysia, 2012.

Abdul-Rauf, Muhammad. *The Islamic View of Women and the Family*. Robert Speller & Sons, Publishers, Inc., 1977.

Abdul-Rauf, Muhammad. *Marriage in Islam*. Exposition Press, 1972.

Adhami, Zaid. *Dilemmas of Authenticity: Inside the Muslim Crisis of Faith*. University of North Carolina Press, 2025.

Ahmad, Iftikhar. "A Closer Look at Judaism." *Pakistan Times*, September 24, 1967.

Ahmad, Irfan. *Islam as Critique*. University of North Carolina Press, 2017.

Ahmad, Shahab. "The Poetics of Solidarity: Palestine in Modern Urdu Poetry." *Alif: Journal of Contemporary Poetics* 18 (1998): 29–64.

Ahmed, Leila. *Women and Gender in Islam: Historical Roots of a Contemporary Debate*. Yale University Press, 1993.

Ahmed, Sara. "Affective Economies." *Social Text* 79, no. 22.2 (2004): 117–39.

Ahmed, Sara. *The Cultural Politics of Emotion*. 2nd ed. Routledge, 2014.

Ali, Kecia. *Marriage and Slavery in Early Islam*. Harvard University Press, 2010.

Ali, Kecia. *The Woman Question in Islamic Studies*. Princeton University Press, 2024.

Alsultany, Evelyn. "Evoking Sympathy for the Muslim Woman After 9/11." In *Evoking Sympathy for the Muslim Woman After 9/11*, edited by Michael W. Suleiman, Suad Joseph, and Louise Cainkar. Syracuse University Press, 2021.

Anderson, Per-Olow. *They Are Human Too: A Photographic Essay on the Palestinian Arab Refugees*. Henry Regnery Company, 1957.

Asfaruddin, Asma. *Striving in the Path of God: Jihad and Martyrdom in Islamic Thought*. Oxford University Press, 2013.

Aydin, Cemil. *The Idea of the Muslim World: A Global Intellectual History*. Harvard University Press, 2017.

Badawi, Jamal. "The Status of Women in Islam." *Al-Ittihad* 8, no. 2 (1971).

Badawi, Jamal. *The Status of Women in Islam*. Muslim Students Association of the United States and Canada, 1972.

Baer, Marc David. *German, Jew, Muslim, Gay: The Life and Times of Hugo Marcus*. Columbia University Press, 2020.

Baker, Deborah. *The Convert: A Tale of Exile and Extremism*. Graywolf Press, 2012.

Banner, Lois. "Biography as History." *American Historical Review* 114, no. 3 (2009): 579–86.

Baron, Beth. *The Women's Awakening in Egypt: Culture, Society, and the Press*. Yale University Press, 1994.

Bayat, Asef. "Islamism and the Politics of Fun." *Public Culture* 19, no. 3 (2007): 433–59.

Berlant, Lauren. *Cruel Optimism*. Duke University Press, 2011.

Berman, Lila Corwin. "American Jews and the Ambivalence of Middle-Classness." *American Jewish History* 93, no. 4 (2007): 409–34.

Berman, Lila Corwin. *Speaking of Jews: Rabbis, Intellectuals, and the Creation of a Public Identity*. University of California Press, 2009.

Beydoun, Khaled A., and Erika K. Wilson. "Reverse Passing." *UCLA Law Review* 282 (2017): 282–354.

Bowen, Patrick. *A History of Conversion to Islam in the United States: White American Muslims Before 1975*. Brill, 2015.

Bowen, Patrick. "Satti Majid: A Sudanese Founder of American Islam." *Journal of Africana Religions* 1, no. 2 (2013): 202.

Bowen, Patrick. "The Search for 'Islam': African-American Islamic Groups in NYC, 1904–1954." *Muslim World* 102, no. 2 (2012): 264–83.

Braslow, Joel. *Mental Ills and Bodily Cures: Psychiatric Treatment in the First Half of the Twentieth Century*. University of California Press, 1997.

Butler, Judith. *Gender Trouble: Feminism and the Subversion of Identity*. Routledge, 2006.

Carlson, John D., and Jonathan H. Ebel. "John Brown, Jeremiah, and Jihad: Reflections on Religion, Violence, and America." In *From Jeremiad to Jihad: Religion, Violence, and America*, edited by John D. Carlson and Jonathan H. Ebel. University of California Press, 2012.

Chan-Malik, Sylvia. *Being Muslim: A Cultural History of Color in American Islam*. New York University Press, 2018.

Chen, Carolyn. "The Religious Varieties of Ethnic Presence: A Comparison Between a Taiwanese Immigrant Buddhist Temple and an Evangelical Christian Church." *Sociology of Religion* 63, no. 2 (summer 2002): 215–38.

Connolly, William E. *Capitalism and Christianity, American Style*. Duke University Press, 2008.

Cook, David. *Understanding Jihad*. University of California Press, 2005.

Correspondence Between Abi-i-A'la al-Maudoodi and Maryam Jameelah. Abul-Qasim Publishing, 1992.

Cottom, Tressie McMillan. *Thick: And Other Essays*. The New Press, 2019.

Curtis, Edward, IV. *Black Muslim Religion in the Nation of Islam, 1960–1975*. University of North Carolina Press, 2006.

Curtis, Edward, IV. *Muslims of the Heartland: How Syrian Immigrants Made a Home in the American Midwest*. New York University Press, 2022.

Davidman, Lynn. *Tradition in a Rootless World: Women Turn to Orthodox Judaism*. University of California Press, 1991.

De Sondy, Amanullah. *The Crisis of Islamic Masculinities*. Bloomsbury Academic, 2014.

Deblinger, Rachel. *Saving Our Survivors: How American Jews Learned About the Holocaust*. Indiana University Press, 2025.

Diner, Hasia. *We Remember with Reverence and Love: American Jews and the Myth of Silence After the Holocaust, 1945–1962*. New York University Press, 2009.

Dinnerstein, Leonard. *Anti-Semitism in America*. Oxford University Press, 1994.

Dollinger, Mark. *Black Power, Jewish Politics: Reinventing the Alliance in the 1960s*. Brandeis University Press, 2018.

Douglas, Mary. *Purity and Danger*. Routledge, 2002.

Eickelman, Dale F., and James P. Piscatori. *Muslim Politics*. Princeton University Press, 2004.

Ellwood, Robert S. *The Fifties Spiritual Marketplace: American Religion in a Decade of Conflict*. Rutgers University Press, 1997.

Esposito, John L., and John Voll. *Makers of Contemporary Islam*. Oxford University Press, 2001.

Euben, Roxanne. *Enemy in the Mirror: Islamic Fundamentalism and the Limits of Modern Rationalism*. Princeton University Press, 1999.

Euben, Roxane. "Killing (for) Politics: Jihad, Martyrdom, and Political Action." *Political Theory* 30, no. 1 (2002): 4–35.

Euben, Roxane, and Muhmmad Qasim Zaman, eds. *Princeton Readings in Islamist Thought: Texts and Contexts from al-Banna to Bin Laden*. Princeton University Press, 2009.

Ferris, Marc. "To 'Achieve the Pleasure of Allah': Immigrant Muslims in New York City, 1893–1991." In *Muslim Communities in North America*, edited by Yvonne Yazbeck Haddad and Jane Idleman Smith. State University of New York Press, 1994.

Furey, Constance. "Body, Society, and Subjectivity in Religious Studies." *Journal of the American Academy of Religion* 80, no. 1 (2012): 7–33.

Gana, Nouri. *Melancholy Acts: Defeat and Cultural Critique in the Arab World*. Fordham University Press, 2023.

GhaneaBassiri, Kambiz. *A History of Islam in America: From the New World to the New World Order*. Cambridge University Press, 2010.

Glazer, Nathan. *American Judaism*. University of Chicago Press, 1957.

Glenn, Susan A. "'Funny, You Don't Look Jewish': Visual Stereotypes and the Making of Modern Jewish Identity." In *Boundaries of Jewish Identity*, edited by Susan A. Glenn and Naomi B. Sokoloff. University of Washington Press, 2010.

Goldstein, Eric L. *The Price of Whiteness: Jews, Race, and American Identity*. Princeton University Press, 2006.

Goldstein, Judith. *Inventing Great Neck: Jewish Identity and the American Dream*. Rutgers University Press, 2006.

Goodman, Nancy, and Marilyn Meyers. *The Power of Witnessing: Reflections, Reverberations, and Traces of the Holocaust*. Routledge, 2012.

Goodwin, Jeff, James M. Jasper, and Francesca Polletta. *Passionate Politics: Emotions and Social Movements*. University of Chicago Press, 2001.

Gordan, Rachel. "The 1940s as the Decade of the Anti-Antisemitism Novel." *Religion and American Culture: A Journal of Interpretation* 31, no. 1 (2021): 33–81.

Gordan, Rachel. *Postwar Stories: How Books Made Judaism American*. Oxford University Press, 2024.

Gordan, Rachel. "The Sin of American Jewish Exceptionalism." *AJS Review* (2021): 1–20.

Gould, Deborah B. *Moving Politics: Emotion and ACT UP's Fight Against AIDS*. University of Chicago Press, 2009.

Grewal, Zareena. *Islam Is a Foreign Country: American Muslims and the Global Crisis of Authority*. New York University Press, 2014.

Gribetz, Jonathan Marc. *Defining Neighbors: Religion, Race, and the Early Zionist-Arab Encounter*. Princeton University Press, 2014.

Griffith, R. Marie. *Moral Combat: How Sex Divided American Christians and Fractured American Politics*. Basic Books, 2017.

Gross, Rachel B., and Sarah Imhoff. "Friends Are the Cream of Life: Mary Antin and Jesse Sampter's Religious Creativity." *Religion and American Culture: A Journal of Interpretation* 33, no. 3 (2023): 354–84.

Gualtieri, Sarah. *Between Arab and White: Race and Ethnicity in the Early American Syrian Diaspora*. University of California Press, 2009.

Haddad, Yvonne [Yazbeck]. "Islamists and the 'Problem of Israel': The 1967 Awakening." *Middle East Journal* 46, no. 2 (1992): 266–85.

Haddad, Yvonne Yazbeck. *Not Quite American?: The Shaping of Arab and Muslim Identity in the United States*. Baylor University Press, 2004.

Haddad, Yvonne Yazbeck and Smith, Jane Idleman, eds. *Muslim Communities in North America*. State University of New York Press, 1994.

Hartman, Andrew. *A War for the Soul of America: A History of the Culture Wars*. 2nd ed. University of Chicago Press, 2019.

Hartung, Jan-Peter. *A System of Life: Mawdudi and the Ideologisation of Islam*. Oxford University Press, 2014.

Hedstrom, Matthew. *The Rise of Liberal Religion: Book Culture and American Spirituality in the Twentieth Century*. Oxford University Press, 2011.

Heinze, Andrew R. "Schizophrenia Americana: Aliens, Alienists, and the 'Personality Shift' of Twentieth-Century Culture." *American Quarterly* 55, no. 2 (2003): 227–56.

Herberg, Will. *Protestant-Catholic-Jew: An Essay in Religious Sociology*. University of Chicago Press, 1955.

Hermansen, Marcia. "Roads to Mecca: Conversion Narratives of European and Euro-American Muslims." *Muslim World* 89, no. 1 (1999): 56–89.

Hillman, Betty Luther. *Dressing for the Culture Wars: Style and the Politics of Self-Presentation in the 1960s and 1970s*. University of Nebraska Press, 2015.

Hirschkind, Charles. *The Ethical Soundscape: Cassette Sermons and Islamic Counterpublics*. Columbia University Press, 2006.

Hirschhorn, Sara. *City on a Hilltop: American Jews and the Israel Settler Movement*. Harvard University Press, 2017.

Hirshbein, Lauren. *American Melancholy: Constructions of Depression in the Twentieth Century*. Rutgers University Press, 2009.

Hoffman-Ladd, Valerie. "Polemics on the Modesty and Segregation of Women in Contemporary Egypt." *International Journal of Middle East Studies* 19, no. 1 (1987): 23–50.

Hole, Judith, and Ellen Levine. *Rebirth of Feminism*. Quadrangle Books, 1971.

Holland, Jennifer L. *Tiny You: A Western History of the Anti-Abortion Movement*. University of California Press, 2020.

Howe, Justine. "Daʿwa in the Neighborhood: Female-Authored Muslim Students Association Publications, 1963–1980." *Religion and American Culture: A Journal of Interpretation* 29, no. 3 (2020): 291–325.

Howe, Justine. "Maryam Jameelah and the Affective Economy of Islamic Revival." *International Journal of Religion* 33, no. 2 (2022): 49–61.

Howe, Justine. *Suburban Islam*. Oxford University Press, 2018.

Imhoff, Sarah. "The Creation Story, or How We Learned to Stop Worrying and Love Schempp." *Journal of the American Academy of Religion* 84, no. 2 (2016): 466–97.

Imhoff, Sarah. *The Lives of Jessie Sampter: Queer, Disabled, Zionist*. Duke University Press, 2022.

Imhoff, Sarah. *Masculinity and the Making of American Judaism*. Indiana University Press, 2017.

Imhoff, Sarah. "My Sons Have Defeated Me: Walter Lipmann, Felix Adler, and Secular Moral Authority." *Journal of Religion* 92, no. 4 (2012): 536–50.

Ingram, Brannon. *Revival from Below: The Deoband Movement and Global Islam*. University of California Press, 2018.

"Interview with Dr. Jamal Badawi: A Pioneer of Islam in America." YouTube. October 15, 2021. https://www.youtube.com/watch?v=RyJ4rrFV2yg.

Iqtidar, Humaira. "Conservative Anti-Colonialism: Maududi, Marx and Social Equality." *Journal of the Royal Asiatic Society*, series 3, vol. 32, no. 2 (2022): 295–310.

Iqtidar, Humaira. *Jama'at-e-Islami and Jama'at-Ud-Da'wa in Urban Pakistan*. University of Chicago Press, 2011.

Iqtidar, Humaira. *Secularizing Islamists? Jama'at-e-Islami and Jama'at-Ud-Da'wa in Urban Pakistan*. University of Chicago Press, 2011.

Jackson, Kenneth T. *Crabgrass Frontier: The Suburbanization of the United States*. Oxford University Press, 1985.

Jackson, Sherman A. *Islam and the Blackamerican: Looking Toward the Third Resurrection*. Oxford University Press, 2005.

Jakobsen, Janet R. *The Sex Obsession: Perversity and Possibility in American Politics*. New York University Press, 2020.

Jamal, Amina. *Jamaat-e-Islami Women in Pakistan: Vanguard of a New Modernity?* Syracuse University Press, 2013.

Jameelah, Maryam. *Ahmad Khalil: The Biography of a Palestinian Arab Refugee*. Muhammad Yusuf Khan, 1968.

Jameelah, Maryam. "A Critique of Islam in Modern History." *Muslim Digest* 10, no. 8 (1960): 187–88.

Jameelah, Maryam. "The Feminist Movement Versus the Muslim Woman." *Al-Ittihad*, fall 1973.

Jameelah, Maryam. *A Great Islamic Movement in Turkey: Badee-u-Zaman Said Nursi*. Muhammad Yusuf Khan, 1976.

Jameelah, Maryam. *Islam and Modernism*. 4th ed. Muhammad Yusuf Khan, 1977.

Jameelah, Maryam. *Islam and the Muslim Woman Today*. Muhammad Yusuf Khan, 1976.

Jameelah, Maryam. *Islam and Western Society*. Adam Publishers and Distributors, 2010.

Jameelah, Maryam. *Islam Versus Ahl al-Kitab*. Muhammad Yusuf Khan, 1968.

Jameelah, Maryam. *Islam Versus the West*. Abul-Qasim Publishing, 1994.

Jameelah, Maryam. *Islamic Culture in Theory and Practice*. 2nd ed. New Crescent Publishing Company, 2006.

Jameelah, Maryam. "Maulana Sayyid Abul Ala Maudoodi and His Impact on My Life." *Young Muslim Digest* 27, no. 6 (2005): 1–5.

Jameelah, Maryam. *The Resurgence of Islam and Our Liberation from the Colonial Yoke*. Muhammad Yusuf Khan, 1980.

Jameelah, Maryam. *Shaikh Hassan al Banna & Al Ikwan Al Muslimun*. Muhammad Yusuf Khan, 1976.

Jameelah, Maryam. *Shehu Uthman Dan Fodio: A Great Mujaddid of West Africa*. Muhammad Yusuf Khan, 1978.

Jameelah, Maryam. *Western Civilization Condemned by Itself: A Comprehensive Study of Moral Retrogression and Its Consequences*. Vol. 1. Muhammad Yusuf Khan & Sons, 1979.

Jameelah, Maryam. *Westernization Versus Muslims*. Muhammad Yusuf Khan, 1978.

Jameelah, Maryam. *Who Is Maudoodi*. Muhammad Yusuf Khan, 1973.

Jameelah, Maryam. *Why I Embraced Islam*. Muhammad Yusuf Khan, 1975.

Jenkins, Janis H. *Extraordinary Conditions: Culture and Experience in Mental Illness*. University of California Press, 2015.

Johnson, Emily Suzanne. *This Is Our Message: Women's Leadership in the New Christian Right*. Oxford University Press, 2019.

Jouili, Jeanette S. *Pious Practice and Secular Constraints: Women in the Islamic Revival in Europe*. Stanford University Press, 2015.

Kallander, Amy Aisen. *Tunisia's Modern Woman: Nation-Building and State Feminism in the Global 1960s*. Cambridge University Press, 2021.

Kaplan, Amy. *Our American Israel: The Story of an Entangled Alliance*. Harvard University Press, 2018.

Kaplan, Edward K. *Spiritual Radical: Abraham Joshua Heschel in America, 1940–1972*. Yale University Press, 2007.

Kashani, Maryam. *Medina by the Bay: Scenes of Muslim Study and Survival*. Duke University Press, 2023.

Kassis, Reem. "The Cruel Calculus of Palestinian Mourning." *Atlantic*, October 11, 2025. https://www.theatlantic.com/family/2025/10/palestinian-grief-grandmother-death/684521/.

Katsch, Abraham. *Judaism in Islam*. New York University Press, 1954.

Katz, Marion Holmes. *Wives and Work: Islamic Law and Ethics Before Modernity*. Columbia University Press, 2022.

Khabeer, Su'ad Abdul. *Muslim Cool: Race, Religion, and Hip Hop in the United States*. New York University Press, 2016.

Khalidi, Rashid. *The Hundred Years' War on Palestine: A History of Settler Colonialism and Resistance, 1917–2017*. Picador, 2020.

Khalidi, Rashid. *Palestinian Identity: The Construction of Modern National Identity*. Columbia University Press, 1997.

Khoja-Moolji, Shenila. *Forging the Ideal Educated Girl: The Production of Desirable Subjects in Muslim South Asia*. University of California Press, 2018.

Khoja-Moolji, Shenila. *Sovereign Attachments: Masculinity, Muslimness, and Affective Politics in Pakistan*. University of California Press, 2021.

Klein, Christina. *Cold War Orientalism: Asia in the Middlebrow Imagination, 1945–1961*. University of California Press, 2003.

Kolbert, Elizabeth. "If You're Thinking of Living in Larchmont." *New York Times*, February 24, 1985.

Kramer, Gudrun. "Anti-Semitism in the Muslim World: A Critical Review." *Die Welt des Islams* 46 (2006): 243–76.

Kranson, Rachel. *Ambivalent Embrace: Jewish Upward Mobility in Postwar America.* University of North Carolina Press, 2017.

Lassiter, Matthew. *The Silent Majority: Suburban Politics in the Sunbelt South.* Princeton University Press, 2006.

Levin, Geoffrey. *Our Palestine Question: Israel and American Jewish Dissent, 1948–1978.* Yale University Press, 2023.

Lewis, Carolyn Herbst. *Prescription for Heterosexuality: Sexual Citizenship in the Cold War Era.* University of North Carolina Press, 2010.

Li, Darryl. *The Universal Enemy: Jihad, Empire, and the Challenge of Solidarity.* Stanford University Press, 2020.

Lipstadt, Deborah E. *Holocaust: An American Understanding.* Rutgers University Press, 2016.

Lorenzini, Sara. *Global Development: A Cold War History.* Princeton University Press, 2019.

Luhrmann, Tanya. Review of *The Protest Psychosis: How Schizophrenia Became a Black Disease. American Journal of Psychiatry* 167, no. 4 (2010): 479–80.

Luker, Kristin. *Abortion and the Politics of Motherhood.* University of California Press, 1985.

Lutz, Catherine A., and Jane L. Collins. *Reading National Geographic.* University of Chicago Press, 1993.

Mace, Emily. "Feminist Forerunners and a Usable Past: A Historiography of Elizabeth Cady Stanton's *The Woman's Bible.*" *Journal of Feminist Studies of Religion* 25, no. 2 (2009): 5–23.

Magid, Shaul. *Meir Kahane: The Public Life and Political Thought of an American Jewish Radical.* Princeton University Press, 2021.

Mahmood, Saba. *Politics of Piety: The Islamic Revival and the Feminist Subject.* Princeton University Press, 2011.

Mahmood, Saba. "Rehearsed Spontaneity and the Conventionality of Ritual: Disciplines of Salat." *American Ethnologist* 28, no. 4 (2001): 4.

Maira, Sunaina. *Missing: Youth, Citizenship, and Empire After 9/11.* Duke University Press, 2009.

Majid, Abdul. "The Zionist Conspiracy." *Pakistan Times,* June 29, 1967.

Malti-Douglas, Fedwi. *Medicines of the Soul: Female Bodies and Sacred Geographies in Transnational Islam.* University of California Press, 2001.

Mamdani, Mahmood. *Good Muslim, Bad Muslim: America, the Cold War, and the Roots of Terror.* Reprint edition. Harmony, 2005.

Manne, Kate. *Down Girl: The Logic of Misogyny.* Oxford University Press, 2017.

Marr, Timothy. *The Cultural Roots of American Islamicism.* Cambridge University Press, 2006.

Masuzawa, Tomoko. *The Invention of World Religions*. University of Chicago Press, 2005.

May, Elaine Tyler. *Homeward Bound: American Families in the Cold War Era*. Basic Books, 2008.

McAlister, Melani. *Epic Encounters: Culture, Media, and U.S. Interests in the Middle East Since 1945*. Updated edition, with a post-9/11 chapter. University of California Press, 2005.

McGirr, Lisa. *Suburban Warriors: The Origins of the New American Right*. Princeton University Press, 2001.

McLarney, Ellen. *Soft Force: Women in Egypt's Islamic Awakening*. Princeton University Press, 2015.

Mehta, Samira. "Prescribing the Diaphragm: Protestants, Jews, Catholics, and a Changing Culture of Contraception." *American Religion* 1, no. 2 (2020): 27–52.

Meijer, Roel. *Global Salafism: Islam's New Religious Movement*. Oxford University Press, 2013.

Mernissi, Fatima. *The Forgotten Queens of Islam*. University of Minnesota Press, 1997.

Metcalf, Barbara, ed. *Making Muslim Space in North America and Europe*. University of California Press, 1996.

Metzl, Jonathan. *The Protest Psychosis: How Schizophrenia Became a Black Disease*. Beacon Press, 2009.

Meyerowitz, Joanne. "Beyond the Feminine Mystique: A Reassessment of Postwar Mass Culture, 1946–1958." *Journal of American History* 79, no. 4 (1993): 1455–82.

Miller, Rasul. "Black Muslim Cosmopolitanism: The Global Character of New York City's Black Muslim Movements, 1929–1990." PhD diss., University of Pennsylvania, 2019.

Miller, Rasul. "Black Muslim Racial Reimagining: Traditions of Racial and Religious Self-Making Among Black Sunni Muslims in the US." *Journal of Africana Religions* 12, no. 2 (2024): 223–51.

Mir, Shabana. *American Muslim Women on Campus: Undergraduate Social Life and Identity*. University of North Carolina Press, 2014.

Moore, Kathleen M. *Al-Mughtaribun: American Law and the Transformation of Muslim Life in the United States*. State University of New York Press, 1995.

Moore, Kathleen M. *The Unfamiliar Abode: Islamic Law in the United States and Britain*. Oxford University Press, 2010.

Moore, Natalie Y. *The South Side: A Portrait of American Segregation*. St. Martin's Press, 2016.

Moore, R. Laurence. *Religious Outsiders and the Making of Americans*. Oxford University Press, 1987.

Moorjani, Angela. "Käthe Kollwitz on Sacrifice, Mourning, and Reparation: An Essay in Psychoaesthetics." *Comparative Literature* 101, no. 5 (1986): 1110–34.

Moreton, Bethany. *To Serve God and Wal-Mart: The Making of Christian Free Enterprise*. Harvard University Press, 2010.

Mullen, Lincoln. *The Chance of Salvation: A History of Conversion in America*. Harvard University Press, 2017.

Muslim Students' Association Women's Committee. *Parents' Manual: A Guide for Muslim Parents Living in North America*. Crescent Publications, 1972.

Nasr, Sayyid Hossein. *The Encounter of Man and Nature*. George Allen & Unwin Ltd., 1968.

Nasr, Seyyed Hossein. *Ideals and Realities of Islam*. 4th ed. George Allen & Unwin Ltd., 2000.

Nasr, Seyyid Vali Reza. *Mawdudi and the Making of Islamic Revivalism*. Oxford University Press, 1996.

"Navigating Differences: Clarifying Sexual and Gender Ethics in Islam." *Navigating Differences*. Accessed November 18, 2025. https://navigatingdifferences.com/clarifying-sexual-and-gender-ethics-in-islam/.

Newfield, Schneur Zalman. *Degrees of Separation: Identity Formation While Leaving Orthodox Judaism*. Temple University Press, 2020.

Ngai, Sianne. *Ugly Feelings*. Harvard University Press, 2005.

Nirenberg, David. *Anti-Judaism: The Western Tradition*. W. W. Norton, 2013.

Noll, Richard. *American Madness: The Rise and Fall of Dementia Praecox*. Harvard University Press, 2011.

Omar, Abdaljawad. "Can the Palestinian Mourn?" *Rusted Radishes: Beirut Art and Literary Journal*, November 27, 2023. https://rustedradishes.com/can-the-palestinian-mourn/.

Orsi, Robert A. *Between Heaven and Earth: The Religious Worlds People Make and the Scholars Who Study Them*. Princeton University Press, 2005.

Orsi, Robert A. "Everyday Miracles: The Study of Lived Religion." In *Lived Religion in America: Toward a History of Practice*, edited by David Hall. Princeton University Press, 1997.

Otterbeck, Jonas. "Battling over the Public Sphere: Islamic Reactions to the Music of Today." In *Religion, Media, and Modern Thought in the Arab World*, edited by Ramez Malouf and Ralph Berenger. Cambridge Scholars, n.d.

Painter, Nell Irvin. *The History of White People*. W. W. Norton, 2010.

Penslar, Derek J. "Antisemitism and Anti-Zionism: A Historical Approach." In *Contemporary Antisemitism: Canada and the World*, edited by Derek J. Penslar, Michael R. Marrus, and Janice Gross Stein. University of Toronto Press, 2005.

Penslar, Derek J. *Zionism: An Emotional State*. Rutgers University Press, 2023.

Pickthall, Marmaduke. *The Meaning of the Glorious Koran: An Explanatory Translation*. Alfred A. Knopf, 1930.

Prell, Riv-Ellen. *Fighting to Become Americans: Jews, Gender, and the Anxiety of Assimilation.* Beacon Press, 1999.

Prell, Riv-Ellen. "Triumph, Accommodation, and Resistance." In *The Columbia History of Jews and Judaism in America*, edited by Marc Lee Raphael. Columbia University Press, 2008.

Purkayastha, Bandana. *Negotiating Ethnicity: Second-Generation South Asian Americans Traverse a Transnational World.* Rutgers University Press, 2005.

Qureshi, Regina Burkhardt. "Transcending Space: Recitation and Community Among South Asian Muslims in Canada." In *Making Muslim Space in North America and Europe*, edited by Barbara Metcalf. University of California Press, 1996.

Rahman, Fazlur. *Islam and Modernity: Transformation of an Intellectual Tradition.* University of Chicago Press, 1982.

Raider, Mark. *The Emergence of American Zionism.* New York University Press, 1998.

Rana, Junaid. *Terrifying Muslims: Race and Labor in the South Asian Diaspora.* Duke University Press, 2011.

Reiss, Tom. *The Orientalist: Solving the Mystery of a Strange and Dangerous Life.* Random House, 2005.

Rock-Singer, Aaron. "The Salafi Mystique: The Rise of Gender Segregation in 1970s Egypt." *Islamic Law and Society* 23, no. 3 (2016): 279–305.

Roediger, David R. *The Wages of Whiteness: Race and the Making of the American Working Class.* Verso, 1999.

Rome, Adam. *The Bulldozer in the Countryside.* Princeton University Press, 2001.

Roof, Wade Clark. *A Generation of Seekers: The Spiritual Journeys of the Baby Boomer Generation.* HarperSanFrancisco, 1994.

Rouse, Carolyn. *Engaged Surrender: African American Women and Islam.* University of California Press, 1998.

Roy, Olivier. *The Failure of Political Islam.* Translated by Carol Volk. Harvard University Press, 1994.

Roy, Olivier. *Globalized Islam: The Search for a New Ummah.* Columbia University Press, 2004.

Rubin, Abraham. "Muslim Identity on the Suburban Frontier: The American-Jewish Context of Maryam Jameelah's Conversion to Islam." *Journal of Jewish Identities* 12, no. 2 (2012): 125–48.

Rubin, Gayle S. "Thinking Sex: Notes for a Radical Theory of the Politics of Sexuality." In *Culture, Society, and Sexuality: A Reader*, edited by Richard Parker and Peter Aggleton. University College London Press, 1999.

Ruderman, Judith. *Passing Fancies in Jewish American Literature and Culture.* Indiana University Press, 2019.

Sadowsky, Jonathan. *Imperial Bedlam: Institutions of Madness in Colonial Southwest Nigeria.* University of California Press, 1999.

Safi, Omid, ed. *Progressive Muslims: On Justice, Gender, and Pluralism*. Oneworld, 2003.

Safi, Omid, and Juliane Hammer, eds. *The Cambridge Companion to American Islam*. Cambridge University Press, 2013.

Said, Edward. "Zionism from the Standpoint of Its Victims." *Social Text* 1 (winter 1979): 7–58.

Sarna, Jonathan. *American Judaism: A History*. Yale University Press, 2004.

Sarna, Jonathan. "Antisemitism in America, 1654–2020." In *The Cambridge Companion to Antisemitism*, edited by Steven Katz. Cambridge University Press, 2022.

Schaefer, Donovan O. *The Evolution of Affect Theory: The Humanities, the Sciences, and the Study of Power*. Cambridge University Press, 2019.

Schaefer, Donovan O. *Religious Affects: Animality, Evolution, and Power*. Duke University Press, 2015.

Schaefer, Donovan O. *Wild Experiment: Feeling Science and Secularism After Darwin*. Duke University Press, 2022.

Schielke, Samuli. *Egypt in the Future Tense: Hope, Frustration, and Ambivalence Before and After 2011*. Indiana University Press, 2015.

Schielke, Samuli. "Hegemonic Encounters: Criticism of Saints-Day Festivals and the Formation of Modern Islam in Late 19th and Early 20th-Century Egypt." *Die Welt des Islams* 47, no. 3/4 (2007): 319–55.

Schmidt, Garbi. *Islam in Urban America: Sunni Muslims in Chicago*. Temple University Press, 2004.

Schultz, Kevin. *Tri-Faith America: How Catholics and Jews Held Postwar America to Its Protestant Promise*. Oxford University Press, 2011.

Scott, J. Barton. *Slandering the Sacred: Blasphemy Law and Religious Affect in Colonial India*. University of Chicago Press, 2023.

Scott, J. Barton, and Brannon Ingram. "What Is a Public? Notes from South Asia." *Journal of South Asian Studies* 38, no. 3 (2015): 357–70.

Sedgwick, Mark. *Against the Modern World: Traditionalism and the Secret History of the Twentieth Century*. Oxford University Press, 2004.

Sedgwick, Mark. *Traditionalism: The Radical Project of Restoring Sacred Order*. Oxford University Press, 2023.

Sharp, Joanne P. *Condensing the Cold War: Reader's Digest and American Identity*. University of Minnesota Press, 2000.

Shehabuddin, Elora. *Sisters in the Mirror: A History of Muslim Women and the Global Politics of Feminism*. University of California Press, 2021.

Sigalow, Emily. *American JewBu: Jews, Buddhists, and Religious Change*. Princeton University Press, 2019.

Silver, M. M. *Our Exodus: Leon Uris and the Americanization of Israel's Founding Story*. Wayne State University Press, 2010.

Simmons, Erika. *Hadassah and the Zionist Project*. Rowman & Littlefield Publishers, 2006.

Solnit, Rebecca. *Men Explain Things to Me*. Haymarket Books, 2014.

Sorkin, David. *Jewish Emancipation: A History Across Five Centuries*. Princeton University Press, 2019.

Spellberg, Denise. *Thomas Jefferson's Qur'an: Islam and the Founders*. Reprint edition. Vintage, 2014.

Spivak, Gayatri Charkravorty. "Can the Subaltern Speak?" In *Marxism and the Interpretation of Culture*, edited by Cary Nelson and Lawrence Grossberg. University of Illinois Press, 1988.

Starrett, Gregory. *Putting Islam to Work: Education, Politics, and Religious Transformation in Egypt*. University of California Press, 1998.

Stephens, Julia. *Governing Islam: Law, Empire, and Secularism in South Asia*. Cambridge University Press, 2018.

Stillman, Norman A. "Antisemitism in the Arab and Islamic World Prior to 1948." In *Antisemitism: A History*, edited by Albert S. Lindemann, and Richard S. Levy. Oxford University Press, 2010.

Stoler, Ann Laura. *Duress: Imperial Durabilities in Our Times*. Duke University Press, 2016.

Swedenburg, Ted. "The Palestinian Peasant as National Signifier." *Anthropological Quarterly* 63, no. 1 (1990): 18–30.

Taji-Farouki, Suha. "Thinking on the Jews." In *Islamic Thought in the Twentieth Century*, edited by Suha Taji-Farouki and Basheer N. Nafi. I. B. Tauris, 2004.

Tareen, SherAli. *Defending Muhammad in Modernity*. University of Notre Dame Press, 2020.

Taylor, Ula Yvett. *The Promise of Patriarchy: Women and the Nation of Islam*. University of North Carolina Press, 2017.

Tibi, Bassam. "From Sayyid Qutb to Hamas: The Middle East Conflict and the Islamization of Antisemitism." In *Global Antisemitism: A Crisis of Modernity*, vol. 4, *Islamism and the Arab World*, edited by Charles Asher Small. Institute for the Study of Antisemitism, 2013.

Tourage, Mahdi. "Performing Belief and Reviving Islam: Prominent (White Male) Converts in Muslim Revival Conventions." *Performing Islam* 1, no. 2 (2012): 2.

Wadud, Amina. *Qur'an and Woman: Rereading the Sacred Text from a Woman's Perspective*. 2nd ed. Oxford University Press, 1999.

Ware, Rudolph, III. *The Walking Qur'an: Islamic Education, Embodied Knowledge, and History in West Africa*. University of North Carolina Press, 2014.

Warner, Michael. *Publics and Counterpublics*. Zone Books, 2002.

Warner, Stephen R., and Judith G. Wittner, eds. *Gatherings in Diaspora: Religious Communities and the New Immigration*. Temple University Press, 1998.

Weisenfeld, Judith. *Black Religion in the Madhouse: Race and Psychiatry in Slavery's Wake*. New York University Press, 2025.

Weisenfeld, Judith. *New World A-Coming: Black Religion and Racial Identity During the Great Migration*. New York University Press, 2017.

Wenger, Tisa Joy. *We Have a Religion: The 1920s Pueblo Indian Dance Controversy and American Religious Freedom*. University of North Carolina Press, 2009.

Wilford, Hugh. "American Friends of the Middle East: The CIA, US Citizens, and the Secret Battle for American Public Opinion in the Arab-Israeli Conflict, 1947–1967." *Journal of American Studies* 51, no. 1 (2015): 93–116.

Winder, Alex. "Nakba Diaries: Unsettling the Scale and Temporality of Historical Writing." *AlMuntaqa* 2, no. 2 (2019): 24–39.

Yang, Fenggang, and Helen Rose Ebaugh. "Religion and Ethnicity Among New Immigrants: The Impact of Majority/Minority Status in Home and Host Countries." *Journal for the Scientific Study of Religion* 40 (September 2001).

Zaman, Muhammad Qasim. *Islam in Pakistan: A History*. Princeton University Press, 2018.

Zaman, Muhammad Qasim. "The Sovereignty of God in Modern Islamic Thought." *Journal of Royal Asiatic Society* 25, no. 3 (2015): 389–418.

Zaman, Muhammad Qasim. *The Ulama in Contemporary Islam: Custodians of Change*. Princeton University Press, 2002.

Zeghal, Malika. *The Making of the Modern Muslim State: Islam and Governance in the Middle East and North Africa*. Princeton University Press, 2024.

Zeller, Benjamin E. "American Postwar 'Big Religion': Reconceptualizing Twentieth-Century American Religion Using Big Science as a Model." *Church History* 80, no. 2 (2011): 321–51.

INDEX

A NOTE ON THE TYPE

This book has been composed in Arno, an Old-style serif typeface in the classic Venetian tradition, designed by Robert Slimbach at Adobe.